UNDERSTANDING THE
FRONTAL LOBE
OF THE BRAIN

UNDERSTANDING THE FRONTAL LOBE OF THE BRAIN

Fractioning the Prefrontal Lobes and Associated Executive Functions

by

Henry V. Soper, Tonya Comstock, Robin E. Kissinger, and K. Drorit Gaines

Fielding University Press is an imprint of Fielding Graduate University.
Its objective is to advance the research and scholarship of Fielding faculty,
students and alumni around the world, using a variety of publishing platforms.

For more information, please contact Fielding University Press, attention
Dr. Jean-Pierre Isbouts, via email to jisbouts@fielding.edu, or via postal mail to Fielding
Graduate University, 2020 De la Vina Street, Santa Barbara, CA 93105. On the web at
www.fielding.edu/universitypress.

Library of Congress Cataloging-in-Publication data
Understanding the Frontal Lobe of the Brain
1.   Neurology – Neuroscience. 2. Neuropsychology

TABLE OF CONTENTS

INTRODUCTION

Providing an explanation of brain-behavior relationships specific to the frontal lobes continues to be a major focus within neuropsychology. Various methodologies from lesion studies to statistical models have been utilized toward the aim of explaining frontal lobe behavioral or executive functions. Still, without an understanding of the underlying processes of executive functions we will remain at a loss to fully appreciate this unique brain-behavior relationship. Adding to the problem, within the field of neuropsychology, the construct of executive functions is not universally agreed upon. Given the variety of ideas regarding this construct, there is no consensus regarding theoretically based assessments or treatment. Executive functions are described in overlapping subcomponents that do not address how information is processed. Others have sought to explain executive functions using factor analyses, which results in one too many factors. These factors also describe observations, but do little to explain the underlying processes.

Some in the field have concluded that the complexity of the frontal lobes – in relation to executive functioning – is so complex that it cannot be understood as separate from processes that involve multiple areas of the brain. Understanding executive functions as a prefrontal lobe phenomenon, our first objective, will benefit the field in developing cohesive theories and assessments that consider how information is processed, rather than continued efforts to correlate observed deficits in specific brain areas. We will then discuss anatomical and physiological mechanisms of the frontal lobes and then fractionate them, structure-by-structure and unit-by-unit, in order to describe these basic processes. Four parallel functional networks will be delineated: dorsolateral, ventrolateral, orbital, and medial/ACC. Fractionation of these networks sheds light on the unique and essential contribution that each makes to frontal lobe executive functions as a whole.

Our desire to understand the relationship between the brain and behavior has captured our attention for at least 5,000 years (Darby & Walsh, 2005). Documentation of this quest came some time later, perhaps one of the first being Aristotle's elaborate explanation of the mind and matter dating back to 300 BC (e.g., Crivellato & Ribatti, 2007). However, it was not until 390 AD that Bishop Nemesius of Emesa (Syria) first linked physical characteristics of the brain to behavior (Finger, 2001). Specifically, his theory of ventricular localization attempted to connect physical structures of the brain (cerebral ventricles) with human functions, which may have been one inspiration for Franz Gall's science of phrenology (Finger, 2001).

Phenology as developed by Gall and Johann Spurzheim represented an early nineteenth century attempt to relate neuroanatomy to behavior. Despite the many shortcomings of Gall and Spurzheim's theory relating the size of cerebral cortical regions to human functions (Benjamin, 2009), it is thought by some to be among the first to suggest that anterior regions of the brain control complex functions, as well as suggesting that the brain comprised distinct functional units (Simpson, 2005). Some authors suggest that the ideas of phrenology sparked a new direction in brain science, which has been supported in part by modern behavioral neuroscience (e.g., Darby & Walsh, 2005; Simpson, 2005).

Interestingly, hundreds of years before phrenology, behavioral descriptions hinted at ideas strikingly similar to later notions of executive functions (e.g., Darby & Walsh, 2005; Finger, 2001). The first specific reference to *higher order functions* likely did not appear until the Renaissance era or later (Finger, 2001). One example is apparent in Thomas Willis's work in 1664, in which he discusses "volitional" behaviors as controlled by certain brain regions (Finger, 2001; Sironi, 2011). Although Willis's theories were eventually disproven, he is credited with advancing behavioral neuroscience (e.g., Finger, 2001; Katon, 2010). Subsequently, Emanuel Swedenborg, in 1740, began to integrate various schools of thought, to hypothesize that the brain was made up of "distinct functional units" that controlled behavioral characteristics, such as motivation (Armistead, Strawn, & Wright, 2009). Nearly 100 years later, Francois Chaussier definitively delineated the frontal lobes, naming them "lobus frontalis" (Filley, 2009). The term prefrontal cortex was not introduced until some 50 years later (Finger, 2001).

Many credit John Hughlings Jackson as being the first to recognize that the frontal lobes are responsible for higher order functions (Benjamin, 2009; Franz & Gillet, 2009; Luria, 1966). Jackson's work is thought to have influenced great minds of the time including Sigmund Freud and Aleksandr Luria (Benjamin, 2009; Finger, 2001). In fact, some suggest that Jackson's work (among others) was an inspiration to Freud, sparking his lifelong quest to find a physiological explanation for the inner workings of the mind (Benjamin, 2009).

Luria admired the work of Freud, though ironically he criticized Freud's approach for being too scientific (Sacks, 1990). Sacks provides a fascinating account of these two complex, fascinating, and brilliant thinkers. He suggests that Freud and Luria both occupy a unique position in the history of science, simultaneously straddling the world that seeks to explain the reasons for events (i.e., classical sciences), and one that seeks to describe (romantic sciences). To Luria, the brain and behavior can only make sense when one simultaneously considers the more qualitative and quantitative aspects of science (Sacks, 1990).

Among Luria's contemporaries, his theories, explained in prolific prose, were criticized and thought to collapse under the weight of scientific scrutiny (Sacks, 1990). In reality, much of Luria's thinking and suppositions continue to influence and impact modern neuropsychology (Darby & Walsh, 2004; Fuster, 2008) and most certainly helped to inform our conceptualization of frontal lobe processes. As but one example, Luria (1966) described the complexity of higher cortical systems by drawing an analogy to other functional systems in the body (e.g., the respiratory system). He enlightens the reader, providing a scientific and poetic description of how the system works together or "concertedly," likening this anatomical and physiological respiratory system to the brain and its capacity for the most complex functions (Luria, 1966).

"Like the functions of a CEO, the functions of the frontal lobes defy a soundbite definition. They are not invested with any single, ready-to-label function" (Goldberg, 2001, p. 23). However, the importance of the frontal lobes cannot be overstated regarding human experience and functioning. Research on frontal lobe functioning proliferated in the 1990s; even so, scientific effort to understand the frontal lobes and particularly the prefrontal cortex remains elusive and, for lack of specificity, "we often lapse into poetic metaphor" (Goldberg, 2001, p. 24). Wasserman and Wasserman (2013) assert that progress in this area has not made appreciable gains since the mid-1990s. They describe the concept of executive function as composed of "a patchwork of skills and populations with some assessments focusing on neuropsychological correlates and others focused on manifest behavior" (Wasserman & Wasserman, 2013, p. 88).

Specifically, while the principles of other areas of the brain whose function is the processing of sensory or motor information are straightforward and generally agreed upon (Luria, 1966), the function of the prefrontal lobes refuses to adhere to our consensual understanding (Stuss & Benson, 1986). Thus, difficulty ensues when the straightforward theories of other brain areas are applied to the frontal lobes, specifically the prefrontal areas.

Some understand brain-behavior relationships through the lens of focusing on observable deficits (Lezak, Howieson, Bigler, & Tranel, 2012). Basically, the patient is assessed for what they are *not* able to do, which provides clues as to the area of dysfunction in the brain. While this approach is intuitively valid when dealing with areas of the brain that have somewhat discrete functions, it provides misleading information when applied to the prefrontal area. For example, for over a hundred years the functions of the parietal lobe have been measured after deficits observed the following trauma to certain areas there (e.g., the apraxias. aphasias, and agnosias). Moreover, the underlying assumption is that other areas of the brain will remain constant in their functioning rather than compensating for the damaged area. In fact, what we are looking at with this approach is the rest of the brain doing what it can without the critical functions (areas) which are now missing.

The frontal lobes constitute a substantial portion of our brains, but they are composed of distinct subsections. Some, such as the primary motor and premotor areas (e.g., Brodmann's areas 4 and 6), are generally not associated with executive functioning (Fuster, 2008; Goldberg, 2001). However, the tertiary, prefrontal areas of these lobes are (Luria, 1973). They have been defined as the projection areas of the nucleus medialis dorsalis of the thalamus (e.g., Fuster, 2008). Most often in this review the term frontal will actually refer to prefrontal.

Introduction to the Job of the Frontal Lobes

The seat of behaviors associated with consciousness such as self-awareness, self-regulation, and intentionality is thought to reside in the frontal lobes (Perecman, 1987). Like any good CEO or general, the prefrontal area is central in selecting goals, strategizing a plan of action, determining the cognitive skills required to implement behavior, coordinating those skills, and ordering behavioral output (Goldberg, 2001). Moreover, the responsibility of evaluating the feedback regarding success or failure as compared to our intentions also rests in the frontal lobes (Goldberg, 2001). A. R. Luria (1973) went so far as to describe the frontal lobes as fundamental in facilitation and maintenance of conscious activity.

Executive functions have been equated with frontal lobe functions by those who study such matters (Soper, Wolfson, & Canavan, 2008). The frontal lobes, which include the prefrontal area, can be thought of as the "action cortex" without primary sensory functions (Fuster, 2008, p. 2; Stuss & Benson, 1986). In essence, the frontal cortex is dedicated to movement, reasoning, expression of emotion, speech, and other actions regarding stimuli that have been sensed and perceived by other areas of the brain (Fuster, 2008). The executive functions, also known as frontal functions, involve incorporating all the available information into a decision prior to acting. It includes aspects such as planning and organizing material, problem solving, and maintaining goal-directed behavior. People with deficits in this area tend to act before they take everything relevant into account.

The Problem with Executive Function as a Construct

First we will discuss executive functioning as a concept, as a frontal lobe concept. Lack of agreement on the definition of the construct of executive functions leaves the field of neuropsychology at odds regarding theoretically based assessment and treatment (Wasserman & Wasserman, 2013). Ideas range from executive functions being attributable to one factor, namely planning (Anderson, 2002), to two factors including perceptual processing speed and reasoning (Salthouse, 2005), to myriad and yet to be determined factors (Koziol, 2013). Moreover, the conceptualization that executive functions need to be differentiated from metacognitive functions, such as planning, as different from control of emotional behavior, has also entered the fray (Ardila, 2013). In short, some in the field are advocating for fractionating executive functions and correlating them to brain areas, while others push to consider executive functions as solely an integrated and whole brain phenomenon. Neither of these approaches furthers the development of the understanding of how information is processed, which stymies the development of theoretically based neuropsychological assessments and treatment. What is needed is clarification of *how* a patient is having difficulty processing information to inform neuropsychological theory and the development of assessments and treatment.

To further elucidate the concept of executive functioning we will begin with a discussion of the frontal lobe functions, coalescing in a theory of executive processes revealed via the fractionation of frontal lobes structure-by-structure and unit-by-unit. Our goal is to demonstrate the underlying processes of executive functions through careful examination of the functional-structural relationships between specific units or circuits in the frontal lobes and behavior. We will identify cortical surface areas and subcortical structures that comprise or are closely related to the frontal lobes. We will discuss the evolution of the frontal lobes as well as their development in an individual person, examining the structural-functional changes in the frontal lobes that occur before birth and continue through adulthood.

Then we will examine the structures that connect each of the functional units and how they communicate with other units and brain regions, and we will consider the role of neurotransmitters in facilitating communication within and between the functional-structural units. Then we will focus on unique processes of the four functional-structural frontal units (i.e., dorsolateral, ventrolateral, orbital, and medial/ACC), which interact in a manner such that an individual can take into account all relevant affective, sensory, memory, and reinforcement information in order to produce the most appropriate motor behavior given the information available. Finally, we have included a number of anecdotes of human behavior, which we believe add richness to the discussion and perhaps narrow the gap between science and daily life.

1.

DEVELOPMENT OF THE PROBLEM

Overgeneralization of Structure/Function Correlations

The first attempt at linking observations of complex behavior with specific brain areas was taken on by Joseph Gall (Luria, 1973). Gall, who was an anatomist, reasoned on the assumption that human capabilities were located in specific areas of the brain, and if particularly robust in an individual would result in a protrusion of the brain, and hence the skull overlying that area (Luria, 1973). Maps were created correlating the bumps on people's heads with functionality. Lesion studies provided the basis for differentiating areas of function, which were mapped and termed phrenology (Luria, 1973).

While certain areas of the brain have been associated primarily with certain types of behavior and functioning, it is not prudent to localize structure to function when it comes to the frontal lobes. If the frontal lobes are thought of as the action cortex of behavioral, cognitive, skeletal, vegetative, and ocular action then the prefrontal cortex is entirely executive in nature (Fuster, 2008). With the exception of possibly executive visual attention, no area of the frontal lobes is thought to work independently (Fuster, 2008). However, some interpretations of research findings are "reminiscent of phrenology" in their desire to associate a function with a particular brain area (Fuster, 2008, p. 173).

By the mid-20th century research specific to executive functioning relied heavily on methods that studied groups (Burgess, 1997). Many of these studies of large groups strived to correlate damaged brain structures with some behavioral manifestation (Burgess, 1997). Some in the field are skeptical of such methods and believe that linking brain structures to behavior and researching groups is inadequate for theoretical development (Shallice, 1988). Those of this mindset, at times called ultra-cognitive neuropsychologists, adhere to the thought that the use of double dissociation yields more accurate data (Burgess, 1997). However, even those who advocate for double dissociation recognize that the information can be misleading (Shallice, 1988).

Dissociation and Double Dissociation. Dissociation in neuroscience has focused on correlating deficits of those with frontal lobe lesions to measurable impairments in functioning to build an understanding of how a normal brain works (Goldberg, 2001). Traditional methods of deciphering neuropsychological functioning of the frontal lobes in animals relied heavily on dissociation of function. In other words, if the assumption is that a certain function is related to an area of the brain, then a lesion of that area should impede the behavior associated with that area (Fuster, 2008). The thinking is that a single case with a dissociated symptom is theoretically more informative than many cases with multiple associated symptoms even though the vast majority of neuropsychological patients present with multiple associated impairments (Bishop, 1997).

Thus, neuropsychological theory is built on unusual and rare cases (Bishop, 1997).

Using this method, it was thought that brain function could be determined by the absence of behavior related to an area that has been removed (Fuster, 2008). This method is prone to misleading conclusions because there may be multiple neurological avenues that could manifest the same behavioral deficit (Dubois, Pillon, & McKeith, 2007).

Some years ago the lesion method in neuroscience was compared to lofting bombs into the telephone company, And then the scientist would dial numbers to see what damage had been done.

Soper (1983) states that the conclusions drawn from this evidence are quite clearly false. The reasoning goes along the line that people with lesions in their left hemispheres tend not to be happy, so happiness must reside in the left hemisphere. Moreover, people with lesions in their right hemispheres feel better than they should, and therefore depression must lie in the right hemisphere. Both conclusions are clearly wrong.

Kevin Walsh (1985) commented on how this faulty logic has been applied to current neuropsychological assessment and theory. Using the Wisconsin Card Sort Task (WCST) as an example, he argued against the logic that just because the frontal lobes are *usually* involved in successful performance on the WCST that those who fail it must have damage to the frontal lobes. This would be true only in the case of pathognomic symptoms when there is one and only one reason for failing the task. Thus, many studies have incorporated double dissociation as originally proffered by Teuber (1955, 1959) to try to bolster validity and reliability.

The concept of double dissociation – to some extent – further validates the concept of the localization of brain function in the neuropsychological field. If a lesion in one area of the brain is correlated to a deficit, it is not prudent to assume that the behavior is localized to the affected area, because the area may be part of a hierarchical structure responsible for the cognition or behavior, rather than being localized in the impacted area (Goldberg, 2001). What is needed is a completely separate loss of function from another area that does not impact the original loss of function (Teuber, 1955).

A crude example to illustrate the concept is as follows: Damage to area A results in loss of function X, but not function Y in a group of people. Damage to area B results in deficits in function Y, but not function X in another group of people. Given the double dissociation of function it is more robust to attribute some aspect of a function to a particular area of the brain, or at least to assume that it is localizable and not a global deficit. Another aspect of this discussion to keep in mind is that when looking at a damaged brain, we are not looking at the damage, but the rest of the brain doing what it is still able to do.

Burgess (1997) argues that when it comes to executive functions, double dissociation can be misleading because the measures for such functions are "less pure" than for other types of functioning. In other words, measurement of an executive function may not be fractionated from the hierarchical process that underlies the behavioral deficit (Burgess, 1997).

During the development of neuropsychological theory, some areas of the brain have lent themselves to distinct functions. For example, it has long been understood that areas such as the lateral areas of the temporal lobes specialize in processing auditory information and relaying it to sensory association areas where higher level processing takes place (Luria, 1973). These structure/function relationships – while not infallible – have facilitated development of a general way to understand how a normal brain works, but this approach breaks down when applied to the prefrontal areas (Jacobsen & Nissen, 1937).

Neuropsychological theory regarding language illustrates that the idea of how structure equals function is sometimes misleading, even in more well understood areas of the brain. It is well known that, in 1861, Broca was the first to catch the attention of the scientific community regarding speech being localized to areas in the left hemisphere (Boring, 1957). Geschwind and Levitsky (1968) added that the planum temporale is larger in the left hemisphere in 65% of people, larger in the right hemisphere in 11% of people, and the same size in 24% of people. This information was used to demonstrate hemispheric dominance with respect to language functioning. Given the structural variation among individuals, it is generally imprudent to state for certain that a behavioral deficit is localized to a particular brain area in part or in whole. This problem is magnified when applied to the prefrontal areas. This planum temporale anomaly also exists for certain other great apes, yet we have never had a good conversation with an orangutan.

Variability in Anterior Frontal Regions
While the sensory-motor areas of the frontal lobes adhere to more traditional ideas regarding brain organization, the anterior portion of the

frontal lobes has increased variability among individuals (Luria, 1966). Variation in the development of the frontal lobes due to factors such as individual experience precludes that every person processes information in a uniform manner. In other words, we can learn to accomplish similar tasks by processing the information in ways that differ from each other. For example, some people may utilize the frontal lobes to shift sets between stimuli while performing the Trail Making Test B (connect the circles from 1 to A to 2 to B and so on to the end). Others may use sensory areas to "just see" which letter or number comes next and do not need to engage the frontal lobes to accomplish the task. The task then is no more complicated than Trail Making Test A (connect the circles from 1 to 2 to 3 to 4 and so on to the end), which consists of numbers only.

Evidence also suggests that the organization of the prefrontal cortex is different than other areas of the brain. For example, electrophysiological evidence exists that demonstrates a high level of sensory motor organization dependent on genetic factors (Ravich-Shcherbo, unpublished investigation, as cited in Luria, 1966). However, individual external – or "paratypical" – experiences more heavily influence the development of the frontal lobes (Luria, 1966, p. 261). This further demonstrates the idiosyncratic nature of the development and utilization of the frontal lobes as well as explaining the myriad behavioral deficits seen in those with dysfunctional frontal areas.

Inconsistent behavioral manifestation muddies the clinical picture because assessment is based on the assumption that "brain damage always implies behavioral impairment" (Lezak et al., 2012, p. 101). At times, a person may behave impulsively, such as getting on a train going the wrong direction, while at other times the same person may show great restraint inhibiting behavior such as not interrupting a boring conversation. In the first instance, the stimulus of the train is quite strong and the person did not consider all of the available information prior to acting. In the second scenario, the person processed the essential available information – such as hurting the feelings of another or being considered rude – and responded in a socially appropriate manner. Each of these abilities would rely on different pathways and thus would present dependent on the context. In a third or fourth case a given stimulus may be responded to differently, as in at another time the person does ignore the train going in the wrong direction or does interrupt the boring person.

Localizing a particular function to a specific brain area when it comes to the frontal lobes could be misleading if not considering the role of the frontal lobes. This is because no part of the prefrontal cortex separately or as a whole performs a specific function by itself (Fuster, 2008). Rather, the architecture of the area is involved in determination of function or, more accurately, process. Specifically, the architecture of the primary motor and sensory areas consists of modules and columns with efferent and afferent connections that are discrete, making the functions of these areas somewhat discrete (Fuster, 2008). In contrast, the prefrontal lobes consist of overlapping networks of connections with many afferent and efferent connections to other areas of the brain (Fuster, 2008).

Taking a look at some of the information presented above, it is clear that there can be, and is, great variability among individuals in prefrontal organization and function/process. Certainly experience plays a role in such individuation, but Luria (1976) himself showed the effect of culture on such cognitive processing.

Frontal Processing and Culture. Given the capacity of the frontal lobes to create mental representations of outside objects and systems (Damasio, 2003), language can be used to verbally create mental representations that a person has not experienced directly (Luria, 1976). Thus, we are exposed to representations of how previous generations have organized their experience (Luria, 1976). To further examine the influence of culture on thinking, Luria (1976) examined a mountain and a village community at the turn of the century. One portion of the population – the villagers – was exposed to radical changes in their economic and political structure, while the other portion – mountain dwellers – was not (Luria, 1976). Unfortunately, given the scope of the study it is unrealistic to replicate, but it does much to describe the response in information processing of one sample of people subjected to radical social and cultural differences.

Data support the premise that as humans master literacy and fundamental knowledge, cognitive processes such as reasoning, imagination, and perception are changed (Luria, 1976). These changes are not limited to a simple widening of opportunity, but involve the restructuring of motivation and thinking (Luria, 1976). Interviews with more socially primitive citizens revealed a reluctance to engage in classification or abstract reasoning (Luria, 1976). People tended to think about objects in concrete ways in which they could utilize the object (Luria, 1976). For example, when asked how a fish and a crow are similar, mountain dweller interviewees would respond that they were not similar because fish can be eaten and crows cannot. Also, a crow can peck a fish, but a fish cannot do anything to a crow (Luria, 1976). The underlying category of "animal" held no value for real-life problems and was thus resisted. Further, people were resistant to engage in hypothetical thinking that did not apply to concrete problems of daily living (Flynn, 2013). The villagers had no such difficulty.

Changes in culture correlate with changes in thinking. Current day adolescents are capable of making abstract reasoning consistent – by using logic – to the extent that they are able to completely ignore symbols while engaging in analogies (Flynn, 2013). For example, modern day high school students can correctly answer the following problem: two circles followed by a semi-circle – two 16s followed by what? The answer to this problem is 8 because 8 is half of 16. Thus, given advances in technology and culture, modern day people are taught to categorize objects – such as we do in science – to use logic to make abstractions consistent, and to think seriously about the hypothetical (Flynn, 2013).

These increasing cognitive abilities manifest in current day assessments that are designed to be free of culture (Folger, 2012). Flynn has identified a systematic trend of increasing IQ scores averaging .3% per year in industrialized societies (Folger, 2012). Upon closer investigation, employing standardized and widely used intellectual assessments such as the Wechsler Intelligence Scale for Children (WISC), scores on crystalline knowledge remained constant. Information such as vocabulary and arithmetic, which we would learn in school are not increasing, but gains are being made by subsequent generations in abstract types of reasoning (Folger, 2012). These are the types of skills that involve the prefrontal area.

Myriad Presentations for Similar Lesions

It has long been recognized that dysfunction in the frontal lobes presents complications due to the "indefinite nature of the deficits associated with injury of this region" as opposed to the more discrete functioning of motor or sensory areas (Jacobsen & Nissen, 1937, p. 3). The behavior of those with frontal lobe difficulty manifests abnormalities in various ways and can become quite confusing if interpreted through observations in animal research. Soper (1983) has compiled, from various sources, some human clinical examples that illustrate myriad ways that these difficulties can present.

A 12-year-old hospital patient repeatedly takes candy and other items from the bedside tables of other patients. The thefts seem unplanned and often the owner of the goods is watching him at the time. When asked why he stole the items he simply states that he was hungry.

Another hospital patient responded to the salient stimulus of a big red call button that just begged to be pressed. So, in stereotypical fashion, he pressed it and was at a loss for words when the nurse showed up at his room.

During rehabilitation for a frontal lobe wound, a patient was working in the carpenter's shop of a hospital. While planing a piece of wood, he went past the place he wanted to stop and continued to plane the wood until it was gone. He then began planing the workbench itself!

A minister who underwent a procedure to remove a significant portion of his frontal lobes appeared to have recovered to the point that his parish was returned to him. All was well until he began telling dirty stories at a funeral (Soper, 1983, pp. 8-9).

Interestingly, such variations in symptomology can present even with lesions in the same brain area between and within patients given the variety of how the information is processed. In each of these cases the person was processing most of the information, but not some of the critical aspects, even though they knew the information not being processed. The young boy did know that the candy belonged to someone else, but he did not use that information. He was hungry, so he ate something, but what he did not process was that it did not belong to him, and therefore he should not have eaten it. The button for the patient felt good to press, but the person did not take into account that a nurse would be summoned if he pressed the button. The carpenter was planing the wood appropriately, but he did not take into account that he was to stop when he got to a certain point. Not processing that information, he continued to plane. In the case of the minister, most people do look sad after a funeral. Being sad generally is not good, so to make someone feel better one might tell jokes and make them laugh, and many of the best jokes are dirty jokes. However, he certainly knew it was after a funeral, he officiated at it, but he did not use that information when he decided what to do to help the situation. In these cases at one level the bizarre responses make sense, but only if you do not use a piece of information, even though you are aware of it.

The Issue of Fractionization

Executive functions as defined here are dependent on the integrity of other functions such as language, memory, visuospatial skills, and praxis, but these are in and of themselves separate functions (Miller & Cummings, 2007). For example, it would be difficult to think abstractly about a proverb – assigning multiple meanings to the same words – in conjunction with a primary language deficit. The task is compromised with either a language or an executive deficit, and hence the etiology of the dysfunction is different. Thus, failure on a test of executive function can occur for many reasons and it is difficult to rule out supportive functions (Chan, Shum, Toulopoulou, & Chen, 2008).

In other words, failure on a test of a certain function will occur if the correlated brain areas are damaged; however, the failure can be caused by other reasons as well (Luria, 1973). Therefore, in the assessment of executive dysfunction it is prudent to first rule out impairment of supportive functions as much as possible (Miller & Cummings, 2007).

Considering how the person processes information rather than measuring specific behavioral deficits can help make this differentiation. However, given that higher order executive functions are dependent on lower order functions, some in the field have come to believe that our understanding of executive functions needs to be "broad enough to include anatomical structures that represent a diverse and diffuse portion of the central nervous system" (Alvarez & Emory, 2006, p. 19).

Riva, Cazzaniga, Esposito, and Bulgheroni (2013) define executive functions as "the capacity to coordinate multiple cognitive tasks to attain a specific goal. This implies simultaneous control and integration of a set of task-or goal-relevant cognitive operations to reach that goal in the most economic, efficient way possible" (p. 97). They believe that such complex tasks necessitate a distributed network of brain circuitry interconnecting various specialized areas throughout the brain. They describe the concept of equating the prefrontal cortex and executive functions as antiquated and overly simplistic given the complexity of the task (Riva et al., 2013). However, this approach is a more complex version of naming specific functions and correlating them to particular brain areas without addressing how the information is being processed.

History of Neuropsychological Theory

Looking back to the development of neuropsychological theory provides clues to how the structure/function relationship garnered such a prominent position in the field. Various schools of thought emerged during the development of neuropsychology as a field. One adhered to the structuralist approach, which sought to correlate observed behavior with localized brain pathology. By contrast, others strove to develop a theoretical understanding of the interactions among brain areas and the sequelae of associated observable syndromes of behavior. The perceived differences between these two approaches to neuropsychology are fundamentally based on the structure versus functional/process paradigms (Adams, 1980).

United States Neuropsychology. The development of clinical neuropsychology, at least in the American tradition, relied heavily on neurology, behavioral science, academic psychology, and particularly on psychometric measures (Luria & Majovski, 1977). Examples of neuropsychologists in the United States that exemplify this approach include Muriel Lezak, Ralph Reitan, Nelson Butters, and Arthur Benton (Luria & Majovski, 1977). Their work included clinical and diagnostic examination of brain injury in humans as well as research on humans, which they applied directly to rehabilitation (Luria & Majovski, 1977).

Burgess (1997) says that clinically it is likely that the only people who will manifest deficits in executive processes are those with highly localized frontal lesions. Thus, researchers have tended to gravitate towards using localization of brain lesions in the frontal lobes as selection criteria (Burgess, 1997). While these methods had challenges given the idiosyncratic nature of the brain damage of each participant (Reitan, 1964), when trying to conceptualize generalizations, humans could describe phenomenological details about cognitive and emotional experience not possible for non-human primates (Fuster, 2008).

In the United States, scientists strove for reliability in predicting organic brain disturbance (Filskov & Goldstein, 1974) and in identifying the nature of such dysfunctions. Batteries of standardized tests were developed in pursuit of these goals, including what was the most known of these assessments, the Halstead-Reitan Neuropsychological Test Battery (Reitan & Davison, 1974).

Experimental Neuropsychology. Another approach to the development of neuropsychology included the experimental neuropsychology camp with scientists such as Karl Pribram and Roger Sperry. Experimental neuropsychologists were primarily concerned with discovering fundamental tenets of brain-behavior relationships, irrespective of their clinical applications (Luria & Majovski, 1977). This work was mostly based on studies of animals in highly controlled experiments. The assumption was made that this method would reveal greater generalizability than observations in natural environments (Luria & Majovski, 1977).

Russian Neuropsychology. In contrast, there were those who deemed the association between an individual behavior and brain lesions as "static neuropsychology" (Glozman, 1999, p. 33). Rather than noting identified correlations in a rigid manner, neuropsychologists subscribing to the Russian – sometimes referred to as Lurian – theory of neuropsychology strove to understand the interactions between the brain and resultant behavior (Glozman, 1999). The dynamics of how cortico-subcortical and interhemispheric areas interact were thought to be the foundation to qualitatively explain and build theories around resultant syndromes of behavioral deficit (Glozman, 1999).

In the Lurian tradition, methods such as performing an initial screen to identify problematic areas were done to identify areas that needed more in-depth investigation (Luria, 1966). This method was touted as a balanced integration of structuralism with functionalism, which strove to consider how the information was being processed (Adams, 1980). This assertion included the caveat that Luria's observations were subjective in nature and not systematically studied (Adams, 1980). However, this approach provided a base of understanding of how people were processing information, which led to their various observable behavioral deficits.

2.

HISTORY OF ANIMAL RESEARCH

Introduction

Research that provided the basis for many current theories on neuropsychological functioning of the frontal lobes began with investigation of animals during the period of 1870 to 1890 (Luria, 1966). Methodology included examination of the changes in an animal's behavior during electrical stimulation or after extirpation of various areas of the frontal lobes (Luria, 1966). Luria (1966) reports that around the turn of the 20th century Bianchi (1895) was one of the first to systematically study the impact of frontal lobe ablation in animals. He subscribed to the idea of a hierarchical structure of motoric activity, with the most complex behavior associated with the frontal lobes. This was accomplished because the frontal lobe served the function of integrating sensory information from other parts of the brain and was involved in determination of a response (Stuss & Benson, 1986). He found that extirpation of both frontal lobes led to disorganized behavior that impeded the ability of the animal to adapt to new circumstances.

These early studies of neuropsychological functioning, which were largely based on behavioral observations of animals with frontal ablations, were replete with "anthropomorphic interpretation" (Fuster,

2008, p. 126). Researchers faced difficulties when inferring motives and feelings in observations of pre- and postoperative animal behavior (Fuster, 2008). While these observations may tell us what area a particular function may be – at least partly – associated with, it does little to explain how the process works (Fuster, 2008).

Hyperactivity

Studies of frontal ablations in monkeys in the 1930s evidenced hyperactivity in the form of what initially appeared to be aimless movement (Jacobsen, 1931; Miller & Orbach, 1972; Richter & Hines, 1938). However, studies were conflicting across species and researchers (Fuster, 2008). The occurrence of hyperactivity is observable at times with lateral prefrontal lesions, but more consistently with orbital frontal lesions, even when the head of the caudate is preserved (Davis, 1958; Mettler & Mettler, 1942; Richter & Hines, 1938; Villablanca, Marcus, & Olmstead, 1976), which is important because damage to the head of the caudate can cause hyperactivity on its own. Ocular motility has also been shown to be impaired with lesions in Brodmann's area 8 (Fuster, 2008). Ferrier (1886) understood ocular motility as being vital to spatial attention.

Disinhibition

As hyperactivity was studied further, it became apparent that it was reducible by limiting external stimuli, especially light (Gross, 1963; Isaac & DeVito, 1958; Mettler, 1944). Interpretation of this observation clarified that hyperactivity was actually secondary to a *hyperreactivity* to external stimuli (Fuster, 2008). The effects of hyper-responsiveness to irrelevant stimuli on attention can be devastating. The deficient ability to ignore extraneous stimuli and inhibit a behavioral response was observed, especially in animals, with ventral or orbital lesions (Fuster, 2008).

More specifically, animals with orbitofrontal lesions have difficulty not orienting to almost any external stimuli, causing rapid and frequent shifts in attention (Fuster, 2008). Conversely, a learned behavior that was once useful in obtaining a reward is difficult to extinguish, especially in those with lesions in the limbic portion of the orbital frontal cortex (Butter, 1969). The behavior will persist past its utility in gaining the reward.

Dysfunctional inhibition is problematic because irrelevant behavior interferes with goal oriented behavior if there is any delay in the spatial or temporal components in the environment (Fuster, 2008). In other words, if a behavior needs to be inhibited in service of a higher order goal, the frontal lobe animal will struggle (Goldberg, 2001). This can cause difficulty in reaching goals in which attainment of the goal depends on the inhibition of a hierarchically lower task. For example, if an animal is rewarded at stimulus A only after a trial in which it responded to stimulus B, and is rewarded at B only after responding to Stimulus A (delayed alternation), the animal with frontal ablations will likely be unable to inhibit responding to the most recently reinforced stimulus and fail the task.

Discrimination

Frontal animals – a term generally used to describe animals that have been subjected to significant frontal ablation procedures – have minimal difficulty performing motor responses learned preoperatively, even if complex (Fuster, 2008). If the stimuli associated with a behavioral output are presented simultaneously, the frontal animal is usually able to respond correctly, but as soon as the stimuli are presented separately in time the animal demonstrates dysfunction. This occurs whether or not the animal learned the task before ablating occurred. The animal will also struggle when required to discriminate between stimuli that require an action and those that require no response, a condition known as go/no-go (Fuster, 2008). Usually the frontal animal will demonstrate an inability to refrain from responding when any stimulus is presented and may even respond in between stimulus presentations (Soper, 1974).

The frontal animal is capable of learning new discrimination tasks if they are presented simultaneously and not in successive order, but once learned the response is not amenable to modification or change. When the learned response no longer produces the desired effect it is not altered. In other words, there is no reversal of the discrimination demand (Gross, 1963; Irle & Markowitsch, 1984; Teitelbaum, 1964). This difficulty in reversing discrimination demands applies to not only *what* the stimulus is but also *where* it is (Fuster, 2008; Soper, 1974). An example is the perseveration of a frontal animal searching for a reward in a location that no longer contains the reward. Instead of searching elsewhere, the frontal animal continues acting on the previous location, perseverates, and does not seem to learn from this experience (Warren, Coutant, & Cornwell, 1969; Warren, Warren, & Akert, 1972).

Attention

Attention is a twofold process, including the ability to focus cognitive resources on a stimulus and to inhibit or exclude non-relevant stimuli (Fuster, 2008). The first component is called set and will be explained further below. It is the ability to focus attention on recent events as well as prospective events (Fuster, 2008). This enables the animal to prepare for a choice or action given the mind's ability to project outcome into the future. In animals that have been trained to discriminate between lines and figures, induced lesions of lateral or orbital prefrontal cortex produce different difficulties with attention (Dias, Robbins, & Roberts, 1996a, 1996b, 1997).

In these experiments, the monkeys with lateral prefrontal cortex damage had difficulty shifting sets from the previously learned task to a new one. Given the nature of set, such as working memory, there is a "time sensitive" or temporal component to attention to internal representations (Fuster, 2008, p. 135). By contrast, monkeys with orbital ablations demonstrated dysfunction in inhibiting previously learned responses. Damage to either of these frontal areas has demonstrated impairment in selective attention in animals.

Delayed Reaction

Delayed response is one of the most intensely studied and well-documented deficits related to frontal lobe ablating procedures in the field (Fuster, 2008). While no one frontal lobe task can explain deficits in delayed reaction, at least two frontal lobe functions have been presumed to be involved: These are working memory and inhibitory control (Fuster, 2008). With respect to this discussion, working memory is defined as "the temporary retention of information – sensory or other – for the performance of a prospective act to solve a problem or to attain a goal" (Fuster, 2008, p. 138).

Jacobsen (1935, 1936) performed a series of experiments on monkeys who were subjected to frontal lobe ablations. After ablating procedures, the monkeys demonstrated deficits on tasks that required them to hold information in memory over a period of time. For example, after having been exposed to a stimulus that was paired with a reward, the monkey's view of the stimulus was blocked for five seconds. When once again exposed to the stimulus, the monkeys with frontal lobe ablations initially performed no better than chance at identifying the stimulus associated with the reward (Kolb & Whishaw, 2009).

Pribram (1952) and his associates expanded the work of Jacobsen (1936) on delayed reaction tasks. These were tasks in which animals were taught a behavior and then required to hold the information in their minds over time until provided with an opportunity to act on the learned response. Deficits in delayed reaction were reliable in identifying primates with frontal lobe lesions (Pribram, Ahumada, Hartog, & Roos, 1964).

Bekhterev (1907, as cited in Luria, 1966) contributed an interesting observation to the differentiation of frontal lobe functioning. He noted that dogs with extirpated frontal lobes do not consider the results of their behavior (Luria, 1966). Also, there seemed no attempt to match new outcomes with past experience. Given the lack of this ability, behaviors in the present are not analyzed in terms of their effectiveness in obtaining present goals (Bekhterev, 1907, as cited in Luria, 1966). Indeed, Lawicka, Mishkin, and Kreiner's (1966) study of dogs with extirpated frontal lobes (proreal gyrus) found that the dogs were impaired on various delayed response tasks. Specifically, dogs with bilateral ablation of the proreal gyrus demonstrated impairment in delayed response, especially when the delay was accompanied by distraction. The length of the delay did not further contribute to the deficit (Lawicka et al., 1966).

The important thing to note about the work of Lawicka (1966) is that a high percentage of dogs would select the correct of the two remaining stimuli after an initial mistake. Lawicka initially suggested that the dogs' difficulty was related to a memory issue – not remembering where the reward was after a period of time. However, given the high percentage of correct selection after failure, it is not that the animals did not remember where the stimulus was, but rather had difficulty with the executive aspects of the task. In other words, they had difficulty by impulsively responding without reference to the clue indicating the correct stimulus.

Because observations of individuals with prefrontal lobe lesions or ablations manifest no clear dysfunction in motor movement, auditory, visual, or tactile disturbance (Luria, 1966), the prefrontal lobes were given an insignificant role in the development of brain organization theory (Goldberg, 2001). While no clear-cut sensory or motility deficits were observed, animals with prefrontal lobe extirpation were definitely impaired. They demonstrated purposeless behavior and were impaired in goal-directed action (Luria, 1966).

With the development of neuroimaging techniques in the 1990s it has been established that the frontal lobes are activated in nearly all cognitive activity and are thus hardly silent (Burgess, 2013).

3.

HISTORY OF HUMAN RESEARCH

Introduction

Clinical observations of *frontal lobe humans* – a term used for individuals with frontal lobe lesions – resulted in conceptualizing similar impairments as those seen in animals. These patients demonstrated no disturbance of gnosis, speech, or praxis, but complex functioning was impaired (Luria, 1966). They were able to carry out habitual behavior, but planning complex purposive action was impaired. They also demonstrated a lack of motivation to initiate action and became inactive (Luria, 1966). Moreover, they seemed to have lost the ability to evaluate their behavior in service of achieving a goal (Luria, 1966).

Human frontal lobe patients also demonstrated dysfunction in ceasing a behavior that no longer had utility in achieving a goal, but would instead persist in acting in a way that no longer produced the desired outcome (Luria, 1966). Interestingly, these patients made no attempt to modify the ineffective behavior and demonstrated no distress about continued failure. In fact, they demonstrated indifference or even euphoria, presumably due to losing the ability to be critical of the result of their ineffective behavior (Luria, 1966).

These observations led neurologists in the mid-20th century to conceptualize the frontal lobes as an "association zone" (Luria, 1966, p. 247) involved in complex psychological functions, making them difficult to describe with physiological language (Fulton, 1943). Subsequently, a combination of biological, psychological, and social interplay became the cornerstone of Lurian theory of brain organization (Glozman, 2007).

Phineas Gage

The history of the study of clinical neuropsychology in humans harkens back to Harlow's (1868) observations of the survivor of a freak accident. Phineas Gage sustained massive damage to his frontal lobes; specifically, his left orbitomedial prefrontal cortex was destroyed when a tamping iron was launched through his skull (Gould & Pyle, 1896). The projectile was 3 feet, 7 inches long, 1.25 inches in diameter, weighed 13.25 pounds, and was pointed on one end.

The pointed end entered Gage's head under his left zygomatic arch and fractured portions of the sphenoid bone. It then penetrated the left orbit and passed through the left anterior cerebrum. The iron proceeded through the coronal and sagittal sutures breaking the frontal and parietal bones. A considerable amount of brain matter was destroyed in the path of the object and his left eye ended up pushed forward almost half of its diameter. Immediately following the horrendous accident, Gage momentarily convulsed, after having been thrown backward. He was taken to a nearby hotel for treatment and maintained some level of consciousness through the whole ordeal.

With minor complications, such as a period of delirium and the loss of vision in his left eye, Gage demonstrated no paresis, aphasia, or loss of bodily function with the exception of his vision (Harlow, 1868). Although initially thought to have made a full recovery, Mr. Gage underwent profound personality changes subsequent to his injuries (Siddiqui et al., 2008). Prior to the accident, Gage was described as smart, shrewd, and capable of executing goal-directed behavior (Gould & Pyle, 1896). Subsequent to his injuries, "The equilibrium or balance, so to speak, between his intellectual faculty and animal propensities, seems to have been destroyed" (Harlow, 1868, pp. 339-340).

The case of Gage in conjunction with the other work in the field such as that of Paul Broca – a French psycholinguist in the 19th century who developed an understanding of language production as correlated to the frontal cortex – set the understanding of brain-behavior relationships on a new course (Miller, 2007). Prior to Broca's identification of speech being associated with the base of the third convolution in the left hemisphere, no serious challenges to equipotentiality in the cerebrum existed (Boring, 1957). Development of modern theories of human neuropsychological functioning in the frontal lobes was also influenced by clinical observations of changes in the behavior of patients with frontal lobe tumors or injury (Luria, 1966).

Today it is generally agreed upon in the field of neuropsychology that localization of function does exist at some level and particular brain areas are correlated to specific functions, at least in part. However, the assumption that a particular brain area is damaged if certain dysfunctional behaviors are observed breaks down when applied to the frontal lobes. If someone is blind we can make assumptions about the areas of the brain that may be impaired. If someone is demonstrating "frontal" dysfunction we cannot assume with certainty that it is attributable in total or in part to the frontal areas.

Difficulties in Methodology

Single Case Studies. While the case of Phineas Gage is the landmark case of benefiting from behavioral observations, its scientific validity is questionable given the pervasive destruction to brain areas in addition to the left orbitomedial frontal cortex (Damasio, Grabowski, Frank, Galaburda, & Damasio 1994; Fuster, 2008). However, the tragedies of both World Wars as well as the Vietnam War did provide patients with more discrete damage to the frontal lobes for study (Glozman, 2007; Luria 1966; Stuss & Benson, 1986). Other sources of data included those with frontal lobe tumors and those who had undergone lobectomy for tumors or epileptic seizures (Milner, 1964). With the introduction of psychosurgery in the 1930s, another source of information emerged, although this information needs to be viewed within the context of preexisting conditions such as personality and thought disorders and variable response to treatment (Fuster, 2008; Stuss & Benson, 1986).

Evaluation of the extensive research on the frontal lobes using observational methods is problematic due to variability of measured behaviors as well as idiosyncratic lesions (Fuster, 2008; Stuss & Benson, 1986). Moreover, these methods assume that brain function without the input of frontal and prefrontal areas would simply manifest deficits in functioning associated with those areas (Fuster, 2008). Rather, when ablation procedures are enacted, an adjustment of the remaining brain areas occurs, making post-ablation behavior difficult to interpret as correlated to specific brain areas (Fuster, 2008). Despite the difficulty in studying large numbers of individuals or groups of individuals with well-defined frontal lesions (Stuss & Alexander, 2000), the construct of the executive functions as correlating to frontal lobe dysfunction has utility, but requires clarification.

Egas Moniz

Another line of research inspired by the work of Jacobsen – and his colleague Fulton – was that of Egas Moniz (Kolb & Whishaw, 2009; Tierney, 2000). During the Second International Neurology Congress in 1935, Jacobsen noted that one of the chimpanzees, a particularly neurotic animal who had received frontal lobe ablations, was observed to be more relaxed post-surgery.

Prior to the removal of both of her frontal lobes, the chimpanzee, Becky, would at times refuse to enter the testing environment and would become enraged if she made an error and was denied the food reinforcer (Tierney, 2000). Post-surgery, she was docile and displayed no frustration despite making more errors than she did pre-surgery (Tierney, 2000). This led Moniz to the question of whether similar procedures would relieve behavioral problems in humans (Kolb & Whishaw, 2009). By 1936, Moniz was attempting to treat the symptomatology of mental illness by severing the neural connections between the frontal lobes and other areas of the brain (Tierney, 2000). This procedure quickly became routine and by the late 1940s was used to treat severely mentally ill patients who did not respond too less invasive interventions (Tierney, 2000).

Moniz (1937) honed and eventually coined his procedure

"leucotomy," after the instrument, a leucotome, used to sever neuronal tissue. Generally speaking, the instrument was inserted anterior to the tragus – the small pointed portion of the exterior of the ear immediately in front of the ear canal – and within three centimeters of the midsaggital line (Moniz, 1937). Incisions were made at depths of 4.5 cm, 3.5 cm, and 2.5 cm from the surface of the brain (Moniz, 1937). The leucotome was then reinserted at an "anteromesial direction" at a depth of 4 cm and three incisions were again made one inch apart toward the surface of the brain (Moniz, 1937, p. 1380).

By today's standards it is clear that the scientific evidence supporting Moniz's work was "flimsy at best" (Tierney, 2000, p. 22). For example, his studies lacked controls as well as rigorous outcome measurement (Tierney, 2000). Procedures were performed "blind," leading to great variation in brain damage among patients as well as documentation of serious side effects (Tierney, 2000). History has not looked kindly on this procedure or those involved in its implementation; but if it were solely detrimental, why would Moniz win a Nobel Prize for this work in 1949 (Tierney, 2000)?

At that time in history, treatment for the severely mentally ill included insulin-coma, electroconvulsive shock, and metrazol convulsion, all of which were associated with severe side effects, including death (Tierney, 2000). Moreover, conditions in asylums fostered desperation and hopelessness for patients and staff alike (Tierney, 2000). Prefrontal leucotomy offered hope that a modicum of peace may be attainable. By the end of the 1940s, psychosurgery had become a routine clinical procedure and was at the height of its popularity, engendering a Nobel

Prize in 1949. Simultaneously, articles were coming out describing observations of deleterious side effects from the procedure (Tierney, 2000). Such observations included amotivation, child-like behavior, flat affect, docility, and other dulling effects (Hoffman, 1949). By 1951, tens of thousands of persons had been lobotomized.

Ralph Reitan

Reitan and Davison (1974) expanded the work of Halstead (1947) in quantifying "biological intelligence" (Luria & Majovski, 1977, p. 960). As such, selection of subtests was based on a compilation of empirical data from individual testing cases. The following inferences were deemed important in the selection process: (a) level of ability reflected in observable behavior, (b) signs of specific pathognomonic deficits, (c) differences in scores and patterns of demonstrated ability, and (d) comparing how well the two sides of the body worked (Reitan & Davison, 1974). Initially the tests were chosen for their ability to distinguish among frontal lobe patients, patients with lesions in other brain areas, and healthy controls (Luria & Majovski, 1977).

In an attempt to remain objective, the neuropsychologist would rely solely on information from the testing session rather than be privy to patient information such as the presenting problem, medical history, or neuroradiological testing results (Luria & Davison, 1977; Reitan, 1964). The tests were meant to reflect various psychological abilities that had been associated with certain brain areas, but as such were not based in a theoretical organization of brain functioning (Luria & Davison, 1977). Reitan (1974) associated the use of "blind assessments" with increasing the validity of neuropsychological testing in its ability to identify areas of brain damage in the individual patient (p. 201).

Investigation into the correlation between neurological diagnosis and determination of diagnosis based on neuropsychological testing revealed that the location and type of lesion was statistically highly correlated between the neurologists and neuropsychologists (Reitan, 1964). However, when considering within-group differences, those identified with psychological testing who had focal cerebral vascular lesions, closed head injuries, and extrinsic lesions were problematic when identifying correct localization. Reitan (1964) highlights areas of this research to be interpreted with caution. For example, clinical opinion in the neuropsychologist condition was forced choice, thus limiting diagnostic options. Reitan describes being unimpressed with the results of his study, owing to his own experience of having made diagnostic decisions based on minimal psychological evidence. While he advocated for further study – with larger groups – of the utility of neuropsychological testing in diagnosis and treatment decisions, he posited that long-term and intense training would be needed to interpret such psychological information.

Brenda Milner

In the search for deficits correlated to the frontal lobes, Milner (1964) concurred with Hebb (1945) and Teuber (1959) that patients with frontal lobe lesions demonstrated less impairment on current assessment instruments of IQ than those with lesions in posterior areas. In an attempt to further understand frontal lobe deficits, Milner (1964) assessed sorting behavior in patients with surgical excisions using the Wisconsin Card

Sorting Test. Patients with dorsolateral prefrontal cortex excisions consistently demonstrated impairment in card sorting and thus were made an experimental group with all other participants with damage in other brain areas forming the control group.

In those with superior frontal lesions, it was observed that they had difficulty with perseveration (Milner, 1964). Participants would continue to place cards in a category long after having received feedback that this category was incorrect. While those with superior frontal lobe damage did worse postoperatively on perseverative errors, those with posterior lesions demonstrated the normal response of changing categories when given feedback of an error when tested after surgery. Interestingly, many of the dorsolateral patients would verbalize an understanding of the various categories and yet continue to place cards in the established category demonstrating an inability to utilize verbalized information to guide behavior – the dichotomy between what they say, or know, and what they do (Milner, 1964). This is in contrast to those with hippocampal lesions who also demonstrate difficulty learning, presumably due to defective memory (Milner, 1964).

Delayed Comparison. As with animals, research has demonstrated difficulty with time delays in man as well. When required to remember a stimulus and identify whether a second stimulus is the same or different after a temporal delay, persons with frontal lobe lesions struggle (Milner, 1964). Frontal lobe patients do not have trouble discriminating between stimuli of varying sensory modalities when presented immediately after each other, but when a time delay is introduced, errors increase with the increase in time between stimuli (Milner, 1964). Having ruled out memory problems given good performance on tests of memory, Milner posits an inability to concentrate only on the pre-delay stimulus to the exclusion of previous trials' stimuli. This interpretation was consistent with other observations of frontal lobe behavior.

Word Fluency. One area in which there is a differentiation of which frontal lobe hemisphere is impacted is in word fluency. Patients with left hemisphere prefrontal lobe lesions in which Broca's area is spared evidence no lasting dysphasia; however, spontaneous speech is negatively impacted (related to transcortical motor aphasia, Milner, 1964). When required to generate various words beginning with a certain letter under a time constraint, left inferior frontal patients demonstrate deficits not seen in those with right superior frontal or left temporal lesions (Milner, 1964). Those with left temporal dysfunction struggled with recalling word pairs and verbal information, especially after a delay. Moreover, patients with right frontal damage did not struggle on verbal tasks, but as mentioned above showed impairment in sorting tasks. The double dissociation of these findings was thought to increase the validity of the conclusion that these areas are associated with their respective functions (Milner, 1964).

4.

THEORIES

Modern theories of prefrontal function could be said to have started with those of Alexandra Luria, who might be considered the father of modern neuropsychology. Much of his work was not available outside of Russia until the translations became available. Then Muriel Lezak made great contributions in both the theory and application of neuropsychological testing. Then was Edith Kaplan who emphasized the information processing in understanding the brain, rather than the content of what the various areas were involved in. The work of Elkhonon Goldberg, a student of Luria's, made the prefrontal areas comprehensible to many clinicians. Let us now follow a path in the development of theories of prefrontal functioning.

Luria's Theory of Human Frontal Lobe Functioning

Dissatisfied with the scientific explanation that the brain was organized as a "series of passively responding devices, whose work was entirely determined by *past* experience," Luria (1973) offered his own understanding (p. 13). Utilizing then current scientific information, Luria developed an understanding of frontal lobe function as integrative in nature. Basically, the frontal lobes imbue sensory input with meaning and develop a "provisional basis of action" (Luria, 1966, p. 248). Moreover, the development of complex behavioral responses is also within the purview of the frontal lobes.

Functional systems theory – Luria's conceptualization – seems based in the ideas of Krol (1912, as cited in Glozman, 2007), who posited that different brain systems are simultaneously integrated and differentiated when engaged in various functions. Luria's conceptualization is also considered cybernetic or systemic in epistemology (Christensen, 1996), a result of various brain regions linked together that specialize in aspects of functioning (Luria, 1973). Within each region, aspects of functioning are arranged in a hierarchy and there is flexible interaction between areas that are modified based on the person's current interaction with the environment (Christensen, 1996). Conscious activity requires the involvement of all three units of function for successful performance of an action (Luria, 1973). Within the anterior and posterior cerebral units, a hierarchical organization of cortical zones was posited. Flexibility in the interaction between and among units allows for development and the restructuring of abilities after injury (Luria, 1973).

Maintaining Arousal. Luria (1973) describes the first unit of function as "regulating tone or waking" (p. 43). In order for man to receive and process information, he must be awake with an "optimal level of cortical tone" (Luria, 1973, p. 44). The area of the brain found to help regulate the balance between excitation and inhibition lies below the cortex in the brain stem and subcortex (Luria, 1973). Areas of the brain involved in this unit include the brain stem as well as the diencephalon and the medial portions of the cortex (Luria, 1973). This unit obeys a "law of strength" in which biologically salient events produce a strong response while weaker stimuli evoke weaker responses (Luria, 1973). The system as a whole works as a sort of neural net, with the ability to respond to stimuli with gradations of intensity (Luria, 1973). However, afferent and efferent connections exist, with the cortex providing information about the intensity of tone. They are also regulated by input from the higher areas (Luria, 1973).

Receiving, Analyzing, and Storing Information. Unlike the first unit, which does not have direct contact with receiving or processing external information, the second functional unit is primarily concerned with "obtaining, processing and storing information arriving from the outside world" (Luria, 1973, p. 43). Location of this system includes the posterior portions of the lateral regions of the neocortex – the occipital, temporal, and parietal regions (Luria, 1973, Figure 2.1). A very small percentage of cells in the primary areas of the secondary unit are organized as a non-specific neuronal network interested in maintaining tone as in the first unit (Luria, 1973). The second unit consists mostly of "isolated neurons," which obey an all-or-nothing law (Luria, 1973, p. 67). In other words, some of the cells in this unit receive discrete sensory input and relay it to other groups of neurons (Luria, 1973).

Figure 2.1

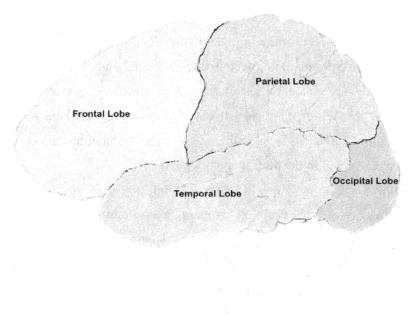

Major divisions of the cortical surface area of the human brain.

Each of the primary areas specializes in processing certain types of stimuli such as auditory in the temporal lobe, vision in the occipital lobe, and kinesthetic sensation in the parietal lobe (Luria, 1973). In essence, the primary or projection area of the second unit receives information and organizes it into elemental components.

Within the secondary portion of the secondary unit there are multidimensional cells that respond to various types of stimuli within a given modality (Luria, 1973). Short axon cells in layers II and III seem designed to synthesize afferent information from layer IV (Luria, 1973). This is where the various components are synthesized into a functional organization, a process that Luria (1973) refers to as gnostic (p. 74).

Planning and Organizing Behavior. The third functional unit specializes in "programming, regulating and verifying mental activity" (Luria, 1973, p. 43)/ The tertiary zones of the third unit consist of overlapping zones of neurons that work in concert to analyze sensory information (Luria, 1973). It is these functions that play an "executive" role that Luria tied to the prefrontal cortex (Ardila, 2008).

These integrative zones for the second unit are located at the boundaries between the occipital, temporal, and inferior parietal region of the post-central cortex (Luria, 1973). This is where sensory information is transmuted from sensory representations to a synthesized symbolic whole. The integrative zones, or tertiary areas, for the third zone, the prefrontal areas, lie anterior to the primary and secondary motor areas. In addition they lie in the orbital and midline regions of the frontal lobes as well as the anterior cingulate area.

Figure 2.2

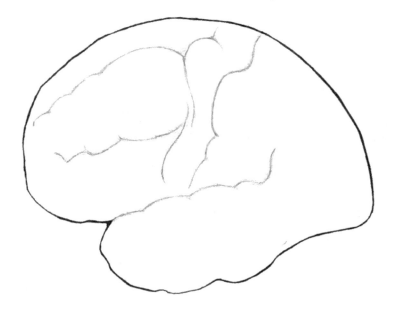

Lateral surface divisions with major sulci and gyri.

Luria's view of brain organization conceptualized overlapping functional systems that worked together in varying combinations to accomplish tasks (Korkman, 1999). While Luria's assessment of dysfunction strove to evaluate the component parts of more complex processes, determining specific deficits was difficult due to the potential involvement of many sub-processes (Korkman, 1999). Thus, an organizational theory to guide findings of what underlies the deficit was needed, which was provided in the development of "syndrome analysis" (Korkman, 1999, p. 90). Finding the primary reason for deficits as well as the secondary manifestations of the etiology of the deficit was paramount in this approach (Glozman, 2007). In other words, we should look at the cluster of associated primary deficits and deficits secondary to the primary ones when differentiating dysfunction.

Application of the Theory

Assessment of these methods began with an initial screening of various functions, such as attention, motor, and memory, and a determination of the primary cause of a cluster of symptoms was made (Glozman, 2007). These hypotheses were formed based on demonstrated difficulties with screening tasks, which informed areas that were subjected to more in-depth assessment. This paradigm of hypothesis testing was individual to the patient and his or her presenting problems (Korkman, 1999). Next, the assessor determined which functions were preserved, and tailored a rehabilitation regimen based on the patient's strengths that attempted to build new networks to restore the function (Glozman, 2007).

Luria believed that if the term "function" referred to the localization of specific function to cerebral tissue, the total functional system cannot be localized to a specific area, but must be a distributed network of coordinating areas (Christensen, 2009). Thus, when attempting to localize lesions in people, neuropsychologists need to analyze the disturbance of higher level cortical processes and their interactions, rather than simply identify that a defect does indeed exist (Christensen, 2009).

Figure 2.3

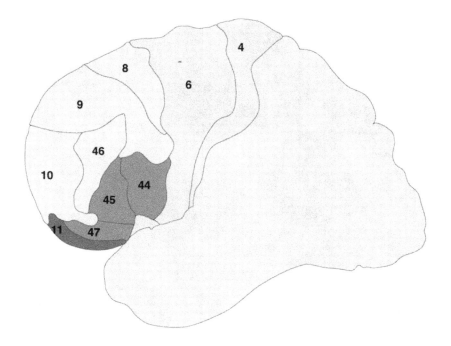

*Lateral view of cortical surface areas of frontal lobes delineated by
Brodmann's areas.*

Luria's conceptual organization of the frontal lobes has undergone
modification through time. Stuss and Benson (1986) reworked Luria's
classification system by positing that the prefrontal cortex was composed
of three major areas. These areas consist of the orbitofrontal or basilar-
orbital, cingulate or medial, and dorsolateral (Miller & Cummings, 2007;
Stuss & Benson, 1986) (Figures 2.3 to 2.5).

Figure 2.4

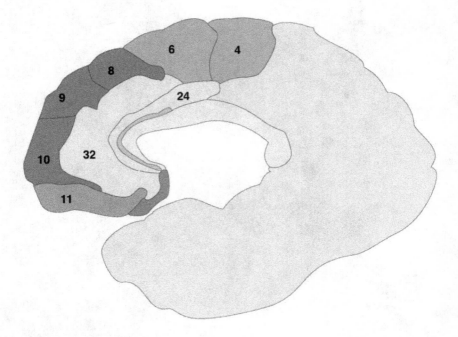

The medial surface area.

Fuster (2008) has incorporated modern neuroscience with Lurian thinking and believes that a cohesive theory is needed to understand various cognitive abilities as separate distributed neural substrates. An important component of Fuster's theory is that neuronal networks are physiologically consistent, but the cognitive processes that use the networks are variable.

Figure 2.5

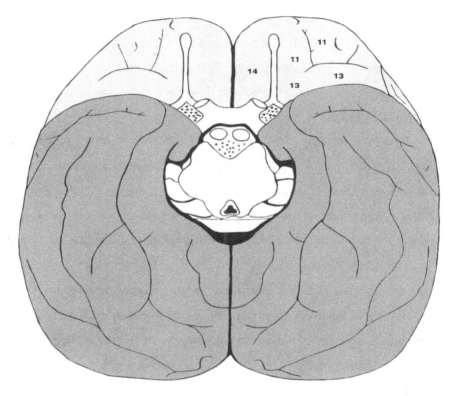

Orbital surface area of the frontal lobes.

Other theories based on the work of Luria include Goldberg and Costa (1981), who add hemispheric specialization to the flexibility of the functional systems posited by Luria. Christensen and Luria (1975) attempted to translate Luria's theory and methods into clinical application. Since that time, the sphere of Luria's theoretical influence has reached German, Spanish, Japanese, and Zulu neuroscientists (Christensen, 2009).

In the United States, the theory was standardized and applied to the Luria Nebraska Neuropsychological Battery (Golden, Hammeke, & Purisch, 1978), which soon surpassed the original publication in popularity. American scientists felt this battery was theoretically consistent, easily administered, flexible, and very thorough (Kolb & Whishaw, 1990).

However, criticism of the battery cited subjective scoring, the extensive amount of training needed to interpret the results, and no validation studies (Christensen, Goldberg, & Bougakov, 2009). Critics of Luria's (1966) methodology also note Luria's resistance to increasing the reliability of his assessment approach through operationalization (Adams, 1980). Luria's resistance to standardization of his methods stemmed from concern that unqualified personnel might misuse testing in lieu of developing a nuanced understanding of neuropsychological principles, which is a concern of all neuropsychologists who reveal their methods (Adams, 1980).

Further, critics of Lurian methodology expressed concern regarding the heavy reliance on pathognomonic signs of brain pathology (Reitan, 1974). The methodology of identifying pathognomonic signs, while flexible in nature, was reliant on the subjective interpretation of the neuropsychologist and vulnerable to "false negative errors" (Adams, 1980, p. 512). The inconsistency among patients increases the opportunity for exacerbation of the weaknesses of the pathognomonic method; namely, lack of reliability and objective measurement (Adams, 1980).

This in essence would negate the contributions of neuropsychology to behavioral neuroscience (Adams, 1980).

Even so, study of groups of people with clusters of symptomatology will help to determine anomalous presentations from more common neuropsychological difficulty (Bishop, 1997), which will in turn inform neuropsychological theory from a process perspective. Despite resistance to Luria's approach to neuropsychology, his critics opined that his approach opened a new way to understand the interrelationships and nature of dysfunction rather than measuring skills (Reitan, 1976).

Lezak's Theory of Human Frontal Lobe Functioning

Conceptualization of executive functions according to Lezak, Howieson, Bigler, and Tranel (2012), incorporates the following four subcomponents: (a) volition, (b) planning and decision-making, (c) purposive action, and (d) effective performance. Each component is deemed necessary to facilitate appropriate and effective adult conduct within our societal constructs (Lezak et al., 2012). According to this line of thinking, cognitive functioning and executive functioning can be differentiated by the types of questions that we ask about these areas. When considering executive function, the questions address *how* a behavior will be engaged, while cognitive questions lean towards *what* and *how much* do you know or do (Lezak, 1983). So the question becomes, "How do these premises inform the construct of executive function?" To begin, we will first consider the subcomponents that make up executive functions as defined by Lezak.

Volition. The ability to determine one's needs or wants, and then to derive a plan of action to attain such goals using intentional behavior, sums up the construct of volition (Lezak et al., 2012). Further, the ability to project the need or desire into the future is a cornerstone of this ability.

An important precursor to volition is the motivation to initiate activity (Lezak et al., 2012), which is necessary to determine and plan attainment of the future goal. Deficits in self-initiation of behavior are thought to be impacted by disruption of affective and cognitive processes that accompany lesions in the frontolimbic or frontal/subcortical circuitry, which is also seen in frontal lobe dementia (Barrett, 2010; Stuss, Van Reekum, & Murphy, 2000). According to Lezak, those lacking in this ability may very well just not think of anything to do – or may require detailed instructions to follow through with – even simple behavior such as eating with utensils (2012).

Despite potentially having considerable ability to perform complex actions, those with impaired volition are unable to engage in abstract or long-term goals because they are unlikely to initiate engagement in new activities (Lezak et al., 2012). Interestingly, routine and previously learned activity is usually preserved (Lezak et al., 2012).

Another component necessary for successful volition is self-awareness, which can be broken down into social awareness, physical awareness, and awareness of self and others (Lezak et al., 2012). It is not unusual for those with moderate to severe brain damage to demonstrate dysfunction in one or more of these areas (Bach & David, 2006 as cited by Lezak et al., 2012).

Planning and Decision-making. Generally speaking, planning is the ability to identify and organize the skills and resources needed to accomplish a goal or fulfill an intention (Lezak et al., 2012). Many component abilities are necessary for successful planning. One such component requires the ability to conceptualize prospective changes from the current situation. Also, the ability to understand the environment and one's relationship to the environment objectively is needed for planning (Lezak et al., 2012). Without being able to engage in an "abstract attitude" and see the big picture, those with frontal lobe damage interpret objects, experience, and behavior in concrete and literal ways (p. 99). This deficit impairs the ability to engage in foresight, goal-directed behavior, and planning.

Other abilities vital to planning include being able to produce various alternative scenarios and solutions, consider the alternatives and select a choice, and organize tasks in a hierarchical order to create a structure or plan with direction (Lezak et al., 2012). Being able to remember the plan and to inhibit irrelevant or tangential impulses also help keep the person on track to accomplishing the goal. Attention is another needed ability to sustain goal-directed behavior. If one or more of these abilities is impaired, planning and decision-making are compromised (Lezak et al., 2012).

Purposive Action. Transitioning a plan into action requires a person to be able to initiate, switch actions, maintain an action, and to be able to stop actions in an organized fashion (Lezak et al., 2012). Dysfunctional programming of behavior can preclude reasonably planned behavior despite preserved motivation, knowledge, or high levels of skill (Lezak et al., 2012). Unfortunately, difficulty in programming behavior does not impede impulsive actions, which do an end-run around planning and action sequence processes (Lezak et al., 2012). In this way, an important differentiation is made between impulsive and deliberately chosen action.

Purposive action is required for new and non-routine behaviors, but is not important for previously overlearned and familiar tasks. Thus, damage to the brain, especially the frontal lobes, is less likely to impact routine and automatic actions despite the level of complexity for example, getting on and riding a bicycle (Shallice, 1982). People with difficulty in programming action may show great disparity between what they say they will or can do and their actual behavior (Lezak et al., 2012).

Difficulties may be apparent with large-scale purposive behavior as well as the fine-tuning of "discrete intentional acts" (Lezak et al., 2012, p. 684). People with difficulties with discrete actions may also struggle with switching actions, should the context of the situation call for such changes in behavior (Pontius & Yudowitz, 1980). Evidence suggests that criminals with frontal lobe dysfunction have difficulty switching "the principle action" when the circumstances of the situation require such changes (Pontius & Yudowitz, 1980, p. 111).

Effective Performance. Performing effectively relies on a person's ability to monitor the results of the action, initiate corrective measures if needed, modulate the tempo and intensity of the action, and monitor other qualitative aspects of behavioral success or failure (Lezak et al., 2012). Unsuccessful and erratic behaviors are not unusual in frontal brain-damaged persons because many different types of damage can cause difficulty with self-regulation, self-monitoring, and self-correction (Lezak et al., 2012).

Impairments in executive functioning manifest globally and can render an otherwise capable person unable to maintain social relationships, to engage in purposive work, or to live independently despite preserved knowledge and considerable skill (Lezak et al., 2012). When executive functioning fails to work, it can also compromise cognitive functioning ability directly through poor planning, defective monitoring of the result of behavior, initiating engagement in the behavior, or ineffective strategies (Lezak et al., 2012).

An example of executive dysfunction disabling an otherwise functioning individual is a lawyer who sustained trauma to the prefrontal cortex. Her postmorbid intellectual score was 128, she had a great fund of knowledge, and yet she had to live in a controlled environment (board and care) because the trauma rendered her unable to live safely alone. She was unable to remember to turn off the stove, pay bills on time, act appropriately in social or work situations, or plan and organize to keep her environment running smoothly.

Lezak et al. (2012) propose that executive dysfunction can arise from trauma to parts of the brain other than the prefrontal areas. Most would probably agree that the subcortical areas within the prefrontal lobes, including some of those involved in the extrapyramidal systems, are involved in executive functioning, and it is the prefrontal areas which are critical, not just the cortex itself. This would extend along the midline to the anterior cingulate cortex. However, there are problems when people try to include areas unrelated to the prefrontal ones.

The Problem with Content-Dependent Theory. Volition, as described by Lezak, contains the ability to determine, plan, and organize intention. This is in accordance with the definition of executive function as including the ability to consider all of the available information, and to choose and plan goal-directed behavior before engaging in a behavioral output (Soper et al., 2008). There is general agreement in the field that these types of "executive" tasks mainly involve the frontal areas. However, as defined by Lezak, volition includes other constructs that may involve the frontal lobes, but are not executive in nature. In spite of this, non-executive abilities are subsumed under the umbrella of volition. For example, Lezak contends that motivation is an important precursor for volition. Many would agree that this is true, but motivation can be impaired by myriad etiologies and is not itself executive in nature.

Loss of motivation due to impairment of emotion, intellect, or level of consciousness is clinically a symptom of apathy (Marin, 1991). Apathy can arise from abulia or anergia (Lezak et al., 2012), and although both of these can be called frontal lobe functions, one would hardly call them executive functions. The difficulty in abulia is not an inability to process all of the available information and choose an action, but rather an inability to will the self into action, to produce the most appropriate motor output (Barrett, 1991).

Taking the example of volition, it is clear that inclusion of constructs that are non-executive – such as motivation – in the definition of a subcomponent of executive function simply creates a label for an observation. In other words, the content of the observed deficit is used to explain the observed difficulty. When applied to the frontal areas, this approach requires more complex ideas and theories to describe phenomena. Simply describing outcome measures without addressing how the information is being processed is not adequate. In addition, using this procedure compromises identification of which area a person is struggling with.

When dealing with areas of the brain that have more discrete functioning, such as sensory or motor areas, measurement of observed deficits provides useful information regarding pathology and treatment. Unfortunately, when solely applying this strategy to the prefrontal areas the resultant information becomes less useful. Due to the inconsistency of the observed deficits and the idiosyncratic nature of information processing (Luria, 1976), assessing outcome behavior is informative, but not sufficient when discussing the functions of the frontal lobes.

Many of the tasks addressed by Lezak, within the construct of planning and decision-making, can be described as executive when using the definition being described in this argument. Skills such as fluency of thinking, selection of a goal, and organizing behavioral output are all components of considering all of the available information prior to acting.

The concept of attention is difficult, for it is one word with many meanings in neuropsychology. An extensive discussion is beyond what we want to do here, but a few examples will serve. A person may be very tired and not attending to many areas of his environment. Due to this he may make errors in behavior. This is not an executive dysfunction, but a sensory one. Another person may not attend to all the information she or he has, but may jump to a behavior prior to processing all the available information. This would be a result of an executive deficit.

With respect to the construct of effective performance, people with pathological inertia may understand and even describe errors in their actions and yet be unable to do anything to correct their actions (Lezak et al., 2012). For example, in the Block Design subtest, the person is able to see the errors made, but cannot figure out how to correct them. The task is compromised not from an inability to see that the behavior is ineffective, but rather from dysfunction in planning and implementing an effective resolution to the problem. Thus, in this example we can further identify that the problem does not lie in the sensory or attentional aspects of the task, but rather with the executive aspects. These are different impairments even though the resultant behavior is similar. Without a way to increase understanding of the basis of how the person is dysfunctional, neuropsychological assessment is limited to confirmation that a problem does indeed exist.

Executive functions control and regulate information from other parts of the brain, and it is possible that trauma to other areas could mimic executive dysfunction, causing people to fail tasks that have been labeled "executive" or "prefrontal" in nature. For example, trauma to many areas can cause someone to fail the Wisconsin Card Sort Task, the Category Test, and Trail Making Test B. However, just because they failed "executive" tasks does not mean there is an executive dysfunction. The dysfunction should be relegated to the sensory, attentional, emotional, or whatever domains are disrupted and causing the deficits in performance. Damage to limbic structures can cause dysfunctional behavior that mimics executive dysfunction, but the etiology is quite different. The emotional aspect itself is disrupted, and not the organization of this information to direct motor movement. Further discussion along these lines requires introduction of the contributions of Edith Kaplan.

Process Approach of Edith Kaplan

Edith Kaplan developed the Boston Process Approach in part in an effort to ameliorate reliance on a single total achievement score (Possin & Kramer, 2013). She advocates for paying attention to not only how many, but when people make errors during neuropsychological testing, and what kinds of errors they make. Analyzing errors adds valuable information when trying to differentiate executive from non-executive errors and the underlying neuroanatomical substrates (Possin & Kramer, 2013). The errors often can be very informative about what is going wrong, and why. Certain types of errors, such as rule violations or repeated errors, are thought to be more indicative of executive (frontal lobe) information-processing dysfunction. For example, the idea is that a rule violation or repetitive errors may indicate trouble with working memory (Possin & Kramer, 2013). Thus, errors are analyzed and compared to normative processing to determine the nature of the dysfunction.

Delis, Kaplan, and Kramer (2001) sought to address the difficulties with fractionating how people fail "tests of executive function" between executive and non-executive reasons. They have built Kaplan's theory into the Delis Kaplan Executive Function System (D-KEFS), in which tests are designed specifically to isolate "lower" (e.g., sensory processing) cognitive functions from executive functions. This approach is designed to address the difficulties inherent in interpreting one test score which is the result of multiple functional abilities (Delis et al., 2001). Many tests of executive functioning assess other non-executive processes as well, such as color discrimination.

Toward this goal, various abilities, executive and non-executive, have been operationally defined in an effort to tease them apart. This approach is definitely a valiant attempt to consider and fractionate the various abilities needed for the specific problem solving and to identify the appropriate construct of executive function. They are trying to resolve the fundamental problem of identification of dysfunctional executive functioning and what causes a failure on executive function tests, which at times can be failed for non-executive reasons. Thus, clarity regarding the construct of executive function as the ability to consider all of the available information prior to choosing a behavioral response would help differentiate prefrontal from more posterior, sensory, non-executive dysfunction.

Kaplan is credited with increasing the ability to differentiate executive functioning using behavioral markers elicited by the D-KEFS (Moes, Duncanson, & Armengol, 2013). For example, in the Stroop paradigm, Kaplan identified that a fourth condition of the test had utility to identify difficulty with switching sets. Thus, failure on that portion of the test could lead to conclusions that a person is deficient with the executive aspects of the test due to a set-shifting problem. Although increasingly fractionated, this is the same line of logic in which failure on a test is attributed to a single construct, as if there is only one reason that a person could fail the task. This is what investigators such as Walsh (1985) and others have been arguing against for decades.

For example, many clinicians have noticed that those with inferotemporal lesions, and even monkeys with pulvinar lesions (Soper, 1982), fail the Wisconsin Card Sort Test, not for executive function reasons, but for sensory processing reasons. The end result is still a failure but, as Walsh (1985) says, such tests are complex, and there are many reasons for failing them.

While difficulty with a test of executive function may provide a piece of information to further investigate an area of functioning, it does not by itself determine how or why the person fails the task. For example, some research has found correlations between higher repetition errors on design fluency tasks in patients with the behavioral variant of frontotemporal dementia (bvFTD; Possin et al., 2012). Moreover, the total number of correct designs did not differentiate the bvFTD group from groups with other types of dementia. The bvFTD group, which made the higher repetition error rate, also had atrophy in anterior areas, but not posterior areas (Possin et al., 2012). However, not all people with atrophy in the anterior areas make these types of errors, and some without atrophy do.

Caution is indicated regarding clinical interpretation of analyzing error patterns on the D-KEFS (Possin & Kramer, 2013). Rather, this information should be considered within the context of multiple tests and observations, to aid determination of how a person is making mistakes in information processing when interpreting test results.

A relatively recent finding by Soper addresses another problem in this area, and is related to process analysis. Soper noticed that in the clinic many individuals of high intelligence who obviously have frontal trauma do not do poorly on many "tasks of executive function." Although in life and on some tasks they show obvious impairment due to executive dysfunction, on many other tasks there is no such difficulty. The suggested conclusion is that for such individuals the problems are so easy that they can be solved either totally through non-frontal (non-executive) processing or with minimal such processing. For example, on the Trail Making Test B, alternating between numbers and letters does not involve much "problem solving" ability because it is so easy for such highly intelligent people. Similarly the requirements for the Wisconsin Card Sort Task, called the "gold standard of executive-function tests" (Delis et al., 2001), can be so easy for very intelligent individuals that even those with serious frontal compromise can succeed without difficulty. Obviously, here we have an example of solving this problem through non-frontal, non-executive, means. Although the sensory information is processed, all the information available does not need to be organized to produce the appropriate motor response. Simple sensory processing is sufficient in this case. The person just "sees" or appreciates the solution, he or she does not have to work it out, to solve it.

The contribution resulting from the Kaplan process approach is substantial, and has permitted us to look more in the correct direction of finding and identifying the process of executive dysfunction in our patients. Once it was believed that if someone was not deficient on an "executive functioning task," such as verbal fluency, they could not have trauma to the executive portions of the brain. Now we know how untrue such a statement is.

However, Delis et al. (2001) discuss the skills needed for their various tasks used in their battery. For example, they say that Trails B skills include visual scanning, number sequencing, letter sequencing, and motor speed (p. 4). These are all content descriptions and do not address the process involved. For example, visual scanning takes into account where the scan has been, what the conditions are for the next item to be looked at, and the pathway to get to that target, organizing this information, and then producing the motor movement – the scan – that is most appropriate. One can see why individuals with executive deficits would have difficulty with the Picture Completion subtests of many of the Wechsler tests.

When discussing their Sorting Task, Delis et al. (2001) talk about the higher-level skills (versus the lower-level skills of sensory and similar processing) needed, such as initiation of problem-solving behavior, verbal concept-formation skills, nonverbal concept-formation skills, transfer of concepts into action, abstract expression of conceptual relationships, flexibility of thinking, and flexibility of behavioral response. These skills refer more to goals or descriptions of what is to be done rather than to the processes involved.

Despite these last few comments, the Kaplan process approach has really helped us come to understand the process of thinking that is disrupted by brain trauma, rather than just what the person can and cannot do.

Goldberg and Soper Theory of Frontal Lobe Functioning

Introduction. Goldberg (2001, 2009) and Soper (Soper et al., 2008) adhere to the understanding of executive function as a phenomenon of the prefrontal cortex despite various opposition in the field. It is clear that difficulty ensues when pathology is observed because there is no clinical condition that is easily limited to dysfunction solely in the frontal lobes (Stuss & Alexander, 2000). This confusion has a long history, as initial investigators thought of the frontal lobes as "the silent lobes" because they are not easily correlated to any single function (Goldberg, 2001, p. 24). Those with frontal lobe dysfunction or significant ablation may retain many abilities such as language, object recognition, memory, and mobility; however, "like a leaderless army, cognition disintegrates and ultimately collapses with the loss of the frontal lobes" (Goldberg, 2001, p. 23).

Given the profuse connections between the frontal lobes and other areas of the brain, the prefrontal areas are ideally positioned to integrate and coordinate the work of other brain areas (Goldberg, 2009). Moreover, the prefrontal areas are singularly suited to combine input from other brain areas to create, for example, never observed associated ideas (Goldberg, 2009). For example, the frontal lobes are not needed to form a mental representation of a horse or a man, but they are needed to form a mental image of a combination of the two – namely a centaur.

This unique ability and position in the brain allows the prefrontal areas to receive all of the available information that is salient to the task at hand, to analyze it prospectively, and to choose an appropriate behavioral response (Soper et al., 2008). It also provides an explanation as to why people with frontal lobe dysfunction tend to "act before they take everything relevant into account" (Soper et al., 2008, p. 698). This line of thinking also sheds light on the clinically confusing phenomenon of inconsistent deficits between and within patients. If the executive task is to utilize available information in order to choose, plan, and organize a response, it makes sense that – depending on what information is processed – in any given situation the behavioral output will vary. At times a person may exhibit dysfunction (get on the wrong train at the station), while at other times function perfectly fine (get on the correct train at the station).

Given the leadership position and executive function of the prefrontal areas, damage or disease processes anywhere in the brain may emerge in difficulty with executive "tasks" (Goldberg, 2009). This is not to say that the observed dysfunction is executive in nature, but rather that the executive task is compromised for a variety of reasons. The executive aspects of the frontal lobes do not directly support cognitive function, but rather provide an organization of cognitive processes (Goldberg & Bougakov, 2000). Poetically speaking, "Injury to the leader will disrupt the activities of many units in the field, producing remote effects. Equally, the functions of the leadership will be disrupted if the lines of communication from the front to the leader are cut off" (Goldberg, 2009, p. 149).

Physiological evidence supports the vulnerability of the frontal lobes, given their profuse connectedness throughout the brain. Measurements of regional cerebral blood flow (rCBF) demonstrated that, irrespective of the location of a tumor in the brain, blood flow to the frontal lobes was particularly disrupted (Lilja et al., 1992). Other studies have shown that cerebral blood flow is disrupted in the frontal lobes in people who are depressed (Nobler et al., 1994), receive electroconvulsive therapy (in the temporal lobes; Risberg, 1980), or were given a cholinergic antagonist (Horner, Prohovnik, Smith, & Lucas, 1988). Thus, the frontal lobes are highly susceptible to dysfunction for any number of reasons and have a very low "functional breakdown threshold" (Goldberg, 2009, p. 150).

Language and Theoretical Development. Since the heyday of phrenology – a precursor to neuroscience – the field of neuropsychology has encountered a paradigmatic modification (Goldberg, 2009). As with other sciences, language must be developed that transcends everyday explanations of scientific principles. Whereas common language explains the world in discrete units that are apparent through observation, scientific language describes the world through organizing principles that are not readily apparent to the observer (Goldberg, 2009).

This is the state in which the science of the brain currently finds itself. Theorists such as Milner (1964), Reitan (1964), and Lezak et al. (2012) have done much to identify individual units of structure/function relationships as well as burgeoning constructs such as executive functions. However, these observations of outcome behavior, as correlated to damaged brain areas, are lacking theoretical underpinnings to explain the observations (Soper et al., 2008).

Given that the field makes the assumption that there is *some* relationship between brain structure and function, the morphology of the brain does aid neuroscientists in identifying gross correlations. For example, the occipital lobes are linked to processing visual information. However, the task for neuropsychology now becomes deciphering how these structures work in concert to produce the array of observable output (Goldberg, 2009). Developing cohesive language to describe these types of explanatory constructs – such as executive functions – will further development of neuropsychological theory.

Building on the Past. Building upon Luria's functional systems theory, Goldberg and Costa (1981) opined a conceptualization grounded in the idea that hemispheric specialization further explained information processing (Goldberg & Bougakov, 2009). In addition to functional systems working together to process information, hemispheric specialization is understood as having more to do with the novelty or familiarity of the information at hand (Goldberg & Bougakov, 2009). Novel information is primarily processed by the anterior regions and the right hemisphere in flexible rather than static or rigid ways (Goldberg, 2009). Once familiarity is established, the bulk of cognitive control for those tasks is taken over by the posterior and left hemispheric areas (Goldberg & Bougakov, 2009).

In an effort to assess how information is processed by an individual in everyday life – at times called ecological validity – Goldberg and associates designed a task called the Cognitive Bias Task (Goldberg, Harner, Lovell, Podell, & Riggio, 1994). Research using this more ambiguous task of selecting a preferred shape and color from an array of two colored shapes, and one target-colored shape demonstrated cognitive selection styles. While overlap did exist between sexes, a robust correlation between cognitive style and behavioral response was present. Males, on the one hand, gravitated toward context-dependent preferences, meaning they tended to prefer choices that were close to the target stimulus. Females, on the other hand, preferred context-independent stimuli such as a particular color or shape.

Gender differences in neuroscience have a history of being tip-toed around so as not to "poke the bear" and bring on an onslaught of fervent rejection. Thus, research has tended to treat people as "a homogenous mass," which reduces information about how people go about making decisions about what they experience (Goldberg, 2009, p. 126). Thus, neuroscience misses an opportunity to further understand how information is processed. Using the example of gender differences, historical research has focused on measuring who is better than whom on vertical cognitive skills where there is a correct response to the stimulus (Goldberg, 2009). There are many studies reporting evidence that males are better at spatial and mathematic skills, while females are superior at language skills. What is missing in these conclusions is measurement of more ambiguous or adaptive information processing. In our daily lives there is rarely a single correct response to a given situation. Thus, as a field we are missing an opportunity to study a general approach to processing individuals that could inform neuropsychological theory. This is where the error analysis of the process group mentioned above becomes important, for the important question here is how do the genders process information differently, not whether and under what circumstances one gender or the other makes fewer or more errors.

Back to executive functioning, given what we know, just what is it, and what is the Soper theory? The neuroanatomy, the behavioral observations, the results of formal testing, and the research all concur. Executive functioning is a process whereby all the available information is organized and integrated by the frontal areas from which the most appropriate motor response is elicited. If the frontal areas, due to trauma, arousal problems, or anything else, cannot integrate and organize the available information, the response, if made at all, will be made only on the basis of that information which was processed. With reference, for example, to the minister who told dirty stories at a funeral, it was clear that he was not processing all of the available information, but was responding to only some of it. The line of logic could follow in this manner. How do people act at a funeral? Sad. Is this good? No. So what do you do? Make them laugh. How do you do that? Tell jokes. What are the best jokes? Dirty stories. There was a rhyme and reason for what the minister did, but he did not take into account that he was at a funeral and that he was a minister. Was the information available? Certainly, he had officiated at the funeral. So what happened was that he made a response not taking into account all the available information, and hence it was not (hardly) the most appropriate response. At another time, another piece of information might not have been processed, and a different, not fully appropriate response, would manifest. It is also possible that at a third occasion he might process sufficient information so that the response was fully appropriate. Although this would most often happen due to trauma to the frontal areas, one could see a similar output from lesions of the longitudinal fasciculi.

5.

SUBCORTICAL STRUCTURES

In this chapter, we continue to fractionate the frontal lobes and turn our focus to the subcortical structures that seem most integrally involved in the processes of executive functions. As such, we will focus on the nuclei of the basal ganglia, the thalamus (and hypothalamus), structures of the limbic system, and the brain stem. While we have parceled out the aforementioned structures, by virtue of the *interconnectivity* and *interdependence* among the structures, we will get a sense of their *functional interrelatedness*. As Hughlings Jackson prophetically claimed decades earlier, we cannot rely on the anatomy or location of a structure alone, as it is only one aspect and may not be the most important one (York & Steinberg, 2011). Certainly this seems to be the case when considering the processes of frontal lobe functions. The findings that will be discussed seem most relevant to humans, even if they were originally found in studies with animals.

Subcortical Structures Involved in Frontal Lobe Functions

 Basal Ganglia. The basal ganglia are a group of subcortical nuclei that share connections with many of the general cortical regions, including the limbic system (e.g., Kandel, Schwartz, Jessel, Siegelbaum, & Hudspeth, 2013; Koziol & Budding, 2009; Noback, Strominger, & Demarest, 2005). Each of the functional structural units (i.e., dorsolateral, ventrolateral, orbital, medial/ACC) is connected to the basal ganglia.

What role do the basal ganglia play? In the simplest of terms, the basal ganglia help to control movement (i.e., behavior). In relation to executive functions, this includes behaviors such as initiating, monitoring, correcting, and inhibiting movement (Kandel et al., 2013; Noback et al., 2005). Some of the most identifiable nuclei of the basal ganglia include the *caudate, putamen, globus pallidus, substantia nigra, and subthalamic nuclei* (STN). Admittedly, the STN are part of the ventral diencephalon and not anatomically part of the telencephalon (Noback et al., 2005; see Figure 3.1). However, in terms of function, they belong to the basal ganglia. As such, it is fitting to include them in this part of the discussion.

Figure 3.1

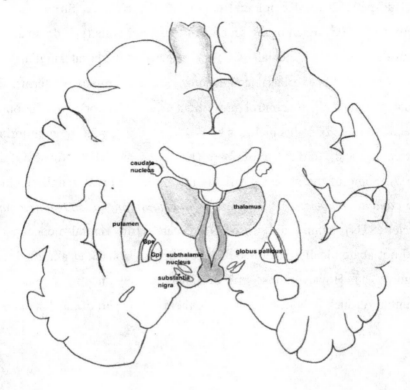

Coronal view of the nuclei of the basal ganglia.

Striatum. The "striatum" (i.e., caudate nucleus and putamen) is an all-inclusive term referring to the dorsal and ventral structures that lie in the subcortical forebrain and midbrain regions (Koziol & Budding, 2009). However, this term, often used in the literature on executive functions, is too general and overshadows the uniqueness of each functional unit. The nuclei in this region serve different functions, depending on their connections with the cerebral cortex, and are essential to our understanding of executive functions. In the next several paragraphs we will discuss the specific nuclei of the dorsal and ventral portions of the basal ganglia.

The caudate nucleus and putamen comprise the dorsal basal ganglia. These nuclei receive sensory and motor information from nearly the entire cerebral cortex. The caudate nucleus has input from post-Rolandic sensory association areas and prefrontal association regions. The putamen receives input largely from cortical somatosensory and motor areas. In contrast, the ventral part of the basal ganglia, which includes the *nucleus accumbens*, plays a larger role in affective and reinforcement responses. The ventral basal ganglia are also connected with other basal ganglia nuclei the globus pallidus, ventral pallidum, and substantia nigra pars reticulata (Noback et al., 2005).

Globus pallidus. The globus pallidus (i.e., pallidum) comprises three sections: medial, lateral, and ventral. The medial aspect makes up the *internal segment of the globus pallidus* (GPi), whereas the lateral aspect encompasses the *external segment of the globus pallidus* (GPe). The internal and external aspects of the globus pallidus will be discussed in greater detail in Chapter 7, where part of the focus will be on the thalamocortical loops. In the meantime it is useful to know that the various segments of the globus pallidus serve unique functions.

For example, one of the roles of the GPi (and the substantia nigra pars reticulata) is to send inhibitory messages to the thalamus, which typically hinder initiation of movement (Koziol & Budding, 2009). By contrast, the main function of the GPe is to inhibit (and disinhibit) the subthalamic nucleus (Koziol & Budding), which plays a role in stopping (or inhibiting), grading, and moderating movement.

These nuclei receive limbic (and reward) information from the orbital region, which is sent to the ventral GPi/nucleus accumbens, and, in turn, information is sent from the ventral GPe (ventral pallidum) to the cortex (via the intralaminar and motor thalamic nuclei) (Gunzler, Schoenberg, Riley, Walter, & Maciunas, 2011). This means that messages regarding initiating behavior and grading behavior, which are salient in terms of emotion and reward, are dependent on the functional capacity of this system, particularly in terms of higher cortical functions.

Substantia nigra. The substantia nigra is divided into the *pars reticulata* (SNpr) ventrally and the *pars compacta* (SNc) dorsally (Noback et al., 2005). The SNpr works in conjunction with the pallidum to regulate motor movement. The SNc is essential in dopamine synthesis, as well as in releasing dopamine to the striatum (Koziol & Budding, 2009; Noback et al., 2005). Dopamine affects frontal lobe functions that are related to motivation, reward, learning, and memory. (The role of neurotransmitters in frontal lobe functions will be addressed in detail in Chapter 6.)

Thalamus. Among its diverse functions, the thalamus plays a role as an intermediary between the cerebral cortex and the reticular activating system (brainstem; Mesulam, 1985). There are three types of thalamic nuclei: specific; association; and nonspecific. The specific nuclei can be further categorized as sensory or motor. The specific sensory nuclei receive information from sensory receptors and send it to sensory areas of the cerebral cortex. Similarly, specific motor nuclei receive information from the basal ganglia (principally the globus pallidus), which is then relayed to the cortical motor regions. The association nuclei receive sensory, motor, affective, and reward information from a wide range of cortical and subcortical regions, which is relayed to various areas of the cerebral cortex including the prefrontal cortex.

Nonspecific thalamic nuclei receive input from the brainstem, reticular formation, other thalamic nuclei, and ventral tegmental nuclei. We are not quite sure about the functions of the nonspecific nuclei, hence the name. To the best of our understanding, information comes from areas throughout the brain and then goes to the frontal cortex. For example, input from the reticular formation raises the level of arousal so that relevant information can be attended to in order to make the most appropriate behavioral response. If there is too low or conversely high levels of arousal, executive functions will shut down. The thalamus has been very slow to reveal its secrets, and what was thought to be true twenty to thirty years ago has been found not to be true.

Hypothalamus. The *hypothalamus* is located between the cerebrum and the brainstem (Noback et al., 2005), beneath the thalamus, and between the optic chiasm and the mammillary bodies. It shares connections with these regions, and receives information from the reticular formation, limbic region, thalamus, and olfactory pathway. The hypothalamus is closely linked to functions governed by the autonomic nervous system that can affect executive functions. For example, it is very difficult to think clearly and work through a challenging problem, or even a relatively simple problem, if we are concerned about our personal safety or have not eaten all day.

Limbic System. The limbic system consists of several neural structures, some of which include the cingulate gyrus, parahippocampal and dentate gyri, hippocampal formation, septal area, amygdala, and portions of the diencephalon (Jääskeläinen, 2012). Paul Broca coined the term "limbic" because the structures lie around the edge, or limbus, of the medial wall of each hemisphere (Jääskeläinen, 2012).

Figure 3.2

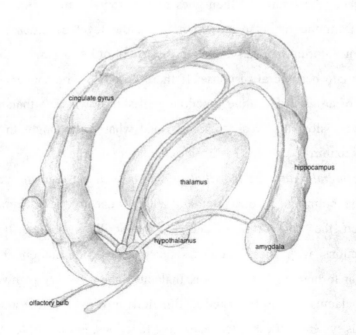

Structures of the limbic system.

In the case of listening to a favorite song the limbic regions receive highly processed sensory information and information related to memory, which contributes to the affective response to the music.

Hippocampal formation. The *hippocampal formation* includes the hippocampus, the dentate gyrus and the subiculum (Kandel et al., 2013). The subiculum comprises the intermediate structures between the hippocampus and the entorhinal cortex. As discussed in Chapter 2, it shares many connections with the neocortex. These connections are integral to the transition from short-term to long-term memory.

Amygdala. The *amygdala* lies rostral to the hippocampus. Along with other parts of the limbic system, it helps regulate feelings, expression of emotions, and emotional memories (e.g., Cozolino, 2002; Offringa et al., 2013). The amygdala influences emotional awareness and the emotional connection to sensory input (Pessoa, 2009). In addition, it communicates with the brainstem, which plays a role in mediating unconscious responses to danger and conscious awareness of fear (Liddell et al., 2005). Stimulation to this area in humans (Wortis & Maurer, 1942) of this area in humans and animals (Kennard, 1945) can cause sham rage. Similarly, insult to this area (also in animals [Akert, Gruesen, Woolsey, & Meyer, 1961] and humans [Miller, Cummings, McIntyre, Ebers, & Grode, 1986]) can cause Kluver-Bucy syndrome, which is characterized by the inability to inhibit sexual behaviors, emotional dullness, and amnesia (e.g., Hayman, Rexer, Pavol, Strite, & Meyers, 1998). We can see how the amygdala, which is essential for processing these types of affective information, which is indispensable for emotionally nuanced aspects of executive functioning.

Brainstem. The *reticular formation* is found at the core of the brainstem; it extends from the lower *medulla oblongata* to the upper portion of the midbrain. In addition, it sends projections to all other regions of the neocortex (Luria, 1966). However, this is not a direct route, as information is sent through thalamic nuclei (Mesulam, 1985) and other subcortical structures such as the hypothalamus (Rempel-Clower, & Barbas, 1998) and the amygdala (Jacobson & Trojanowski, 1975).

Sleep, arousal, muscle tone, attention, movement, and vital reflexes are also regulated by information from the reticular formation (Luria, 1966). Its neurons allow for brief periods of excitation, which permits the reticular formation to have a gradual influence in regulating the nervous system. Activation of the ascending reticular activating system (ARAS) increases during REM sleep, when in pain, or when our attention is immediately needed elsewhere (Mesulam, 1985).

Of course it is easy to see the importance of the brainstem reticular formation, especially the ascending component, in executive functioning. However, by the same token it is particularly important for all cerebral functioning, as Luria describes through his first zone of information processing.

Tegmentum. The *tegmentum*, the floor of the cerebral aqueduct, includes the *rostral portion of the reticular formation nuclei, periaqueductal gray matter, red nucleus, substantia nigra*, and *ventral tegmental area* (Noback et al., 2005). In humans, the periaqueductal gray matter is related to pain control (Noback et al., 2005). The red nucleus receives input from other motor nuclei and the cerebral cortex and sends projections to the cerebellum and spinal cord (as part of the extrapyramidal system). The tegmentum receives a substantial amount of input from the ventral pallidum, which allows for the limbic region to influence this portion of the striatum through dopaminergic projections. The ventral tegmentum, of course, also sends heavy projections to the nucleus accumbens to serve reinforcement.

Conclusion

Consistent with other controversies related to defining and measuring executive functions, there is no shortage of disagreement when it comes to agreeing on how to delineate the subcortical structures involved in executive functions (e.g., Chow & Cummings, 2007; Pribram, 1987). Admittedly, this categorization and description of subcortical structures is not exhaustive in number or detail. Still, it provides an indication of the critical contribution of subcortical structures in carrying out executive functions.

Indeed, the structure-function conundrum of cortical and subcortical structures speaks to the challenge of understanding frontal lobe functions. (As we saw in Chapter 2, the gyrus rectus is anatomically located in the orbital region, however its functional relationship, via cortico-subcortical pathways, is stronger with the medial/ACC. The subcortical structures discussed in this chapter are involved in a) the cortically originating extrapyramidal system(s) (COEPS); b) contributing emotional, memory, and reward information to these systems; or c) both functions. (The COEPS will be discussed in greater detail in Chapter 7.)

To illustrate, Ivan Divac (Srebro, 1999), around 1967, found that lesions in the caudate nucleus in monkeys and cats had the same effect as lesions of the overlying prefrontal cortex. Thus, it would not be unreasonable to assume that disease or damage to the dorsomedial thalamus, pallidum, or the like, would result in executive dysfunction, despite the fact that the prefrontal cortex is entirely intact, demonstrating the interregional dependency of executive functions.

In conclusion, it seems rather apparent that in order to understand executive functions, we must focus on the functional relationship among the various cortical and subcortical structures, which suggests that a discussion limited to the prefrontal cortex provides a decidedly narrow understanding of frontal lobe functions. Thus, executive function involves frontal subcortical systems and not just the cortex.

6.

EVOLUTION OF THE FRONTAL LOBES

Despite the limitations of Charles Darwin's *Theory of Evolution*, his suppositions still permeate our thinking about the evolution of the human brain. According to Darwin (1871, 1896), the human brain evolved through *natural selection*. According to Darwin's theory our primitive ancestors who were capable of learning behaviors, which extended beyond basic instincts, were more likely to survive in order to pass along their genes. The learning of new behaviors was thought to act on the brain, resulting in increased brain size. In turn the increased size meant greater complexity, which eventually resulted in the evolution of an ape-like brain into a human-like one. Of course, this line of reasoning is Lamarckian, a perspective that has permeated the lay community but recently is reemerging with some strength in academic settings.

Some suggest that bipedalism and tool-making capacity are the behavioral hallmarks of human evolutionary advancement (Wynn & Coolidge, 2008). Still others argue that our capacity for language (Schoenemann, 2006), pro-social behavior (Hoffman, 2013), and the ability to develop unique cultural traditions (Ardila, 2008) unmistakably mark the evolution of the human brain (although recent evidence indicates that language as we know it, and our level of social behaviors emerged long after the advent of humanity). Arguably, the aforementioned behaviors are indicative of evolutionary advancement; still they are not exclusive to humans (Montgomery, 2013).

In terms of biology, some suggest that changes in the olfactory bulbs of humans may be linked to evolution of the frontal lobes. For example, for many primitive mammals olfaction was essential to safety, sustenance, and mating (Kaas, 2005). However, during the course of human evolution the olfactory bulbs of primitive mammals continued to advance, while in humans the olfactory bulbs lagged behind compared with other aspects of brain and sensory development (Miller & Cummings, 2007). Some investigators suggest that the olfactory bulbs of humans are one-third smaller than predicted by estimates of brain size (Schoenmann, 2006).

Let us see if we can get an idea of the development of the prefrontal cortex. Fish, amphibians, reptiles, and birds do not have neocortices, let alone prefrontal regions. However, they do process complex information and move successfully through their environments defending themselves and performing other behaviors necessary for survival. In fact, they can be quite successful despite not having expansive neocortices or executive functions. Let us take a closer look at what they do have neurally.

The best place to start with the development of the prefrontal cortex in particular and executive functioning in general is with the triune brain model of Paul D. MacLean (1990). His model proposes that the human brain is composed of three different structural and functional parts, the first of which he calls the R-complex, or the "reptilian brain." He proposed that the reptilian complex is responsible for species-typical instinctual behaviors such as aggression, dominance, territoriality, and ritual displays (i.e., numerous behaviors with an affective component).

If one looks at the various brain parts in this category, sensory ones are apparent, These include the olfactory bulbs and the optic and auditory tecta as well as certain diencephalic areas including portions of the pulvinar of the thalamus. Some suggest the pulvinar functions as an association area within the thalamic nuclei (Augustine, 1996). Indeed, these latter areas are certainly involved in sensory integration, specifically in what Trevarthen (1968) calls the secondary systems, processing much of what we would term ambient sensory information. The brains of the animals mentioned above (fish, amphibians, reptiles, birds) contain these basic structures. The paleomammalian complex or the "limbic brain" is the second part of the triune brain. This is composed primarily of older systems, ones found in fish, amphibian, reptile, and bird brains. These would include the septum, amygdala, hypothalamus, hippocampal complex, and the cingulate area. By their very name one can see that this is the portion of the brain responsible for affect and emotional responses. All vertebrate animals, including fish and amphibians, show either precursors to the basal ganglia or these ganglia themselves.

The neomammalian complex or the "neocortical brain" is the third and most advanced portion of the brain in the MacLean model. This most recent step in the development of the mammalian brain provides the substrate for the abilities of language, abstraction, planning, and advanced perception. Of most importance here is the prefrontal cortex, which is essential for executive functioning. With this neocortical brain, sensory and affective information from the two more primitive parts of the brain can be processed and integrated to contribute to producing the most appropriate motor response. There is evidence that the earliest mammals had neocortices (Buzzell & Amaral, 2007), but none that pre-mammals had such structures, although some certainly had pallial structures that later may have developed into neocortex, or at least neocortical layers.

Perhaps the best way to get an idea of the development of these most important areas would be to look at animals whose prefrontal cortices are just developing. These currently would be best represented by the monotremes and their close relatives. Just how did we come to develop our neocortices, and the prefrontal neocortex in particular? Some of the work of Freidrich Sanides (1968) offers not only a conceptualization of the anterior corticalization of mammals, in primates in particular, but also offers insight into the functions of these areas. He attributes the groundwork for much of his theory to the early research of Abbey (as cited in Schiebinger, 1993) on monotremes and marsupials. Sanides observed a duality of the architectonic progressions in the neocortex, one arising from the parahippocampal moiety and the other from the parapiriform moiety. Functionally, the terms *sensory moiety* and *affect moiety* might be used to better understand the development of the functions of the prefrontal lobes. What Abbey did, through his cytoarchitectural and myeloarchitectural studies, is subdivide the entire echidna and platypus neocortex into two major components, one related and adjacent to the hippocampus, the sensory or archicortex, and the other one to the piriform cortex, the affective or paleocortex. He proposed that progressive evolutionary differentiation takes place in both major components through thickening of the cortex, accentuation of the lamination, and eventually the appearance of granular cells. Abbey stated that different architectonic fields represent successive waves of differentiation and evolution, commencing from the hippocampus and from the piriform cortex, respectively.

These two evolutionary moieties appear to meet at the principal sulcus in Old World monkeys (e.g., macaques) and at the inferior frontal sulcus of humans which, as we have discussed before, appears to be the demarcation line for the types of information processed by the prefrontal cortex. More sensory information is processed by the dorsal-lateral or hippocampal aspect and more emotional (limbic) by the more ventral aspect. A potential problem arises here, for quite clearly human expressive language includes areas (e.g., Broca's area) beneath the inferior frontal sulcus, which would suggest a strong motor component arising from the limbic or affective moiety. Vocalizations, throughout most of the animal kingdom, occur as a result of a change in affect, and are in fact an affective response. So it should not be surprising that expressive language would have a strong affective component (prosody). This proposal of a limbic or affective basis for language was proposed earlier by Rousseau (1754; 1992) and Herder (1772; 2007). Some researchers have suggested that the different cortical layers find their origins in different pallial structures. However, whether or not this is true the overall conceptualization remains the same.

Ambient information processing

Animals without neocortices can of course survive and even thrive in many environments. But there are many things that are beyond their ken.

For example, if you place a desired object on one side of a fence with fencing to the sides (the bypass, or detour, problem), submammalian animals cannot determine that in order to obtain the desired object, the animal must first move away from the object to go around the fence to get to it. Dogs and other animals with neocortices are able to solve this problem easily, but geese and other animals with much more primitive brains will not figure out the solution.

It is clear that without a neocortex an animal cannot have executive functioning or, according to some, even thinking. Such an animal can learn, as through classical or operant conditioning, but cannot formulate a solution and then perform it, in the manner of higher primates. Assuming that the prefrontal cortex plays a key role in this process, the amount of such cortex may be related to the efficiency of executive functioning. Rather than Jerison's (1990) encephalization quotient, the proportion of prefrontal cortex in relation to weight or brain size may be most important. For example, the tree shrew, a primitive primate, has a miniscule prefrontal cortex, especially when compared to higher primates. By contrast, the dolphin has a very large brain, but the amount devoted to prefrontal cortex is relatively limited. (The dolphin has massive temporal lobes, probably for processing the sounds it receives.)

Just what kinds of information can be processed without a neocortex? The mammalian visual system is substantially different from that of other animals, such as fish, amphibians, reptiles, and birds. We have come to think of the mammalian primary visual system as that which courses from the retina to the lateral geniculate body of the thalamus, and then on to the dorsal and ventral portions of the calcarine area of the occipital lobe. This primary visual pathway is complemented by retinal projections to the superior colliculi (optic tectum), then to specific areas of the thalamus (e.g., the lateral pulvinar). Fortunately, Colwyn Trevarthen (1968) has opened a window into this area of inquiry. Trevarthen discusses two mechanisms of vision in primates, one that involves the neocortex and one that does not. The two do interact, but they process visual information in quite different manners, to some extent handling different information. The anatomically older mechanism exists in all vertebrates and consists of retinal projections to the superior colliculus of the mesencephalon. This has come to be known as the secondary visual system, even though it was functional long before the development of the other one now known as the primary visual system. This anatomically newer system projects to the lateral geniculate of the thalamus after temporal visual field fibers cross at the optic chiasma. This lateral geniculate body then projects to neocortical areas of the occipital lobe.

Trevarthen (1968) described functional differences between the two visual systems. He stated, "I examine the visual mechanisms of the brain to test the idea that vision involves two parallel processes; one ambient, determining space at large around the body, and the other focal, which examines detail in small areas of space." The focal, or primary, system is often somewhat easier to understand. Much of the information in this channel is processed through the portion of the fovea concerned with central vision, permitting the animal to study a visual object in detail. The other visual system in humans is not as easy to comprehend, but those of us who have worked with cortically blind people have seen it in action. These people cannot describe the details of stimuli through their visual system, yet some aspects of vision seem to be intact. Similar findings have been observed in monkeys. Unlike those who are blind from eye problems, these people walk around to a certain extent but do not walk into large objects. When asked about it they become confused and just say there is something there. Often they can tell if an elevator is open or closed, yet they cannot go into detail about finer visual details. (Supposedly cortically blind macaques, but not humans, can differentiate between colors.)

What these individuals are processing is what Trevarthen referred to as ambient information, that is, nonspecific information about the space around them. They pick up enough information so that they do not walk into the large objects or the door of the elevator, but process very little detailed information beyond that. Similarly, when students walk around a crowded classroom they tend not to bump into people or desks, yet can tell you little about what they saw as they went around large objects (e.g., how many backpacks there were).

Imagine that a monkey brachiating through trees had to stop and focus on each branch; it would quickly slam into the trunk of a tree. However, if it could draw in enough ambient information, where the branches are and whether the branches can bear its weight, it could move fairly quickly through the trees. Similarly, an ungulate running away from a lion does not spend a lot of time studying the terrain, but processes just enough so it can take the fastest route. Its focal vision would still be concerned with the lion, but its ambient vision would help guide the best path for escape. One wonders if the shifty halfback in football or the wing in hockey is particularly adept at using their ambient vision. Much as focal vision tends to draw on information from the central fovea, ambient vision is adept at processing information from the periphery. Another point made by Trevarthen is that the ambient visual system can bring information into the fovea (more accurately, into focal vision). Thus a still lion in the ambient and peripheral vision of the ungulate can be brought into focal vision, first by having the eyes directed precisely toward it.

As humans, we tend not to walk into doors or fall down stairs, but process large-scale ambient information to facilitate our movement. We may not remember the color of the door or the rug on the stairs, or even if there was one, because so little, if any, focal information is being consciously processed.

We may wonder how animals with eyes on either side of the head can process information, but if most of what they process is ambient information, it is easier to understand. Fish, amphibians, reptiles, and birds do not have cerebral cortices, and hence cannot process visual or other information at that level, but they do have large optic lobes to varying degrees, better referred to in these animals as superior colliculi. Thus, it is expected that they would be very proficient in processing ambient information.

In terms of human brain development our primitive ancestors likely were reliant upon "the smell brain." As the frontal lobes developed through the course of evolution, we became less reliant on our olfactory capacity to inform us about the world and selection of behavioral responses. Still, others disagree, indicating that the change in the olfactory bulbs is on par with other changes in the evolution of the frontal lobes (Jerison, 2007). What is unique to the evolution of the frontal lobes of humans? How is this evident in executive functions? We will return to this line of inquiry later, but first we will consider past and current theories as well as approaches that inform our understanding of how the human frontal lobes evolved.

Darwin and Beyond

Theories explaining the evolution of the human brain are often divided between natural selection and adaptation. For example, Stephen Stanley (1992) asserts that our primitive ancestors began to walk upright in order to care for their offspring. This adaptation afforded our (formerly tree-swinging) ancestors greater motility. According to Stanley this enabled humans to accommodate a larger brain. Prior to that, the greater motility allowed them to move when the climate became inhospitable increasing their chance of survival. Others offer a similar rationale when arguing for natural selection. Balsters and colleagues (2010) suggest that *Homo sapiens* could withstand dramatic changes in the environment because natural selection increased the ability to find more adaptive solutions. In other words, natural selection afforded *Homo sapiens* the ability to problem-solve (Balsters et al., 2010).

Another argument that favors adaptation as a means of surviving environmental conditions considers a slightly different motor capacity than bipedalism. Wynn and Coolidge (2008) argue that sensorimotor abilities of *Homo sapiens* led to evolutionary advancements in brain functioning (Wynn & Coolidge, 2008). According to their supposition, the increased sensorimotor capacity resulted in increased neural capacity. This improved *Homo sapiens'* ability to plan and strategize in order to find innovative solutions. While certainly it can be argued that sensorimotor abilities have increased over the course of evolution, Jerison (2007) reminds us that the evolution of sensorimotor abilities is common to all primates.

We will consider one more argument related to natural selection and Homo sapiens' capacity to withstand the many challenges of living some 100,000 or more years ago. Schoenemann (2006) asserts that through natural selection, social behaviors increased. The improvement in social behaviors resulted in greater cooperation and working together, which in turn improved Homo sapiens' chances of survival.

How can we make sense of what appear to be competing theories? Jerison (2007) and others (e.g., Montgomery, 2013) suggest a compromise, opining that natural selection and adaptation should be thought of as compatible concepts, not competing ones. Montgomery (2013) explains that the majority of the evidence appears to favor a model wherein the human brain was most likely initially influenced by natural selection, which led to greater adaptive capacity.

Measuring Evolutionary Development of the Frontal Lobes

As we continue our discussion we will consider how arguments on the evolution of the brain are often fortified or refuted by measuring brain size, reorganization of structures, and cortical encephalization. As we will see in terms of the frontal lobes, and the rest of the brain for that matter, size is far less import than other advancements afforded to us by evolution.

Size. Are bigger brains better? Not necessarily. According to Jerison (2007), larger brain size does not always equate to greater intellectual functioning, but most often it is an indication of a greater capacity to process information. By some estimates the size of the human brain is thought to have tripled – if not quadrupled – in the millions of years leading to modern man (Zhang, 2003).Others argue that the size of the human brain has not changed significantly during evolution (e.g., Ardila, 2008; Balsters et al., 2010). Still others contend that the changes in size of the human brain are limited to the frontal lobes (Fuster, 2008).

In terms of uniqueness, some suggest that the frontal lobes of humans do not show a specific advantage in size compared to other mammals (Barton & Venditti, 2013; Hoffman, 2013). Jerison (2007) warns that side-by-side comparisons of the frontal lobes can be problematic for this very reason, because the unique function of the frontal lobes is often discounted. Another aspect often not considered is the individual difference in brain size, volume, and even location of specific brain areas (e.g., Broca's area). Furthermore, the frontal lobes not only vary greatly in terms of topography, but also show considerable differences in functional capacity based on genetics, as well as pre-natal and post-natal environments.

Indeed, many argue that pound-for-pound brain comparisons tell us very little about intellectual or functional capacity (Manger, Spocter, & Patzke, 2013; Schoenemann, 2006). We need only consider the fate of the Neanderthals to know that other factors must be considered when making claims about brain function based solely on brain size, as the Neanderthal's brain was actually slightly bigger than ours (Ardila, 2008;

Banyas, 2007). As such, we need to consider the way the frontal lobes of humans function in conjunction with suppositions based on brain size.

Reorganization. It is also argued that the reorganization of the brain over the course of evolution is a better measure of advancements in the functional capacity of the frontal lobes (Hoffman, 2013). Interestingly, Liu and colleagues (2014) suggest that aspects of brain volume and cranial capacity of humans appear to have decreased during evolution. They argue that the brain became more efficient with cortical and subcortical reorganization, resulting in a more compact, though more efficient, structure (Liu et al., 2014).

As brain capacity continued to expand, the multitude of information being processed required more and more neurons throughout the brain (Kaas, 2005). However, some evolution favors efficiency. Kaas has proposed a model of the brain wherein neurons and their connections endlessly multiplying makes for a very inefficient brain, as each of the billions and billions of neurons would need to connect with all parts of the brain. As such, Kaas and others (e.g., Balsters et al., 2010) suggest that because of evolutionary pressure the brain developed networks, which could process and communicate the information more efficiently. This solved the problem of an ever-expanding number of neurons and the need for longer and longer connections. Some say this allowed for the development of specific functional systems (Balsters et al., 2010; Hoffman, 2013). These functional systems continued to be reorganized and rescaled, which some suggest supplanted the need to form new structures and increase brain size volumetrically (Balsters et al., 2010). In fact, Semendeferi, Damasio, Frank, and Van Hoesen (1997) argue that cortical and subcortical reorganization is one factor unique to the evolution of the human brain. Indeed, brain reorganization, as related to the formation of cortical and subcortical connections, appears to explain more about evolutionary advancement. However, we have yet to consider what many regard as the key to understanding the evolution of the frontal lobes in humans.

Cortical Encephalization. Cortical encephalization appears to be one of the most important measures when considering the evolution of the human frontal lobes (Jerison, 2007; Kaas, 2005; Miller & Cummings, 2007). Areas with more folds or convolutions have a greater concentration of white matter (Balsters et al., 2010; Schoenemann, 2006; Smaers et al., 2011) and are associated with greater capacity for complex functions (e.g., Miller & Cummings, 2007). By some estimates the human brain is approximately five times as encephalized as our nearest living primate relative (Jerison, 2007). Because of the link to white matter growth some suggest that white matter volume (as opposed to brain volume) is a better indicator of human evolutionary strides (Ardila, 2008; Balsters et al., 2010; Semenderferi et al., 2002).

Other investigators suggest that encephalization does not explain the evolutionary advancement of the human frontal lobes. For example, Molnar (2011) has argued that other species show even greater convolutions in terms of cortical topography despite having only rudimentary brain functions. However, his argument shows a limited understanding of cortical encephalization. We need to consider both brain region and brain function when making comparisons to other species (Miller & Cummings, 2007). Such comparisons may obviate the possibility of arriving at the conclusions of certain early experiments involving cortical stimulation that led some scientists to believe that the frontal lobes are nothing more than lifeless blobs or "silent areas" (Luria, 1967).

Mosaic Versus Concerted Neural Structures

In this section, we will consider *mosaic* and *concerted* theories, which are also used to explain the evolution of the human brain. In general, mosaic theory refers to unique cell development within an individual organism, whereas concerted theory concerns the temporality of the development of neural structures. Similar to our discussion of brain size, reorganization, and encephalization, there is considerable disagreement in terms of the viability of each of these theories. Perhaps even more problematic, there is confusion about which suppositions relate to which theory. Some suggest that mosaic theory implies that brain structures evolved independently of each other (Balsters et al., 2010; Bayans, 2007). Furthermore, Hoffman and others (Semendeferi, Lu, Schenker, & Damasio, 2002) opine that mosaic theory explains the development of specific brain systems secondary to evolutionary pressure.

However, some describe concerted theory in nearly identical terms. In fact, some of these definitions have been put forward by those who are rather critical of mosaic theory (Balsters et al., 2010; Banyas, 2007). For example, Balsters and colleagues (2010) suggest that concerted theory explains how evolutionary pressure acted upon "whole functional systems comprising several interconnected parts of the brain."

Perhaps it is best to side-step the mosaic vs. concerted theories debate entirely and consider another perspective that may be more useful in terms of applying evolutionary constructs to executive function and dysfunction. Schoenemann (2006) helps us to simplify matters by categorizing the evolution of brain structures and systems as adaptive or non-adaptive. Accordingly, genetic changes that are adaptive improve functioning, while nonadaptive ones, which may be the result of genetic drift, lead to executive dysfunction.

To illustrate, in the 1980s an acclaimed film depicted a man with autism who also had a highly developed ability to calculate and recall basic math facts. Over the course of the film, the man's neuro-typical brother tries to receive personal gain from his older brother's savant-like skills. We also see that despite the older brother's advanced mathematical abilities, he is unable to independently perform many basic functions.

Perhaps it suffices to say that evolutionary pressures and random changes increased our chances of survivability and resulted in predictable and measurable changes. Arguably some of the most important changes have been cortical encephalization and the organization of structural-functional networks.

Neocortical Evolution

Evolutionary advancements of the cortex and subcortical structures indicate several changes, which distinguish the phylogenetic development of mammalian and nonmammalian vertebrates. For example, the development of a neocortex in mammalian primates reflects similar trends among humans in the formation of the central sulcus and inferior frontal sulcus (Fuster, 2008). These cortical divisions were followed by the development of separate motor and premotor regions (Luria, 1966).

The delineation of regions of the neocortex and greater expansion in specific areas of the prefrontal cortex are also thought to correspond to more complex behaviors. For example, the growth of frontal and lateral convexities aligns with an increased capacity for abstraction and the ability to inhibit responses to sensory and affective stimuli, respectively (Fuster, 2008).

In addition to the aforementioned changes, phylogenetic changes and the development of more complex frontal lobe functions, which coincide with the expansion of the prefrontal cortex, are another important phylogenetic change warranting mention. Increases in connectivity from the mediodorsal nucleus to the prefrontal cortex transpired without corresponding volumetric changes to the latter structure (Fuster, 2008). It has been suggested that the phylogenetic advancement of the PFC be considered in conjunction with changes in cortico-cortical connections and thalamic projections, along with other morphological changes of the frontal lobes (Pandya & Yeterian, 1996).

Conclusion

Petrides (2005) points out that nonprimate mammals have at most two of the prefrontal areas, the orbital and the medial/ACC. He says that the orbital area preferentially responds to external stimuli that are likely to be significant for rewarding. The medial anterior cingulate responds more to information about the body's internal state. Together, he says these two areas contribute to what might be called the emotional aspects of decision-making.

The third prefrontal region, the lateral area, is apparently unique to primates and has developed a granular layer. Petrides (2005) believes that this area is concerned with the rational aspects of decision-making. This granular layer does not exist in other mammals, so it may be that the granular layer is what is unique to primates, or it could be that the lateral prefrontal area is what is unique to primates and part of it is the granular layer. This discussion is ongoing. However, the work of Lawicka (1966) strongly suggests that perhaps the proreal area of cats and dogs, at least, may be homologous to the dorsal lateral prefrontal areas of primates at least with regard to function.

In humans, the ventrolateral area is very important, but a question arises as to whether it is unique to primates, and it certainly seems to be, and if so is it just an extension of the dorsolateral area. The work of Sanides (1968) strongly suggests that this area is derived from the emotional moiety from the orbital areas. However, there is little concrete evidence supporting either theory.

Schneider (2014) takes a slightly different approach. He defines the prefrontal area, as has been done by others, as the projection area of the medialis dorsalis of the thalamus. The medial portion of this nucleus receives information from the limbic forebrain, including the olfactory area, and projects to the ventral lateral prefrontal cortex. The lateral portion of the medialis dorsalis projects to the dorsolateral prefrontal areas. According to Schneider, nonprimate mammals might have lateral prefrontal cortices, but they would probably not have a well-developed granular layer.

Finally, we return to our discussion of the unique aspects of the evolution of the frontal lobes in humans. Admittedly we share many similarities with nonhuman primates in terms of development and behavior (Montgomery, 2013; Smaers et al., 2011). Still, the human brain is not simply an overgrown nonhuman primate brain (Schoenmann, 2006). As such, comparisons of frontal lobe functions in humans to those of modern primates might hold the key to understanding evolution's unique signature in the frontal lobes of humans.

It is possible that the one behavior that appears to be unique to humans and is clearly a frontal lobe function is the ability to anticipate in the abstract. This evolutionary shift in cognition, which coincides with greater elaboration of cortical and subcortical connectivity, allowed humans to utilize other information in responding to stimuli, whether affective or sensory. Evolution afforded humans the capacity to move beyond immediate temporal information to greater levels of abstraction.

According to Fuster (2008) evolution has enabled us to develop and act upon remote and idiosyncratic goals that move beyond instinct and are based on the totality of information included in the past, present, and future (Fuster, 2008). In fact, Berkman and Lieberman (2010) appear to have demonstrated this uniquely human executive function. They compared humans to nonhuman primates with regard to their respective capacities to approach or avoid a desired stimulus (based on an over-arching *abstract* goal) and found that only humans were able to anticipate and plan for achieving an abstract goal (Berkman & Lieberman, 2010).

We may not be able to sing the sweet melodies of a nightingale, jump like a kangaroo rat, or sniff out nourishment like a grizzly bear, but we are able to modulate our behavior in order to reach a goal that might be hours, days, or even years away. Perhaps our ability to utilize foresight in an effort to attain an abstract goal is the ultimate adaptation afforded to us through evolution, with the frontal lobe playing a key functional role.

7.

DEVELOPMENTAL TRAJECTORY OF THE FRONTAL LOBES

After hundreds of years of misconceptions we have come to understand that, like the functional differences of the frontal lobes, the development trajectory also differs from that of other brain regions. For example, it was not until recently that we recognized that frontal lobe development extends beyond the first seven years of life in humans (Luria, 1966). With advancements in static neuroimaging, this timeline was extended into adolescence (Fuster, 2008; Romine & Reynolds, 2005). However, within the last decade we have learned with a good deal of certainty the frontal lobes continue to develop well into the third decade of life (Arain et al., 2013). This protracted development of the frontal areas implies the possibility that much of their eventual organization is based on experience interacting with the outside world, and not a consequence of genetics alone.

We are left with the task of clearly delineating the details of the protracted development of the frontal lobes and how this relates to the maturation of executive functions. Some suggest that at four to five months of age, infants are capable of specific, executive-like, frontal lobe functions (Grossman, Parise, & Friederici, 2010; Mulder, Pitchford, Hagger, & Marlow, 2009). Others argue that an infant's frontal lobes function in a global capacity until sometime later, when topographical organization and reorganization become evident (Huang et al., 2015; Wolff et al., 2012). The neurobiological evidence offers greater support for the latter (Bell & Wolfe, 2007), though the notion of topographical organization is regarded as problematic by many in the field (e.g., Arain et al., 2013; Brocki & Brohlin, 2010).

Nevertheless, there is little question that following birth the frontal lobes demonstrate prolific cortical and subcortical changes (Fuster, 2008). It is largely thought that cortical and subcortical changes result in distinct, functionally and structurally related units (Alexander-Bloch, Raznahan, Bullmore, & Giedd, 2013; Deoni, Dean, O'Muircheartaigh, Dirks, & Jerskey, 2012; Fuster, 2008).

Initially the discovery of cortical and subcortical organization gave rise to different theories as to purpose (Conklin, Luciana, Hooper, & Yarger, 2007). One such theory suggested the units were organized by functional domain for example, spatial and non-spatial Goldman-Rakic, 1995), while another argued that the organization was related to the "process" or function (e.g., selecting, monitoring, attention; Petrides, Alivisatos, Meyer, & Evans, 1993). The latter of the two aligns more closely with our current understanding of functional-structural units and the relationship to the suspected developmental trajectory of executive functions. Before discussing the development of executive functions, we will turn our attention to the postnatal development of the frontal lobes, specifically cortical myelination and the development of functional-structural units.

Myelination of the Frontal Lobes

In the 100 years since Paul Fleschig's mapping of myeloarchitecture (as cited in Arnold & Trojanowski, 1996), it has been repeatedly articulated that the frontal lobes (of humans) are unmyelinated at birth. Nevertheless, the neurobiological antecedents necessary for the eventual development of the frontal lobe structures are present (Hudspeth & Pribram, 1990). Fleschig's work supports the argument that the unmyelinated state enables the infant to adapt to the environment (Arnold & Trojanowski, 1996). Perhaps even more importantly, the unmyelinated state necessitates engagement with the environment (Fuster, 2008).

In relation to the frontal lobes, Darby and Walsh (2006) and others (e.g., Polderman et al., 2007) argue that the term "environment" must be employed broadly to include events in the external environment (e.g., stressors, poverty, injury) as well as influences within the internal environment (e.g., genetics, physiology, nutrition, disease). The two that seem to be of the greatest importance are experience and genetics (Glasser, Goyal, Preuss, Raichle, & Van Essen, 2014; Polderman et al., 2007; Spear, 2013; Trampel, Ott, & Turner, 2011; Wolff et al., 2012).

By observing images of white matter, via resting MRIs and other approaches to neuroimaging, we have learned that myelogenesis parallels histological changes (Blakemore, Burnett, & Dahl, 2010; Dean et al., 2014; Glasser et al., 2014). More recently, functional MRIs have given us more insight into the myelination process and its role in the development of cortical and subcortical units. At a basic level, and in response to neuronal activity (Demerens et al., 1996), the myelin sheath wraps around the axons. This creates the white matter bundles comprising major neuronal pathways (e.g., fasciculi). The increased insulation facilitates more efficient communication between brain regions (Huang et al., 2015), that appears directly related to an increase in the thickness and degree of white matter development (Alexander-Bloch et al., 2013). This is because myelination dramatically increases the brain efficiency and speed with which areas of the brain can communicate (Gibson, 1991). This is supported by evidence that white matter is particularly concentrated in areas of the frontal lobes that show functional connectivity (Vasung, Fischi-Gomez, & Huppi, 2013). Efficiency of communication has caused many to focus on improvements in processing speed (Arain et al., 2013; Bell & Wolfe, 2007; Ferrer et al., 2013). While increases in processing speed are likely related at least initially to myelination, arguably a more important effect of myelination is the ability to inhibit responding (Decety, 2010; Soper, 2014). That is, with the development of white matter and the corresponding maturation of functional structural units of the frontal lobes, there is an increased capacity to control affective responses. Many link this to the development of the orbital unit, which in part mediates responses to affective information by the process of affective appraisal (Decety, 2010; Solbakk et al., 2014). For example, after myelination should we have the grave misfortune of encountering a black widow spider in our briefcase, we would likely feel startled or even fearful, but then move into action to safely remove the spider from our briefcase. It is less likely that we would scream and run out of the room.

In other words, the process of myelination improves communication, so that we are better equipped to inhibit responses to affective, sensory, and mnemonic information in order to make the most appropriate response.

Sketching a timeline. Most agree that at the beginning of the second year of life (roughly between 12 and 16 months), myelination of the frontal lobes rapidly increases (Deoni et al., 2012; O'Muircheartaigh et al., 2014). According to some, the pace becomes noticeably slower around the sixth year of life (Arain et al., 2013; O'Muircheartaigh et al., 2014). Others argue that the pace slows immediately after the initial surge (Deoni et al., 2012). By most accounts, myelination in a five-year-old child is about 80% that of an adult (Dean et al., 2014; Deoni et al., 2012). While there is continued myelination in subsequent years, this finding corresponds to behavioral evidence of notably greater self-control evident in typically developing children by around seven to eight years of age (Hale & Fiorello, 2004; Soper, 2014).

It is now largely accepted that the growth of the frontal lobes continues until about 25 years of age. However, what that growth consists of remains a matter of debate. For example, some suggest that the structural complexity of an adolescent's frontal lobes is comparable to that of an adult, although some refinement of these structures continues into early adulthood (Fuster, 2008; Romine & Reynolds, 2005). Others contend that a second "growth spurt" evident in specific axonal connections of basic structures begins in adolescence and then continues to be refined as the structures become myelinated (Arain et al., 2013; Spear, 2013). For example, some suggest that structural growth of axonal connections becomes the foundation of specific neuronal networks

(Vasung et al., 2012). Clearly there is some debate as to whether myelination during adolescence is more about fine-tuning existing structures (e.g., Arain et al., 2013) or forming new functional networks (Vasung et al., 2012). Still, there are several points of agreement in terms of what affects the process of brain development, in general, between adolescence and adulthood.

For example, there is consensus that efficiency of the neuronal networks (i.e., structures) becomes more efficient as a result of increased myelination (Arain et al., 2013; Spear, 2013). Many agree that functional structural development continues to be mediated by experience and environment (e.g., Glasser et al., 2014; Vasung et al., 2012; Wolff et al., 2012). However, others suggest that the environment may not be an important factor at this stage in development (Ferrer et al., 2013; Polderman et al., 2007). In reality it is difficult to separate experience from environment, as availability and access to various experiences largely depend on the environment one is in, which includes culture, economic factors, stress, and the like (e.g., Spear, 2013). Regardless of what constitutes these external factors, it is agreed that how one uses or abuses the brain during this latter stage of development continues to be formative as well as predictive of later functioning (Arain et al., 2013). Myelination is said to reduce brain plasticity (e.g., Glasser et al., 2014; Wolff et al., 2012), though the payoff is the strengthening of neuronal connections, which results in increased efficiency (Spear, 2013; Steinberg, 2005).

This reworking or refinement process is evident in an interesting (though probably more frustrating to parents of adolescents) functional lag between adolescents and adults. To explain, it appears that adolescents are often able to perform similarly to adults in some measures of executive functions (Huizinga, Dolan, & van der Molen, 2006). They are also quite capable of explaining the codes and conduct of acceptable behavior. However, when faced with an emotionally charged situation in the real world, adolescents do not fare nearly as well, as they are more prone to impulsive and emotional decision-making (Arain et al., 2013; Spear, 2013; Steinberg, 2005). Encouragingly, by the latter teen years, there is some improvement and a greater capacity for decision-making (Arain et al., 2013; Decety, 2010).

Vulnerability of the frontal lobes. The neural plasticity of the frontal lobes, prenatally and postnatally, also increases vulnerability (e.g., Arain et al., 2013). There is considerable evidence that prenatal teratogens and premature birth cause anomalies in the development of white matter, which are associated with deficits in executive functions (Blakemore et al., 2010; Dean et al., 2013; Edgin et al., 2008; Glasser et al., 2014; Paus et al., 2008; Wolff et al., 2012). Similarly, the postnatal environment poses risks to optimal development. Poor nutrition, and physical and psychological stressors, have been shown to negatively affect myelination (Arain et al., 2013). Adolescence is generally regarded as the third time when there is increased risk of abnormal neural development (Steinberg, 2005). Damage occurring later in development can negatively impact normal functioning (Spear, 2013), whereas damage during the earliest periods of development may prohibit the structure from developing at all (Bell & Wolfe, 2007; Huang et al., 2013; Walsh, Morrow, & Rubenstein, 2008).

Developmental Trajectory of Functional-Structural Units

The development of functionally related cortical and subcortical structures is mediated by the maturation of white matter (Arain et al., 2013; Huang et al., 2015; Raznahan et al., 2011; Spear, 2013). There is considerable evidence that the development of functional-structural units follows the pattern of hierarchical development (Conklin et al., 2007; Luria, 1966). Our current understanding suggests that the orbital and ventral areas myelinate first, followed by the medial prefrontal/anterior cingulate, and dorsolateral regions. We will look at this process more closely by describing the development of white matter tracts in the three general regions.

Orbital and medial circuits. The fornix is one of the earliest of the frontal functional-structural pathways that myelinate after birth (Vasung et al., 2012). By four months of age this major pathway (by way of the anterior commissure) begins to connect the temporal lobes and portions of the olfactory region. This process appears to parallel the myelination of the internal capsule, corpus callosum, and optic radiations, which begins roughly between three and six months of age (Dean et al., 2013; Deoni et al., 2013; O'Muircheartaigh et al., 2014). The internal capsule allows for more efficient communication of messages from the thalamus to all areas of the cortex (Walsh, 2005). As the corpus callosum myelinates, beginning with the splenium and progressing anteriorly to the genu (Deoni et al., 2013; Vasung et al., 2013), connections between the temporal lobes, amygdala, and olfactory regions become more plentiful.

Decety (2010) examined myelination in relation to emotional

regulation and understanding. He found that as the orbital regions, anterior cingulate, and insula become myelinated, the ability to perceive affective states becomes possible. However, responses to input are more involuntary and reflexive at first. At approximately 18 to 36 months of age myelination in the medial region increases (Counsell et al., 2008; Decety, 2010). Behaviorally toddlers become less egocentric and capable of distinguishing between the self and others (Decety, 2010).

Ventrolateral circuit. According to Fleschig (as cited in Bailey and von Bonin, 1951) the ventrolateral circuit shows more prolific myelination around 18 months to two years of age, which coincides with increased language development (O'Muircheartaigh et al., 2014) and greater voluntary control of emotions (Decety, 2010). This further suggests that affective aspects of executive function develop comparatively earlier. It would appear that the first segment of development (in terms of functional units) orients a child to the sensory and relational world via affective mechanisms, which are largely mediated through the orbital, ventral, and medial regions of the brain. Although these circuits are the first to myelinate, the fine-tuning of these networks continues for years to come.

Dorsolateral circuit. It is largely accepted that the dorsolateral region is last to develop. Evidence of the maturation of this region is sometimes discussed in terms of improvements in reasoning ability (Ferrer et al., 2013), performance on tests of executive function (Brocki & Bohlin, 2014; Romine & Reynolds, 2005; Steinberg, 2005), observation of increased emotional regulation (Decety, 2010), and neuroimaging studies (Schmithorst & Yuan, 2010). For example, maturation of this region has been associated with improvements in working memory and other cognition related executive functions (Conklin et al., 2007; Gathercole, Pickering, Ambridge, & Wearing, 2004; Luciana, Conklin, Hooper, & Yarger, 2005). It is also linked with improvement in metacognitive abilities (Steinberg, 2005; Stone, Baron-Cohen, & Knight, 1998). Some investigators suggest maturation of the dorsolateral circuit is also evidenced by increased control of emotions and self-regulation, which happens in conjunction with maturing of the medial/ACC, orbital, and ventrolateral regions, in a bottom-up process (e.g., Decety, 2010). Some suggest this developmental shift coincides with an increase in focal connections (Durston et al., 2006).

Proximity and Plasticity

In terms of cortical and subcortical connections that occur over the course of development, some follow a pattern of proximal to distal development, wherein brain areas with related functions are the first to develop followed by more and more distal connections (Alexander-Bloch et al., 2013). The refining process during myelination follows a similar pattern, wherein the sensory and motor areas become myelinated first, followed by the association areas, and finally connections from the frontal lobes to more and more distal areas of the brain. which are the last to become myelinated (Raznahan et al., 2011; Spear, 2013). This enables highly processed information from these other areas to reach the frontal lobes and help to guide decision-making based on various forms of information. The distal connections allow for more complex processing and advancement of executive functioning (e.g., Alexander-Bloch et al.,

2013; Spear, 2013). As mentioned previously, the tradeoff for the loss in neural plasticity is increased functional capacity, which is facilitated through the development of specific and highly efficient functional structural networks (e.g., Spear, 2013; Wolff et al., 2012). Glasser and colleagues (2014) have a slightly different viewpoint, suggesting that myelination becomes a surrogate for synaptic plasticity in the facilitation of communication between cortical and subcortical areas via the functional structural networks.

As mentioned, the development of these networks is in part dependent on experience (as well as influenced by genetics, biology, and the environment). There is reciprocity in development such that experience helps to develop the functional structural units and development of these units in turn facilitates more complex forms of thinking which further develops the structures, and so on. We see evidence of this in the brains of individuals who are bilingual, where the cortical connectivity leads to increased proficiency in many frontal lobe tasks, such as attention, abstract reasoning, and creative and divergent thinking (Adesope, Lavin, Thompson, & Ungerleider, 2010). However, there appear to be some limitations depending on the age of bilingualism. When there is second language exposure in early childhood, it is associated with the most advantage in terms of cognitive effects, but even those who learn a second language later in life benefit in terms of executive functions (Adesope et al., 2010). In fact, some researchers suggest that individuals who continue to use bilingual language abilities over the course of their lifetime tend to maintain greater integrity of specific white matter tracts that is, superior and inferior longitudinal fasciculi (Luk, Bialystok, Craik, & Grady, 2011).

Development of Executive Functions

It is a notable challenge to track the developmental trajectory of executive functions against the backdrop of developmental and cognitive milestones. As with the milestones that are linked to the posterior regions of the brain, there similarly appears to be a continuum along which these structures and functions develop. There are also considerable individual differences (Horton & Horton, 2008; Raznahan et al., 2011). Furthermore, the challenges that arise when attempting to define and quantitatively measure what constitutes executive functions in adults are only magnified when considering the changes that are simultaneously taking place in cognition (Anderson, 2001; Horton & Horton, 2008; Huizinga et al., 2006; Paus, 2010). For example, Anderson (2001) argues that developmentally appropriate assessment tools can detect executive functions in children as young as six-years-old. In contrast, Huizinga and colleagues (2013) argue that there is too much "task impurity," wherein the current tools cannot tease apart executive functions in order for them to be measured. Segmenting tasks into isolated components is reductionist by nature, and necessarily decreases the construct of executive functions.

Some investigators suggest that executive functions develop in a discrete manner (Huizinga et al., 2006), and are emblematic of developmental stages (Romine & Reynolds, 2005). For example, Anderson (2001) and others (e.g., Alexander-Bloch et al., 2013; Fuster, 2008; Kolb & Wishaw, 2009) suggest that executive functions develop similarly to Piaget's theory of cognitive development following a similar trajectory to cortical myelination. Still others argue that executive functions develop in a non-linear pattern (Deoni et al., 2013; O'Muircheartaigh et al., 2013).

It seems that executive functions of the frontal lobe develop in a multidimensional and multifaceted manner. For example, a child who demonstrates "proficiency" on a task of working memory does not "master" this milestone at six years old, or even at 14 years old. Rather, over the course of development and with experience and exposure to a rich and stimulating environment, the protracted and, in part, reciprocal process of the development of functional structural units affords greater capacity for complex and abstracting thinking and, by virtue, increased capacity for executive functions.

Conclusion

There are several points we can take away from this discussion. The first is that frontal lobe development is a protracted process extending through at least the third decade of life. Second, we have learned that the development of the frontal lobes depends greatly on experience and environment. Third, we recognize that because of the lengthy developmental trajectory and influence of factors other than development there are multiple risk factors that can thwart development (e.g., stress, poverty, illicit substances, lack of stimulation). By contrast, because of this malleability, we also recognize that exposure to a rich and stimulating environment or other experiences (e.g., learning a second language) also create opportunities to increase the efficiency of the functional structural units. Fourth, we recognize that the development of structural functional units follows a general pattern with the furthest frontal regions developing last. Finally, based on our understanding of this developmental process, which is dependent on the formation of functional structural units that are likewise dependent on myelination, we would not expect executive functions to be fully developed and functional prior to structural development.

8.

NEUROTRANSMITTERS

As we continue to fractionate the frontal lobes, we will consider in the current chapter how the four functional structural units (i.e., dorsolateral, ventrolateral, orbital, and medial/ACC) communicate at the cellular level via neurotransmitters. In the simplest of terms, neurotransmitters increase or decrease cellular activity by influencing neurons via direct or indirect communication (Kandel, Schwartz, Jessel, Siegelbaum, & Hudspeth, 2013). Direct influence typically involves a neurochemical binding to or opening the receptor of a neuron, whereas indirect influence involves the interplay of neurotransmitters, where one influences or modulates another (Kandel et al., 2013).

Whether the influence of neurotransmitters is direct or indirect is in part dependent on the location of the neuron, as well as the specific properties of a given neuron (Fuster, 2015; Kandel et al., 2013). For example, acetylcholine (ACh) acts as a neurotransmitter in the peripheral nervous system, but as a neuromodulator in the central nervous system (Amici & Boxer, 2007). In addition to the cell's location, neurons possess unique properties that also influence responsiveness to a given neurotransmitter (Kandel et al., 2013). This is not to say that there is not a relationship between a given neurotransmitter and behavior, but rather it is more telling to consider the effect of a neurotransmitter in relation to location or neurocircuitry (Fuster, 2015; Miller & Cummings, 2007).

Main Neurotransmitters of the Frontal Lobes: An Overview

Neurotransmitters fall into three main classifications, monoamines, neuropeptides, and amino acids (Cozolino, 2002). Monoamines, such as dopamine (DA) and serotonin (5-HT), have been related to specific frontal lobe functions (Carlson, 2012). By contrast, others such as norepinephrine (NE) and ACh are thought to act more globally, mediating the capacity to engage in executive functions. One example of this mediating effect is observed in the interaction of 5-HT and DA, wherein the former facilitates transmission of the latter (Fuster, 2015; Kandel et al., 2013). As we will discuss, some neurochemicals appear integral to specific executive functions, while others seem to serve more of a supportive role. It is important to note that 5-HT (as well as some of the other neurotransmitters (e.g., DA) have many subtypes (as many as 14 according to some investigators; e.g., Homberg, 2012), which are classified in relation to the different types of receptor sites (e.g., Kilgus, Maxmen, & Ward, 2015). However, because these delineations are beyond the scope the present discussion, we will utilize the abbreviation 5-HT to include all of the various substrates.

In addition to monoamines, glutamate and γ-aminobutyric acid (GABA) are the main excitatory and inhibitory neurotransmitters, respectively, and also contribute to frontal lobe functions. They modulate or regulate the brain's responsiveness as a whole by speeding up communication or slowing it down. As one example, glutamate moderates the flow of information between cortical regions and subcortical structures, such as between the dorsolateral unit and the hippocampus (Fuster, 2008). By contrast, GABA also modulates the rate of communication between cells, impacting executive functions in a global way by inhibiting responses to certain information at certain times and facilitating the capacity to limit focus to the most relevant information.

Other factors also influence the effect and effectiveness of neurotransmitters. Aging, for example, has been shown to have a deleterious effect on the saturation of neurotransmitters such as DA, which tends to decrease particularly in the dorsolateral frontal region (Fuster, 2015). The reduction in DA in the dorsolateral region has been linked to impairment or deterioration of executive functions (Fuster, 2015). Fortunately, this DA decrease does not appear to be inevitable but can be positively influenced by continuing to engage in mentally challenging and stimulating activities (Harrison, 2015).

In addition to changes associated with aging, dopamine levels decrease in the process of learning. As learning takes place, the frontal lobes become less involved, shifting responsibility for executing a learned behavior from the anterior regions of the brain to the posterior ones. Thus in this case, too, we see a decrease in the amount of dopamine, but for an entirely different (and benign) reason. Exposure to toxic substances or chronic stress can also change the balance or effectiveness of neurotransmitters. For example, chronic use of alcohol has been shown to decrease the responsiveness of glutamate and GABA (Bhandage et al., 2014). While a detailed discussion of the aforementioned factors is beyond the scope of the present discussion, we certainly get a sense that neurotransmitters and their saturation levels are related to functioning. As frequently cited in the literature, we recognize that too much or too little of a given neurotransmitter (regardless of structural-functional unit) can have deleterious effects on functioning, as in the Yerkes-Dodson phenomenon (e.g., Pennanen, van der Hart, Yu, & Tecott, 2013). Furthermore, due to the brain's plasticity, changes in the concentrations of neurochemicals can continue to alter brain structure throughout the lifespan.

For the remainder of this discussion we will narrow the focus to learn more about the direct and indirect effects of several of the neurotransmitters that appear most involved in executive functions, namely DA, ACh, 5-HT, and NE. We will consider their roles as it pertains to the four structural-functional frontal units, examining each unit in turn. As we will see, a given neurotransmitter in one unit may globally influence executive functions, whereas the effect in a neighboring unit may seem more specific.

Neurotransmitters in Relation to Frontal Units

Dorsolateral unit. To varying degrees DA, NE, 5-HT, ACh, glutamate, and GABA influence the dorsolateral unit. Beginning with global influences, GABA, the brain's general inhibitory neurotransmitter, curbs responding to irrelevant sensory information (Homberg, 2012). This, in turn, facilitates the dorsolateral unit's capacity to focus on relevant sensory information, particularly abstract information (Homberg, 2012). However, GABA does not function alone; it requires DA, acting as a neuromodulator, to trigger its release (Carlson, 2012). DA appears to have the greatest influence in the dorsolateral region, in terms of grading the responsiveness to sensory stimuli and facilitating more cognitive aspects of executive function (Kilgus, Maxmen, & Ward, 2015). As one example, DA appears central to working memory (Miller & Cummings, 2007), presumably by increasing GABA and subsequently inhibiting responsiveness to irrelevant information.

DA in the dorsolateral region is also associated with influencing the consolidation of memories through the hippocampus, which understandably impacts learning (Miller & Cummings, 2007). Thus, when this pair of neurotransmitters is functioning optimally, or more importantly concertedly, DA facilitates the dorsolateral unit's capacity to focus on relevant sensory information, while GABA inhibits the response to information from other functional structural units that would cause interference.

ACh also influences the dorsolateral unit's capacity to attend to relevant sensory information and seems particularly involved when the information is novel (Miller & Cummings, 2007). ACh works globally as well. We see this with the effects of psychostimulant medication, which in the medial/ACC region helps to increase alertness and arousal. However, an overabundance of ACh transmitted via the open circuits of the thalamocortical loops (see Chapter 7) can deleteriously impact the seemingly more specific and focused aspect of executive functions attributed to the dorsolateral unit. Thus, the dorsolateral unit demonstrates a diminished capacity to focus on relevant information, as the focus on irrelevant information becomes disinhibited, allowing irrelevant stimuli to take on greater saliency (Miller & Cummings, 2007).

NE also indirectly affects the dorsolateral circuit, through its interaction with the medial/ACC (Franceschi, Anchisi, Pelati, Zuffi, & Matarrese, 2005). For example, a slight increase of NE in stressful situations (e.g., when taking an exam), can facilitate the capacity to recall information. However, too much of this "stress" hormone will have the opposite effect, causing the information to seem temporarily unavailable. Of course, this can be a vicious cycle wherein even more NE is dumped into the system, further thwarting access to memories and interfering with the capacity to engage in more cognitive aspects of executive function (Fuster, 2015; Zhang et al., 2013). 5-HT, like NE, influences the interplay of affective aspects of executive function, as information is transmitted through the open circuits. Suboptimal levels of 5-HT can create a sense of apathy and subsequently decrease the motivation to engage in more complex dorsolateral frontal lobe functions (Franceschi et al., 2005).

In summary, it seems the more cognitive aspects of executive functions are modulated by the dorsolateral region, which is most notably influenced by DA. GABA, NE, ACh, and 5-HT also affect the dorsolateral unit, although more globally, in that too much of these latter four substances interferes with inhibiting responsiveness to irrelevant sensory information (ACh) or recalling and further processing needed information (NE). Too little can create difficulties with disinhibiting responsiveness to irrelevant sensory information (GABA), and can lead to disinterest in engaging in the most complex of executive functions (5-HT).

Ventrolateral unit. The ventrolateral region helps us judge the relevance of current information, through associations with our previous experiences (i.e., memory) with given sensory and affective information (Homberg, 2012; Petrides, 2005). In other words, we use our memory to make decisions about how to respond in the present. This process is greatly influenced by 5-HT. For example, 5-HT in the ventrolateral unit facilitates our ability to inhibit responses to previously learned information (memory) and modulates our response to information increasing the saliency of information (sensory or affective) that appears most rewarding in the moment (Homberg, 2012).

It is not surprising that several psychological disorders, including schizophrenia, depression, obsessive-compulsive disorder, and substance abuse, have been associated with 5-HT. For example, substance abuse can interfere with 5-HT production and responsiveness, which can have an effect on judgment and mental control (Morey et al., 2011). Instead of the individual being able to inhibit responding to (sensory or affective) information, the information that is strongly tied to a previous experience will have a stronger pull in terms of getting our attention. This information will take on even greater saliency if it is thought to lead to a reward (Morey et al., 2011).

As such, when the ventrolateral unit is not functioning properly, it is more difficult to inhibit a response to information that appears counter to our immediate goals, which can impair the capacity to engage in more cognitive aspects of executive functions (Fitzgerald, 2011; Morey et al., 2011; Stone, 2013). Not surprisingly, increasing the level of 5-HT can decrease impulsive responding to irrelevant sensory and affective information (Fitzgerald, 2011).

Dopaminergic neurons in the ventrolateral regions also factor into reinforcement, based on the evaluation of sensory (i.e., dorsolateral) and affective (i.e., medial/ACC) information (Carlson, 2012) and communication through the open circuits. Substances such as cocaine and amphetamines trigger the release of dopamine in the nucleus accumbens. Anticipation of secondary reinforcement (e.g., money) can also trigger the release of DA there. The release is most pronounced when the stimulus is novel or the reward is unexpected, causing an even more intense and pleasurable response that plays a significant role in the development of an addiction.

Some investigators have suggested that the inability to resist an immediate reward has less to do with the relationship to prior learning than with a diminished capacity to predict negative consequences when presented with specific stimuli (Walker, Robbins, & Roberts, 2009). Perhaps there is an awareness of the negative consequences, as would be the case in substance abuse, but the sensory or affective pull is so rewarding that the logical consequences pale in comparison. Either way, when neurochemicals via the open circuits are unable to inhibit responsiveness to immediate information, the dorsolateral region fails to come online in order to modulate our behavior in a manner more consistent with long-term goals.

In summary, DA and 5-HT are central to functions of the ventrolateral unit, mainly by inhibiting the responsiveness to sensory and/or affective information. This in turn enables the dorsolateral region to engage in the most complex forms of executive functions.

Orbital unit. Damage to the orbital unit is a frequent consequence of many traumatic brain injuries (TBI) and is associated with poor impulse control, increased aggressiveness, and obsessive-compulsive behavior (Atmaca et al., 2011; Franceschi et al., 2005). Many investigators have suggested that 5-HT and DA are the key neurotransmitters linked to functions modulated by the orbital unit (e.g., Homberg, 2012; Miller & Cummings, 2007).

Before continuing, it is necessary to mention that many of the studies (i.e., human and animal) examining the saturation and functional effects of 5-HT and DA in the orbital region often include medial or lateral and ventral areas that we conceive of as part of the medial/ACC unit or the ventrolateral unit, respectively (e.g., Clark, Walker, Dalley, Robbins, & Roberts, 2013; Stein, Miczek, Lucion, & de Almeida, 2013; Yohe, Suzuki, & Lucas, 2012). For example, in a recent review of the role of 5-HT in the orbital region, Fuster (2015) indicates that depletion of 5-HT is associated with the inability to delay gratification and work toward a future reward, while acknowledging the influence of adjacent areas (i.e., orbitomedial, orbitofrontal), which is presumably in relation to open circuits. Others have found a link between the depletion of 5-HT in the orbital region and the capacity to control responses to sensory and affective input, particularly when the input is related to previous experience (Homberg, 2012; Murphy, Smith, Cowen, Robbins, & Sahakian, 2002). Here we might consider Mischel and colleagues' (1972) marshmallow experiment. Mischel et al. presented young children each with a marshmallow, informing them that if they could wait to eat the marshmallow they would be given a second marshmallow. Some of the children were quite successful, while others despite their best efforts and knowledge of a larger reward could not resists eating the treat (Mischel et al., 1972).

Some investigators have linked the depletion of 5-HT in the orbital (and ventral) region to an increase in fear responses in humans (Morey et al., 2011) and aggressive behaviors in rodents (e.g., Stein et al., 2013; Yohe et al., 2012), particular to a specific sensory stimulus that has previously been linked to an affective response. Admittedly, it is difficult to unequivocally tease apart the influence of the orbital and adjacent areas in order to draw distinct conclusions. It seems that 5-HT in the orbital region influences the pull of sensory information, which is in part dependent on the saliency of the immediate reward transmitted via open units from ventral, medial, and lateral frontal structures.

ACh also impacts activity of the orbital circuit. When the level of ACh is too high it can create problems with attending to irrelevant visual information. For example, in studies involving reversal learning tasks, subjects tended to focus on the previously learned stimuli and were less capable of attending to novel stimuli (dorsolateral region) (Miller & Cummings, 2007). By contrast, DA in the orbital unit appears to affect the appeal and thus motivation of responding to sensory information (Miller & Cummings, 2007; Fuster, 2015). We suggest that the greater concentration of DA compared to 5-HT in the orbital unit may support a more limited definition, wherein the "affective" responses attributed to the orbital region may be the result of the indirect influence from ventrolateral and medial/ACC (via the open circuits).

Given our conceptualization of the orbital unit (and in relation to open and closed circuits), we might expect executive dysfunction of this unit to result in difficulty delaying responses to reward. Such difficulty would be further complicated by a tendency to be alerted to, and lured by, sensory information, which can lead to acting in the moment due to an inability to consider consequences. To conclude this section, I will share an anecdote that seems to capture executive dysfunction of the orbital unit rather succinctly. As reported by Soper (2010);

A man with a slowly growing tumor first manifested his illness when, on going to the station one day to catch a train in one direction, he got on the train which happened to arrive first, although it was going in the opposite direction. He did not realize until later that he had acted purely on impulse and had given way to the influence of the immediate situation.

Medial/ACC unit. The medial/ACC unit is also modulated by DA, 5-HT, and NE, which differentially influence the decision-making process (Homberg, 2012). For example, DA in the medial/ACC (ventrolateral and orbital) circuit is tied to behaviors related to reward, which has been linked to addictive behaviors. Food, water, and sex (and drugs) trigger the release of DA. The powerful dopaminergic effect results in greater saliency of sensory information linked with a sensory reward (Fuster, 2015).

5-HT reaches the medial/ACC region via pathways directly from the brainstem. This input influences subcortical structures, including those of the limbic region. At optimal levels, 5-HT helps the medial/ACC unit to moderate physical and affective states, which allows for cognitive aspects of executive functions (i.e., the dorsolateral) to be put to use more effectively (Fuster, 2015; Miller & Cummings, 2007).

NE, like 5-HT, is essential to functions of the medial/ACC, moderating alertness and arousal and facilitating the capacity to engage in more complex executive functions (Fitzgerald, 2011; Marzo, Totah, Neves, Logothetis, & Eschenko, 2014; Snyder, Wang, Han, McFadden, & Valentino, 2012). The locus coeruleus, the main source of NE, is directly connected to the medial PFC as well as to certain subcortical structures (e.g., the hippocampus) (Snyder et al., 2012). NE in the medial/ACC supports the roles of the surrounding functional-structural units (particularly the dorsolateral) by facilitating an individual's capacity to pay attention to the most relevant information while less relevant information fades into the background (Howells, Stein, & Russell, 2012; Smallwood et al., 2012). Essentially, NE in the medial/ACC is part of a signal-to-noise filtration system. Similar to other neurotransmitters, too much or too little NE is problematic for executive functions. For example, some investigators suggest that when the concentration of NE is chronically either too low or too high, it can lead to anxiety or inattentiveness, respectively (e.g., Howells et al., 2012).

However, Smallwood and colleagues (2012) offer a different perspective, and suggest that a chronic overabundance of NE is linked to inattentive features of ADHD (i.e., daydreaming). They suggest that attention is drawn inward to "internal" information, wherein one's own thoughts become more salient than information in the environment (Smallwood et al., 2012). In summary, NE is transported from the medial/ACC to neighboring executive units, influencing the capacity to attend to the most relevant information by minimizing the influence of extraneous stimuli.

As discussed in the preceding paragraphs, deviations from the optimal level of NE in the medial/ACC unit can have deleterious effects on cognitive aspects of executive functions, contributing to under- or over-responsiveness.

Conclusion

To conclude, neurotransmitters affect and are affected by changes in motivation, anxiety, aggression, and cognition, which impact and are impacted by the ability to engage in all facets of executive functions. We know that too much or too little of a neurotransmitter will impact functioning of the specific unit, which is likely to affect executive functions as a whole. Certain of these transmitter substances (e.g., ACh) seem to predominantly raise the level of excitability of many of these areas involved in executive functioning, whereas others (e.g., 5-HT) lower it. In a normal individual, a balance is struck so the most appropriate level of excitability for a given cognitive and environmental situation is established for each structural-functional area.

It seems that each system is influenced (either directly or indirectly) by many of the same neurotransmitters (i.e., DA, 5-HT, NE, ACh, GABA, and glutamate), although not equally. This is due in part to the stream of information communicated via open circuits of the thalamocortical loops. It is also influenced by where innervation originates and terminates (Fuster, 2015). For example, adrenaline serves different functions in the peripheral vs. central nervous system (Carlson, 2012). As such, the function of a given neurotransmitter – (e.g., dopamine in pleasure; serotonin in impulsivity; norepinephrine in vigilance (Kilgus et al., 2009) – seems to depend critically on its location, the concentration of a given type of neuron or receptor in that location, and the interconnectivity with other regions.

DA seems to follow this rule, appearing integral to the precise, cognitively related functions moderated by the dorsolateral unit. However, throughout the frontal lobe DA moderates all aspects of executive behaviors including the capacity to respond to affective, sensory, and memory information. NE also has a global influence on frontal lobe functions, by increasing attention and arousal to certain stimuli (e.g., danger stimuli), which in turn shuts down cognitive aspects of executive functions. By maintaining a steady stream of NE, levels of arousal and alertness remain stable.

However, DA and NE also impact the saliency of information further processed in the orbital and ventrolateral regions, which in turn impacts the capacity of the dorsolateral region to function optimally or at all. DA appears essential to the influence of affective and sensory information via the ventrolateral and orbital units. The effects represent more of a filtration system, turning attention toward or away from given stimuli. 5-HT also influences these regions, impacting behavior more generally, in terms of being able to inhibit responsiveness to sensory (orbital) or affective (ventral) information, which influences the range of behaviors tied to motivation. ACh in the dorsolateral region acts more specifically to increase the saliency of novel sensory information by increasing or decreasing the saliency of information filtered via the ventrolateral and orbital regions, which in turn facilitates or impedes the capacity to make the most appropriate behavioral response.

9.

WHITE MATTER PATHWAYS

Executive functions (or frontal lobe functions) involve the sending and receiving of sensory, affective, memory, and reinforcement information to and from many cerebral cortical and subcortical regions of the brain, and then integrating this information in order to make the most appropriate motor response. The frontal lobe's interdependence with other areas of the brain requires efficient pathways for communicating both basic and higher-order information. Indeed, the frontal lobes share robust connections throughout much of the brain (Bennett, 2014).

Because of these robust connections and the integration of sensory, affective, and other information, the prefrontal cortex has, at times, been referred to as one of the association cortices (e.g., Fuster, 2008). While this designation may not strictly apply, it still serves to emphasize the complex integration that takes place in the prefrontal cortex. Indeed, the frontal lobes integrate massive amounts of information, which is sent and received via multiple pathways throughout the brain (e.g., Chow & Cummings, 2007; Koziol & Budding, 2009; Mesulam, 1986).

In this chapter we will examine two of these major pathways: white matter tracts (i.e., fasciculi) and the thalamocortical loops. In the first part of the chapter we will focus on the white matter tracts or fasciculi. These are thick bundles of neuronal axons, usually wrapped in myelin. The major classifications of fasciculi include: association fibers, projection fibers, and commissural fibers (Jellison et al., 2004). Most of our focus will be on two of the major association tracts, the *superior longitudinal fasciculus* and the *cingulum*. We will also discuss several of the other fasciculi that play a role in executive functions.

The second part of the chapter is devoted to taking a look at the other significant pathways relevant to executive functions by examining key subcortical circuitry. Specifically, we will discuss the role of the basal ganglia thalamocortical loop; first by providing a description of the basic model, including direct and indirect pathways. Then, we will consider variations to the basic model as they relate to the functional units of the frontal lobes (i.e., dorsolateral, ventrolateral, orbital, and medial/ACC). We suggest that examining the anatomy of the major pathways and respective cortical and subcortical connections will set the stage for a broader definition of executive function. This may help address the current conundrum of there being too narrow a definition of the process of executive functioning.

Major Fasciculi

The superior longitudinal fasciculus (SLF) and the cingulum are the two major fiber systems that connect the more posterior regions of the brain with the more anterior ones. Both of these are involved in sending and receiving information related to sensation-perception, memory, affect, and reinforcement. They are also integral to executive functions. Because both fasciculi contain bi-directional fibers (e.g., from sensory association areas to and from various frontal areas), one could imagine the fasciculi simultaneously sending posterior information forward and receiving information from the frontal lobe. Examining their respective anatomies reveals the different types of information they supply to the "executive units" of the prefrontal areas (see Figure 7.1).

Figure 7.1

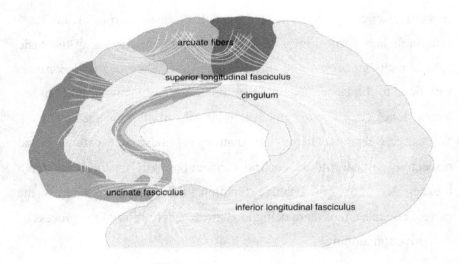

Lateral view of the brain with major fasciculi.

Superior longitudinal fasciculus. The SLF is the largest of the association fibers (Jellison et al., 2004). Extending from the frontal lobes, it arches around the superior aspect of the insula en route to the posterior cortices – that is, the parietal, temporal, and occipital lobes (e.g., Catani, Howard, Pajevic, & Jones, 2002; Jellison et al., 2004; Wakana et al.,

2004). Along with other association fibers (i.e., the uncinate and the fronto-occipital fasciculi) the superior longitudinal fasciculus connects the right and left sides of the frontal lobe with the corresponding (i.e., ipsilateral) hemispheres of posterior cortical areas (Catani et al., 2002). As the SLF courses from the anterior to the posterior regions of the brain, it contains many fibers projecting between multiple posterior association areas and secondary sensory areas, and between the lateral (and dorsal) portions of the prefrontal cortex (e.g., Jellison et al., 2004; Wakana et al., 2004). Its role in executive functioning has been thought to be mainly a mechanism for communicating between lateral sensory and prefrontal areas. However, more recently it is considered to be involved more broadly in aspects of executive function, and to play roles in attention and language, as well as affect and memory (Kamali et al., 2014).

We will consider the work of Kamali and colleagues (2014) and others (Makris et al., 2005) in order to fractionate distinct aspects of SLF. Using various forms of diffusion tensor imaging (DTI), several distinct aspects of the SLF have been identified, which are referred to as SLFI, SLFII, and SLFIII (Kamali et al., 2014; Makris et al., 2005). According to Kamali et al., the SLFI originates in the parietal lobe and extends closely along the cingulate gyri, coursing through myelinated areas of the frontal lobes (BA 4) to the superior frontal gyrus. The SLFI terminates in parts of the dorsolateral unit (BA 8, 9) and supplementary motor area (BA 6; Kamali et al., 2014; Makris et al., 2005). Functionally, the SFLI is associated with higher order motor behaviors, namely those related to application of abstract rules (Markis et al., 2004).

Similarly, SLFII originates in the parietal lobes, in the white matter of the angular gyrus (Kamali et al., 2014). It courses through the central aspect of white matter lateral to the corona radiata and superior to the insula (Kamali et al., 2014; Makris et al., 2005). It connects aspects of the superior temporal region, specifically Wernicke's area (BA 22), to aspects of the dorsolateral unit (BA 8 and 46). En route to the anterior regions of the brain, it passes through parts of the middle longitudinal fasciculus (near the arcuate fasciculus). It then moves through the motor (BA 4) and premotor region (BA 6), before terminating in the dorsolateral unit (BA 8, 46; Kamali et al., 2014: Makris et al., 2005). Makris et al. (2014) suggest this aspect of the SLF is associated with visual spatial attention and spatial working memory (which is likely related to connections afforded by the arcuate fasciculus. We will take this up in a subsequent paragraph).

The SLFIII is the most lateral portion of the SLF. It originates in the parietal lobe, in the supramarginal gyrus, and then courses through somatosensory white matter and the arcuate fasciculus. It terminates in the ventrolateral unit (BA 44) and the premotor area, BA 6 (Kamali et al., 2014; Makris et al., 2004). This portion of the SLF appears to play a role in motor planning, including the motor planning of language (Makris et al., 2014). It seems to also play a role in monitoring facial and hand movements (e.g., Petrides & Pandya, 2002).

The arcuate fasciculus (AF) can also be considered part of the SLF. In fact, at times, the two terms are used interchangeably. The AF is a main connection between the dorsolateral unit and the temporal lobe (Kamali et al., 2014). Unlike the aforementioned aspects of the SLF, the AF originates in the temporal lobe. From there, it courses around the insula and penetrates other aspects of the SLF (i.e., SLFII, SLFIII), before terminating in the dorsolateral unit, BA 8 and 46 (Catani et al., 2002; Kamali et al., 2014; Makris et al., 2005). Similarly to SLFII, the AF also connects to Wernicke's area, BA 22 (Catani et al., 2002). Because of these connections with the parietal lobe, it is thought to play a role in modulating both visuospatial and audiospatial information (Makris et al., 2014). Having established the course of the AF, its role in visual spatial attention and visual spatial working memory may be becoming clearer.

Kamali and colleagues (2014) have distinguished another area of the SLF; the *temporoparietal SLF* (SLF TP). This aspect originates in the parietal lobes, near the origin of the AF. Its fibers course from the temporal lobe to the parietal lobe, and from the parietal lobe through the temporoparietal white matter. Some of the fibers extend to the angular gyrus, whereas other fibers of this pathway extend to the SLFII and *middle longitudinal fasciculus* (MLF; which penetrates the parietal lobe) (Kamali et al., 2014).

Other association fibers. The *uncinate* and the *fronto-occipital fasciculi* are part of a network of association fibers which, along with the SLF, connect the frontal lobes with the ipsilateral hemisphere (Catani et al., 2002). The *uncinate fasciculus* connects anterior aspects of the temporal lobe with parts of the orbital unit and the frontopolar region, BA 10 (Catani et al., 2002). Lateral fibers from BA 10 join the orbital region in forming the uncinate, which hooks anteromedially and terminates in the temporal pole, uncus, hippocampal gyrus, and the amygdala (Catani et al., 2002).

The *superior fronto-occipital (subcallosal fisciculus)* connects to aspects of the dorsolateral unit and the parietal region. En route to the posterior regions, it receives projections from lateral aspects of the prefrontal cortex, that is, the inferior and middle gyri (Catani et al., 2002). The *inferior fronto-occipital fasciculus* connects aspects of the ventrolateral and dorsolateral units with the portions of the temporal and occipital lobes, passing through the external capsule. In considering the multiple connections of the association pathways (beginning with the SLF, to the inferior fronto-occipital fasciculus), we can more clearly entertain Makris's et al. (2004) supposition the that SLFII plays a role in both visual spatial attention and visual working memory.

Cingulum. The cingulum, by contrast, conveys information from more midline brain structures and contains fibers of different length, which extend from the uncus and parahippocampal gyrus to the frontal lobes; nearly making a circle connecting the frontal lobes and cingulate gyrus to the hippocampus and amygdala (e.g., Catani et al., 2002; Kamali et al., 2014; Wakana et al., 2004). It courses along the ventral aspect of the hippocampus until reaching the amygdala (Wakana et al., 2004).

The cingulum connects the medial frontal gyrus, parietal lobe, and cingulate to aspects of the temporal and occipital lobes (Catani et al., 2002). Many shorter fibers "join and leave" the cingulum along its route (Catani et al., 2002). These connections implicate the cingulum's involvement in emotional (affective), reinforcement, and memory functions.

Internal capsule and thalamic projections. As we transition to our discussion of the basal ganglia thalamocortical loops, it may be helpful to know that one of the other white matter tracts, *the internal capsule*, is a major pathway for thalamic projection fibers (e.g., Catani et al., 2002;

Wakana et al., 2004). Of specific interest to our discussion are the fibers in the anterior portion of the internal capsule, which serves as a major connection between the thalamus and the frontal cortex, as well as to parts of basal ganglia and motor areas (Catani et al., 2002; Wakana et al., 2004).

Cortically Originating Executive Systems

Based on the basal ganglia motor circuit loop, Alexander, Delong, and Strick (1986) identified the *basal ganglia thalamocortical circuit,* which has become the prototype for subcortical circuitry (Chow & Cummings, 2007; see Figure 7.2). The basic model of a basal ganglia thalamocortical loop involves direct and indirect connections, most of which begin at the cortical surface of the frontal lobes (Chow & Cummings, 2007). From there, information is sent to the thalamus via the basal ganglia, and eventually back to the cerebral cortex, thus closing the loop (Chow & Cummings, 2007). This basic schema describes the *cortical originating executive system.*

In this system, there are six parallel circuits. Four of them involve the prefrontal areas (i.e., dorsolateral, orbital, ventrolateral, and medial/anterior cingulate cortex) and executive functions, while the other two are more directly responsible for motor responses. They are composed of the Cortically Originating Extra Pyramidal System (COEPS, described below) and the direct cortical spinal and corticotrigeminal systems, in which single neurons extend and carry information from the cortex (predominantly area 4) to the trigeminal nerve (for the head and face) or through the pyramids, down to the motor neurons of the spinal cord.

Figure 7.2

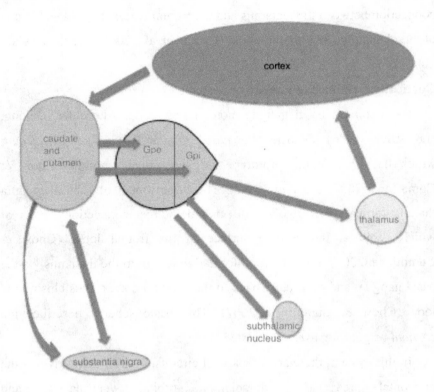

Basic basal ganglia thalamocortical circuit.

In looking at the motor system, we are familiar with the cortically originating extrapyramidal system (COEPS). Fibers from the motor cortex descend to the telencephalic basal ganglia; especially the caudate nucleus, putamen, and globus pallidus, as well as to the lower nuclei, which include the red nuclei and substantia nigra (e.g., Chow & Cummings, 2007). Many of the projections through the telencephalic basal ganglia exit through the ansa lenticularis to the ventral anterior thalamus (e.g., Gunzler et al., 2006). From there, they project back to the cortex via thalamocortical fibers (Chow & Cummings, 2007).

Of course there is much more to the extrapyramidal system than just this executive mechanism, as contacts to the lower nuclei and the reticular formation are also very important. But as we shall see, there are several parallel circuits moving from cortex-to basal ganglia-to ventral anterior thalamus, then back to the cortex; all originate in the prefrontal cortices involved in executive functioning. As opposed to the cortically originating executive systems, the latter are more comparable to the well-known proprioceptor originating extrapyramidal feedback loops (POEPS).

Subcortical Circuits

In general, when sensory information is received through the primary sensory organs it is sent to posterior (i.e., post-Rolandic) regions of the brain to be processed in secondary sensory areas and then sensory association areas. Through the basal ganglia thalamocortical loops, which we will more generally refer to as the subcortical circuitry, information is conveyed to specific pre-Rolandic cortical regions, mostly in the prefrontal and premotor areas, that result in the inhibition or disinhibition of behavior.

The subcortical circuits are most often referred to either by function (i.e., motor, oculomotor) or by the cortical area where the circuit originates, that is, dorsolateral prefrontal, orbital, and medial/ACC (Mega & Cummings, 2001). Each circuit consists of parallel subcortical structures, which include portions of the basal ganglia and the thalamus (Mega & Cummings, 2001). Cortical and subcortical areas communicate via neurotransmitters, which are sent and received through reciprocal or unreciprocated afferent and efferent pathways along each of the parallel pathways (Alexander et al., 1986; Mega & Cummings, 2001). For example, upon receiving information from posterior or limbic areas, an excitatory signal arises from cortical areas in the frontal lobes. Efferent projections convey this excitatory signal to specific areas of the striatum, which are then acted upon by a neurotransmitter, GABA. This results in an inhibitory signal.

Motor circuit. As noted previously, the prototype of the basal ganglia thalamocortical circuit is based on the motor circuit (which we will review in order to frame the larger discussion related to the prefrontal subcortical circuitry). The motor circuit begins with information arising in the motor regions of the cerebral cortex, which then sends projections to the striatum (putamen and caudate nucleus). The direct circuit extends to the globus pallidus interna (GPi) and to the subthalamic nucleus pars reticulara (SNpr), which send information to the ventrolateral (VL) region of the thalamus, before returning to motor areas of the cortex (Alexander et al., 1986).

Projections via the indirect pathway extend to the globus pallidus externa (GPe) which, in turn, projects to the subthalamic nucleus (STN). The STN then sends excitatory signals to the GPi, influencing its output to the thalamus and, ultimately, cortical activity (Koziol & Budding, 2009). These, too, are related to the Cortical Originating Executive System (COES), or the executive mechanism.

Frontal Circuits

Dorsolateral circuit. As expected from its name, the dorsolateral circuit originates in the dorsolateral region, specifically from BA 9 and 10. This circuit sends information from the cortex to the striatum (i.e., dorsolateral head of the caudate nucleus), which is then transmitted to GPi and SNpr along the direct pathway, and to the GPe along the indirect pathway. The direct pathway sends information from the GPi and SNpr to the (parvocellular aspects), medialis dorsalis (MD), and ventroanterior (VA) thalamus, respectively. The MD closes the circuit by sending information back to the dorsolateral unit, specifically to BA 9 and 10 (Mega & Cummings, 2001). Projections from the MD to the prefrontal cortex are unique in that they only project to "nonmotor" areas (Campbell, Duffy, & Salloway, 2001). Information from the VA is also sent to prefrontal cortical areas (e.g., the premotor and supplementary motor areas; Gunzler et al., 2011). The indirect pathway also provides information to these cortical areas. However, it sends the information indirectly from the GPe to the subthalamic nucleus (SN). That information is then sent to the GPi and SNpr and similarly to specific cortical areas (Mega & Cummings, 2001; Gunzler et al., 2011).

The executive circuit parallels the COEPS, both of which are templates for the other frontal executive circuits. A parallel system appears to exist for the circuit that originates in the orbital, ventrolateral, and medial/ACC areas though the zone of influence (e.g., affective or sensory) differs depending on the origin of the pathway.

Orbital circuit. The orbital circuit originates in BA 11. Information is sent to the ventral striatum or nucleus accumbens (e.g., Mega & Cummings, 2001; Zald & Kim, 2001). From here the orbital circuit connects with the globus pallidus prior to reaching the MD thalamus (Mega & Cummings, 2001; Zald & Kim, 2001). Information from the MD thalamus (and to a lesser extent from the VA thalamus) is sent to BA 11 (Zald & Kim, 2001), closing the loop.

Ventrolateral circuit. Based on information from Mega and Cummings (2001), we can also identify a ventrolateral circuit, which is referred to as the lateral aspect of the orbital unit, arising primarily from BA 47. From BA 47, information is sent to the striatum (ventromedial caudate). It is then transmitted to the mediodorsal aspect of the GPi and SNpr. From there, information is sent to specific (magnocellular) aspects of the thalamus (inferomedial) MD and (medial) VA thalamus. This brings the information back to BA 47, closing the loop (Mega & Cummings, 2001).

Medial/ACC circuit. The ACC loop originates in BA 24 and sends information to the ventral or *limbic* striatum (ventral medial caudate, ventral putamen, nucleus accumbens, and the olfactory tubercle) (Mega & Cummings, 2001). From the limbic striatum, information is sent to the Gpi, ventral pallidum, and substantia nigra. An indirect loop may transmit information from the ventral striatum to the GPe (Mega & Cummings, 2001). The GPe sends information to the SN, which is then sent to the ventral pallidum. From there, the circuit is closed via connections from the (magnocellular) MD thalamus to the anterior cingulate (Mega & Cummings, 2001). The anterior cingulate loop seems to be involved in the affective aspects of executive functioning.

Direct and indirect pathways. As mentioned, the basal ganglia thalamocortical loops consist of direct and indirect pathways, both of which have specific roles in regulating behavior (Chow & Cummings, 2007). In the case of voluntary movement, such as executive functions, the direct pathway increases the cortical response. By contrast, the indirect pathway inhibits it (Mega & Cummings, 2001). More specifically, signals via the direct pathway are sent from the cortex to the GPi and SNpr, which then send inhibitory messages to the thalamus. The reduction in thalamic output triggers an excitatory signal to the cortex.

Inhibitory signals are also sent from the striatum to the GPe. Those coming from the GPe act on the STN, increasing its activity. Projections from the STN convey excitatory signals back to the GPi/SNpr. In turn, these signals act on the thalamus to increase activity, which then moderates the signal sent to the cortex via the direct pathway.

Open circuits. Open circuits comprise reciprocal afferent and efferent fibers that send information to those functionally related areas of the brain that are not part of the direct circuitry of a given unit. For example, afferent connections from other areas of the brain (e.g., parietal lobe, temporal lobe, frontal lobe, subcortical structures) are sent via open circuits to specific frontal circuits (Mega & Cummings, 2001). The other type of open circuit sends information from a specific circuit (e.g., dorsolateral) to other brain areas that serve a related function (Mega & Cummings, 2001). In addition to afferent and efferent connections, open pathways include reciprocal connections, such as the major shared connection between the ACC and the dorsolateral unit (BA 8, 9, 10, and

46) (Mega & Cummings, 2001). We will discuss specific open structures as related to the open circuits in the section that follows.

Dorsolateral open circuit. The open circuit of the dorsolateral circuit maintains reciprocal afferent and efferent connections with other cortical and subcortical areas of the brain, which support the functions of the larger dorsolateral unit. For example, the open circuit provides the sharing of information via reciprocal pathways between the supplemental motor area (BA 6), areas of the dorsolateral unit (BA 8, 46), and aspects of the parietal lobe (e.g., Mega & Cummings, 2001, Pandya & Yeterian, 1996). The open circuits of the dorsolateral circuit include robust reciprocal connections between the ACC circuit and BA 8, 9, 10, and 46 (e.g., Mega & Cummings, 2001; Pandya & Yeterian, 1996), enabling the sharing of highly processed affective and sensory input. Information from other cortical and subcortical areas within the larger aspect of the dorsolateral unit, as well as from other prefrontal units (e.g., ventrolateral, orbital), are also shared between specific afferent and efferent connections of the dorsolateral circuit (e.g., Mega & Cummings, 2001).

Ventrolateral open circuit. Based on Mega and Cummings' (2001) description of the lateral open circuits of the orbital lateral unit, we can surmise that these would align with our suppositions of the ventrolateral open circuits. These open circuits appear to share reciprocal connections with the medial/ACC unit, specific aspects of the amygdala, the temporal lobe, and a specific aspect of the supplemental motor area BA 6 (Mega & Cummings, 2001). The ventrolateral circuit receives information from the thalamus, basal ganglia, midbrain tegmentum, and brainstem (Mega & Cummings, 2001). It sends information to the cingulate (BA 33 and 25), including aspects of the anterior cingulate cortex (BA 32). We can see how this would be a particularly rich area for the executive mechanism to integrate various forms of information, especially limbic information.

Orbital open circuit. Based on Mega and Cummings' (2001) descriptions of the medial aspect of the orbital circuit, the open circuit of this unit is thought to share connections with the amygdala, cingulate, insula, and temporal lobe. It receives information from affective regions such as the hippocampus, midbrain, and brainstem, as well as the substantia nigra. The open circuit sends information to the cingulate (BA 33) and aspects of the insular cortex (Mega & Cummings, 2001).

Anterior cingulate cortex open circuit. As mentioned, the ACC circuit shares abundant connections with the anterior cingulate circuit and aspects of the dorsolateral unit (areas 8, 9, 10, 46) (Mega & Cummings, 2001). As mentioned previously, this enables the sharing of sensory and affective information, presumably with each informing the other in relation to respective functions. Reciprocal connections between aspects of the ventrolateral unit (BA 47), key limbic structures (i.e., amygdala, hippocampus), regions of the temporal lobe (BA 35, 36, and 38), and the insula and claustrum are also noted (Mega & Cummings, 2001). Information is sent from aspects of the thalamus, hippocampus, BA 28 and BA 35, midbrain, and brainstem to the ACC circuit (Mega & Cummings, 2001). Open pathways of the ACC circuit send information to specific nuclei of the thalamus and basal ganglia. We can see that these connections allow for sharing of affective and sensory information, as well as information related to autonomic functions.

Conclusion

The major fasciculi serve as an information superhighway. They are involved in the continual sending and receiving of information related to the senses, affect, and memory. As discussed, the dorsolateral region mainly receives highly processed sensory information, which it processes further by integrating it with other relevant types of information. These include affective and mnemonic information from other areas of the brain via the superior longitudinal fasciculi.

The ventrolateral area also receives sensory input from the superior longitudinal fasciculi, and memory and affective information from the cingulum. The orbital area, by contrast, is involved in organizing the information to provide the most appropriate affective output. The cingulum feeds into the orbital cortex, providing it with affective information. This is why, after a disruption to this area following a blow to the head, some people may have trouble controlling their affective output. The medial prefrontal/ACC region also receives mainly affective information from the cingulum, and reinforcement information from nucleus accumbens and ventral tegmentum areas. Damage to this region may cause problems with reinforcement, as well as learning from negative reinforcement.

The thalamocortical circuitry is related to sites we have identified as the four functional-structural units (i.e., dorsolateral, orbital, ventrolateral, and medial/ACC). From these, excitatory impulses are sent to respective areas of the striatum, and then transmitted via direct or indirect pathways. Once received in specific areas of the thalamus, thalamic information is sent, along the direct route, to the cortex and other structures.

Simultaneously, indirect pathways send and receive information between many regions outside of the closed circuit via reciprocal afferent and efferent connections. By fractionating the frontal lobe circuits into four distinct units (in accordance with cortical location, routes, and connections to other structures), we have identified the basis of the functional structural relationship of the frontal lobes.

In the past, there was a tendency to conceptualize executive functions as those more specific to the dorsolateral region, with little mention of the essential contributions of the other regions. However, we are not suggesting there are four independent mechanisms. Rather, there is one overarching mechanism with four different parts that process different types of information; collectively, these underlie executive functions as a whole. This helps to explain why definitions of executive function that attempt to capture the complexity of frontal lobe behaviors in terms of specific tests designed to measure it will always fall short.

10.

EXECUTIVE FUNCTIONS OF THE DORSOLATERAL UNIT

Despite the fact that the dorsolateral region has been studied longer than any of the other functional structural units, and is often the main focus of executive functions, we still lack a common language to describe these functions. However, there seems to be consensus that the dorsolateral prefrontal cortex is implicated in the most complex and abstract aspects of executive functioning. Some investigators have conceptualized these functions in terms of cognitive control, working memory, and behavioral control (e.g., Baeken, Schrijvers, Sabbe, Vanderhasselt, & De Raedt, 2012; Baddeley, 2003; Levy & Goldman-Rakic, 2000), as well as overseeing goal-directed behavior (Miller & Cohen, 2001; Stuss, 2011). Others have focused more specifically on its role in the modulation of motor output (e.g., Callaert et al., 2011; Thorn, Atallah, Howe, Graybiel, 2010). Still others have focused on its capacity to mediate certain cognitive functions (e.g., Barbey, Colom, & Grafman, 2013; Blumenfeld & Rangantha, 2006). Admittedly, there is more work to be done in definitively specifying the functions mediated by the dorsolateral unit (Braddeley, 2013), though there appear to be several points of agreement.

A main goal of this chapter is to consider the areas of consensus regarding dorsolateral functions and fit those together with our understanding of executive functions. Prior to embarking on that lengthier discussion, I will provide an overview of the anatomical aspects of the dorsolateral unit and its cortical connectivity. Next, I will review several prominent theories that have been used to explain the functional capacity of this region. This will be followed by a consideration of specific functions in the context of executive behaviors. Finally, I will briefly consider some of the evidence for laterality of function.

Mapping the Territory

The functional structural dorsolateral unit consists of BA 8, 9, 9/46, 10, 46 and the rostral aspect of BA 6 (e.g., Barbas & Pandya, 1991; Petrides, 2000; Petrides & Pandya, 1999; see Figure 8.1). Pandya and Yeterian (1996) have further divided BA 8 into dorsal (8A) and ventral regions (8B). We will use these architectonic divisions in the present discussion; doing so will provide a context for detailing the cortical connectivity of the dorsolateral region.

It is important to note that when referring to the dorsolateral cortex in Old World monkeys the tissues dorsal and ventral to the principal sulcus are usually included. If the principal sulcus represents the homologue of the inferior frontal sulcus (Petrides and Pandya, 1994, 2001), discussions of this region (in monkeys) include what would be considered the ventrolateral prefrontal cortex in humans.

Figure 8.1

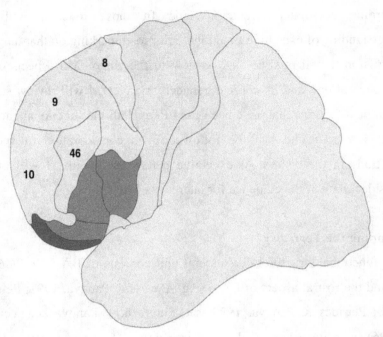

*Lateral aspect of cortical surface areas corresponding
to the dorsolateral functional structural unit.*

In this discussion, we will take this into consideration and focus on the dorsolateral regions in the human as much as possible.

The dorsolateral unit shares rich connections with specific areas within its own boundaries, as well as with the other prefrontal functional structural units and the frontal lobes as a whole. For example, within the dorsolateral unit, BA 8A receives information from BA 8B, BA 9, and 9/46 (Pandya & Yeterian, 1996). This area also receives information from specific aspects of the ventrolateral unit (BA 45). Pandya and Yeterian indicate that a significant source of information for BA 8A comes from the temporal lobes and the insula, as well as (to a lesser extent) from aspects of the parietal lobe. Similarly, BA 8B shares many of these same connections, including a reciprocal connection with area 8A as well as with other areas within the dorsolateral unit, that is, 9, 9/46, 46 (Pandya & Yeterian, 1996). It also receives input from the motor region, as well as from aspects of the other frontal functional structural units (i.e., ventrolateral, BA 45, 47; orbital, BA 11; and medial/ACC, BA 24). Further, BA 8 receives information from information from the paralimbic region (BA 23, 31), aspects of the parietal lobe, the insula, temporal lobes, and occipital lobes (Pandya & Yeterian, 1996).

The lateral portion of BA 9 also receives information from other areas within the dorsolateral unit (i.e., BA 8B, rostral aspect of BA 9), from the orbital region (i.e., BA 11, 13, 14), medial/ACC (BA 24, 32, and aspects of the ventrolateral region, BA 47), the premotor area (BA 6), as well as from lateral and posterior regions of the brain, for example, the temporal lobes and insula (Pandya & Yeterian, 1996). Similarly to other aspects of the dorsolateral unit, BA 9/46 receives input from other areas in the dorsolateral region, such as the ventral and dorsal aspects of BA 8, and BA 46. Information is also sent to BA 9/46 from other functional structural units (i.e., orbital: mainly from BA 11, medial/ACC; BA 24, 32) and the premotor region (BA 6), as well as from posterior structures, the occipital, temporal, and parietal lobes (Pandya & Yeterian, 1996). Connections shared with the ventrolateral unit will be discussed at length in the next chapter.

The most anterior portion of the dorsolateral region, BA 10, receives information from other parts of the dorsolateral unit (BA 9, 46), along with other structural functional units, for example, the orbital and medial/ACC (Burgess, 2010). BA 10 has diffuse connections, which allow it to integrate highly processed information from nearly all other areas of the brain (Bunge, Helskog, & Wendelken, 2009). Finally, the premotor cortex (BA 6) receives input from BA 8B and 9, the supplemental motor area (BA 8A), and aspects of the cingulum (Pandya & Yeterian, 1996).

D'Esposito and Postle (2015) and others (e.g., Averbeck, Lehman, Jacobson, & Haber, 2014; Bunge et al., 2009; Choi, Yeo, & Buckner, 2012; Jarbo & Verstynen, 2015; Pandya & Yeterian, 1996) describe the cortical organization of the dorsolateral unit as part of a functional structural hierarchy. For example, areas above the inferior frontal gyrus (IFG) receive more information from dorsal and medial regions, whereas areas below IFG receive input primarily from ventral and orbital regions (Pandya & Yeterian, 1996). Some investigators suggest that brain regions closer to the top in this hierarchy mediate intrinsic brain functions (e.g., Choi et al., 2012). The more anterior aspects of the dorsolateral region (BA 9, 46) share widespread connections with other cortical and subcortical areas, which some say suggests the capacity for more general functions (D'Esposito & Postle, 2015).

Theoretical Underpinnings

Multiple theories have been developed to explain executive functions. In this section, I will limit the discussion to *domain theories* and the theory of the *central executive* (CE; Baddeley, 2012). (For a more comprehensive review of specific executive function theories such as those of Lezak and Goldman, please see Bennett, 2014.)

Domain theories take two positions in relation to executive functions: *domain general* and *domain specific*. The main postulate of the domain-general theory is that executive functions describe a general pattern of behavior that cannot be tied to a specific area of the brain (e.g., Alsop et al., 1995), whereas domain-specific theories posit that we can link executive functions to specific areas in the frontal lobes (e.g., Levy & Goldman-Rakic, 2000). In terms of the dorsolateral unit, those on the domain-general side such as Alsop et al. (1995) and others (e.g., Alvarez & Emory, 2006; Barbey et al., 2013; Stuss, 2011) argue that the dorsolateral unit mediates general cognitive processes. Conversely, those who agree with domain-specific theories point to links between specific areas of the dorsolateral unit that mediate specific functions, such as spatial and verbal aspects of working memory (e.g., Fried, Moss, Valero-Cabre, & Pascual-Leone, 2014; Levy & Goldman-Rakic, 2000).

Even if we adhere to a specific theory of frontal lobe function, it does not resolve the debate regarding executive functions because these theories seem open to interpretation. For example, some use domain-specific theories to bolster the argument for another theoretical construct, that of the CE (Osaka et al., 2004). Interestingly, one of the most prolific writers on the subject of the CE, Alan Baddeley, argues that domain-specific theories conflict with the basic premises of a CE (Baddeley, 2012). Still others suggest that domain-specific theories are not only in conflict with the notion of a CE, but also provide unequivocal evidence that there is no such thing as a CE (Stuss, 2011). Importantly, Aleksander Luria (1973) provided an alternative viewpoint, positing that the hierarchical organization of the brain provides a structural mechanism for complex brain functions. Indeed, there is considerable evidence that frontal lobe functions are part of this hierarchy, wherein the dorsolateral unit mediates the functions at the top of the hierarchy that fall along a continuum from concrete to abstract.

The Dorsolateral Unit and Executive Functions

Even with an understanding of the hierarchical organization of the brain and its relationship to brain functions, it a considerable challenge to succinctly describe the executive functions mediated by the dorsolateral unit, at least without entering into a debate over semantics, much less theory. One of the challenges often discussed in the neuropsychology literature regards a lack of understanding of the basic processes of the frontal lobes, which then defaults to describing tasks designed to measure complex brain functions (e.g., Stuss, 2011). Some have navigated this challenge by attempting to create a common language to describe frontal lobe functions, with terms such as working memory, cognitive control, goal maintenance, and complex motor planning (e.g., Baeken, Schrijvers, Sabbe, Vanderhasselt, & De Raedt, 2012; Barbey et al., 2013; Barcelo & Knight, 2002). Others prefer more general terms such as "executive" functions (Stuss, 2011). Yet, therein lies the conundrum: how do we allow for enough flexibility when defining frontal lobe functions without being so vague that it is virtually meaningless?

Soper's (2014) definition of executive functions, "the ability to take into account and integrate all of the available information and to produce the most appropriate motor output" seems to provide a much needed middle ground, which enables us to define "executive" without the risk of being so restrictive that we are, once again, describing a task instead of a function. In the following paragraphs we will utilize Soper's definition to examine the functional structural relationship of the dorsolateral unit in terms of the information received, how it is integrated, and the motor output.

The "taking in of information" or receiving of information. Multiple modes of inquiry into frontal lobe functions (e.g., lesion studies, fMRI, cytoarchitectonic-connectional) demonstrate that the dorsolateral region receives highly processed (mostly sensory) information from adjacent cortical regions (e.g., Heekeren, Marrett, Ruff, Bandettini, & Ungerleider, 2006; Stuss, 2011). The sensory information is not "sensory" per se, but rather so refined that it bears no resemblance to the elementary perceptual form; meaning that in the processing of the sensory information it is converted into an abstract representation (Blumenfeld & Ranganath, 2006; Chao & Knight, 1998). The dorsolateral region also receives affective information (again, highly processed), as well as information that has been stored in memory, which is sent from neighboring functional structural units and other areas in the brain (e.g., Burgess, 2010; Stuss, 2011). Thus, the dorsolateral unit "takes in" information from multiple sensory-perceptual and affective areas of the brain, via direct and indirect connections.

Interpretation and integration of information. Examination of anatomical (architectonic-connectional) and functional (fMRI) studies provides compelling evidence of the dorsolateral region's capacity to integrate a vast array of information (e.g., Volle, Gilbert, Benoit, &

Burgess, 2010; D'Esposito & Postle, 2010). Part of this integration process involves ongoing monitoring and manipulation, which is largely moderated by BA 46 and 9/46 (Petrides, 1991, 1994, as cited in Petrides, 2000).

This process is further supported by the capacity to activate previously generated rules (with support of the ventrolateral region) in order to internally produce new rules as a function of activating a relational template (Volle et al., 2010). These rules are used to assimilate information received from widespread regions of the brain (e.g., Volle et al., 2010; Burgess, 2010). Indeed, in order to integrate information, some researchers suggest that a new connection or relationship is made with the information presented (D'Esposito et al., 2000). D'Esposito and colleagues propose that the dorsolateral region requests information from other areas in the prefrontal cortex, while it simultaneously activates rules that are both relationally contingent and consistent with a present goal. (In a subsequent section, it is suggested that this process integrally involves the basal ganglia.)

Thus, in order to engage in abstract reasoning, the dorsolateral region calls upon self-generated rules and/or connections to make sense of current information (Volle et al., 2010). This enables the dorsolateral unit to engage in further processing of information, wherein abstract representations of new information are integrated. This is done through a process of organizing the information by using an existing template or rules (that also exist in the abstract) from which new meaning can be made (Baddeley, 2003). In part, this is due to the unit's capacity to apply rules to reconcile incongruences in the information (Baddeley, 2012;

Heekeren, Marrett, Ruff, Bandettini, & Ungerleider, 2006).

The dorsolateral system appears to create order by integrating information through the production of new self-generated relationships. These relationships are based on the capacity to access and activate previously learned rules (e.g., Baddeley, 2012; Volle et al., 2010).

Contribution to motor output. The capacity to take in information and give it meaning is fundamental to the third aspect of dorsolateral executive functions, that is, the capacity to produce the most appropriate motor response. Knowing that the dorsolateral unit is directly connected to the premotor and, ultimately, motor areas, it is likely no surprise that this region is involved in motor output. Indeed, that is what has been found. The dorsolateral unit, along with its connections to premotor, motor, and subcortical areas, is integral to modulating and monitoring motor output (e.g., Choi, Yeo, & Buckner, 2012; D'Esposito & Postle, 2015). It is also essential for complex motor planning (Baeken et al., 2009; Miller & Cummings, 2007). Notably, it is not only the dorsolateral unit that is involved in this process. Seminal studies by Halsband and Passingham (1982, 1985) and Petrides (1982, 1986) have found that nonhuman primates were impaired in making visuomotor responses when the premotor cortex was damaged, despite there being no impairment in the perception of visual signals or engagement of motor movements. This can be interpreted to mean that the premotor area is involved in making the connection between the information and selection of a motor response congruent with an immediate task.

Indeed, Wallis and Miller (2003) found that abstract rules directly related to intentional motor movement show greater involvement of the premotor region of primates than the prefrontal cortex. This is consistent with neural mechanisms in humans, indicating that the premotor cortex is essential in the planning of motor output (Beurze, De Lange, Toni, & Medendorp, 2007). Other researchers also suggest that the premotor cortex is involved in the selection of rules and planning of given motor output (e.g., Amiez, Kostopoulos, Cham-pod, & Petrides, 2006; Halsband & Freund, 1990; Schluter, Rushworth, Passingham, & Mills, 1998). Furthermore, it has been found that the premotor region is involved in mental operations *even in the absence of a specific motor goal* (Hanakawa et al., 2002), meaning that the premotor area is implicated in representing abstract rules even when the need for a motor movement is absent (Nakayama, Yamagata, Tanji, & Hoshi, 2008). We might think of the premotor region as part of a preparatory mechanism, wherein abstract rules are represented and selected, and as part of larger system involved in executive processing.

Other key structures in this system are the basal ganglia. It is well established that the basal ganglia are involved in integrating information related to motor movement and the processing of information from the frontal cortices (e.g., Alexander et al., 1986; Graybiel, 2008). However, some suggest that the role of the basal ganglia, while essential, may be more limited and specific in terms of executive functions. For example, Hoshi (2015) suggests that the basal ganglia are the center for interpreting motor movement and cueing subsequent behavioral goals, which are maintained and refined further in the dorsolateral and premotor regions. Part of this process involves inhibiting certain movements and facilitating the initiation of other movements via communication in the thalamocortical loops (Mannella & Baldassarre, 2015). The motor cortex (BA 4), which some suggest is part of a mechanism that guides intentional motor behavior (e.g., Abe & Hanakawa, 2009; Rushworth et al., 2005), is also involved in this process. Together, these findings indicate that we need to expand the foci of executive functions by going beyond the prefrontal cortex to the frontal lobe as a whole. Although some investigators disagree (e.g., Stuss, 2012), this strongly suggests that, to a significant degree, executive functions and prefrontal lobe functions can be thought of as synonymous.

Hemispheric Specialization

Many researchers have considered the functional laterality of the dorsolateral unit and some have provide evidence that certain processes are modulated differentially according to hemisphere (e.g., Heekeren, Marrett, Ruff, Bandettini, & Ungerleider, 2006; Colombo, Balzarotti, & Mazzucchelli, 2016). For example, it appears that the nature of the information "taken in" by the left and right hemisphere may differ. Heekeren and colleagues (2006) suggest that the left (posterior) region of the dorsolateral unit is differentially responsive to information that is coherent. It has suggested that the right hemisphere plays an interesting role in evaluative decision-making. For example, Colombo et al. (2016) found that temporary impairment of the right dorsolateral region affects decision-making related to attractiveness, wherein "functional" items were seen as less attractive. Others have examined what might be considered integrative functions. Smirni, Turriziani, Mangano, Cipolotti, and Oliveri (2015) indicate that the right dorsolateral unit appears to increase the accuracy of non-verbal memory by inhibiting episodic memories that may cause interference. Furthermore, Smirni and colleagues speculate that the inhibitory process blocks competing networks, while the facilitatory process may increase activity in the temporal lobe. Still others have examined laterality in motor output. For example, Perach-Barzilay and colleagues (2013) demonstrated differences in the capacity to inhibit aggressive behavior. They found that the left dorsolateral unit plays a larger role in helping to modulate aggressive tendencies.

Conclusion

Indeed, it is common knowledge that that the dorsolateral region is not involved when a task is familiar or routinized (Barbey et al., 2013; Novick, Kan, Trueswell, & Thompson-Schill, 2009). However, when it is necessary to integrate abstract information to form a new meaning or understanding, we rely on the dorsolateral unit. In fact, the more abstract the task, the greater the involvement of the more anterior units along the functional structural hierarchy of the dorsolateral region (e.g., Badre, 2008; Badre, Hoffman, Cooney, and D'Esposito, 2009, Jung & Haier, 2007; Volle et al., 2010).

Furthermore, our understanding of neural networks and connectivity supports a hierarchical structure, wherein information needed to perform complex brain functions is transmitted from areas throughout the brain to the most anterior regions, where it is processed further; some of this information is suppressed, while other information is integrated. As such, this supports the capacity to initiate appropriate behavior (e.g., Burgess, 2010; Stuss, 2011). Despite Baddeley's affinity for the notion of a CE, he offers a line of reasoning that is complementary to hierarchical functions, suggesting that frontal lobe functions may involve a process of co-modulation, wherein "higher order" and "lower order" functions engage in reciprocal co-modulation.

In the next chapter, we will take a closer look at the processes involved in higher order functions, specifically in terms of executive functions and the functional structural relationship of the ventrolateral unit. This will be followed by a similar discussion of the orbital and medial/ACC units. After examining the processes of each individual unit, we will conclude by addressing executive functions as a whole.

11.

EXECUTIVE FUNCTIONS OF THE VENTROLATERAL UNIT

The ventrolateral functional structural unit is involved in many facets of executive functions, including those related to attention, memory, and reasoning. Some refer to the ventrolateral unit as a "cognitive control mechanism," due to its capacity to access mnemonic information to guide goal-directed behavior (Badre & Wagner, 2007). Others have described its functions in relation to specific tasks associated with executive (and cognitive) functions, such as set-shifting, rule learning, rule use, working memory, and analogical reasoning (e.g., Garcin, Volle, Dubois, & Levy, 2012; Geddes, Tsuchida, Ashley, Swick, & Fellows, 2014; Hedden & Gabrieli, 2010).

In the simplest of terms, the ventrolateral unit is tasked with facilitating and inhibiting the range of behaviors necessary for encoding information, remembering the information, and selecting among memories, in order to make the most appropriate behavioral response. In the following discussion we will provide more detail about the specific behaviors moderated by the ventrolateral unit. We will begin by outlining the anatomical details of this unit, in terms of location and connectivity with other cortical and subcortical structures. Then we will proceed to look at the interplay of affective and sensory information, which are further processed by this unit in the storage, recall, or selection of memories. We will also consider the theories that have been put forward in an effort to gain an overall understanding of how this unit processes information. The first, domain-specific theory, suggests that the functions of the ventrolateral unit are distinct. The second, domain-general theory, relates its functions to more global operations of the prefrontal cortex. In the final sections, we will fractionate this unit further, first by considering executive functions that are differentially attributed to the anterior, mid, and posterior regions of the ventrolateral unit. Lastly, we will discuss the role of hemispheric specialization.

Mapping the Territory

Brodmann's Areas. The ventrolateral region comprises BA 44, 45, and 47, which anatomically correspond to the pars opercularis, pars triangularis, and pars orbitalis (Pandya & Yeterian, 1996; Petrides & Pandya, 2002). BA 44 is likely better known as Broca's area. Thus, it is not surprising that there is considerable evidence linking the ventrolateral unit to aspects of language function, which we will address later in this discussion (see Figure 9.1).

Figure 9.1

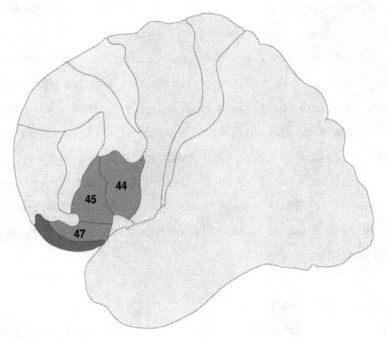

Lateral aspect of ventrolateral unit denoted by Brodmann's areas.
BA 44 corresponds to Broca's area.

Corticocortical connections. The ventrolateral unit shares connections with the three other functional structural units in the prefrontal cortex, other frontal lobe regions related to aspects of motor functioning (e.g., BA 6, supplemental motor area, cingulum), and lateral and posterior brain regions (e.g., association areas and multimodal integration areas; Pandya & Yeterian, 1996). Indeed, the ventrolateral regions are privy to information from secondary sensory areas, association, and integration areas related to olfactory, gustatory, visceral, somatic, and visual sensations (Kohno, Noriuchi, Iguchi, Kikuchi, & Hoshi, 2015) and other aspects of posterior brain regions, that is, information from the temporal, occipital, and parietal lobes (Badre & Wagner, 2007; Fujiwara, Tobler, Taira, Iijima, & Tsutsui, 2009; Garcin et al., 2012). The ventrolateral region also receives considerable input from the limbic system and paralimbic regions, that is, the amygdala, entorhinal, and perirhinal cortex (Price, 1999), which is suggested to play a role in the experience of "gut feelings" (Novick et al., 2009).

Area 44 receives information from aspects of the dorsolateral region (BA 9/46), orbital (BA13), and medial regions (BA 24), the supplementary motor area, as well as the posterior regions of the brain, for example, the inferior parietal lobule and superior temporal sulcus (Panda & Yeterian, 1996). Area 45 receives information from nearly all other areas in the prefrontal cortex, with the exception of BA 9/46 of the dorsolateral region (Pandya & Yeterian, 1996).

BA 47 receives a large amount of information from aspects of the temporal lobe and ventrolateral area (BA 45), as well as (in varying degrees) other aspects of the dorsolateral (BA 8, 9, 10, 46, 9/46), orbital (BA 14, 13, and 11), and medial/ACC regions (BA 32; Pandya & Yeterian, 1996). Other aspects of the ventrolateral unit (i.e., 45, 47) also send information to specific regions in the dorsolateral unit, that is, BA 8, 9 (Pandya & Yeterian, 1996).

Theories Explaining Ventrolateral Functional Processes

Executive functions attributed to the ventrolateral unit are often described in similar terms (e.g., set shifting, rule finding), though the processes underlying these behaviors seem to be often debated. Some investigators argue that various functions are domain-specific and distinctly moderated by the ventrolateral area. Others view ventrolateral unit functions as fulfilling a more general role, in that as task demands increase, more cortical areas are recruited in the facilitation of executive functions. In the next sections, we will describe these respective positions.

Domain general. Domain general is typically interpreted in one of two ways. Dobbins and Wagner (2005) use the term to describe the unit's capacity to select from an array of information stored in memory, ranging from concrete to abstract. In making no further distinction in terms of the "type" of information, the functions are referred to as general, as this unit processes information across the domain hierarchy. Similarly, Novick et al. (2009) consider the capacity to process conflicting information that was recalled from memory as domain general, in that it resolves conflict in the general service of maintaining cognitive control. Hedden and Gabrieli (2010) take domain general further still, suggesting that the ventrolateral unit, like the dorsolateral and medial/ACC regions, is involved in either facilitating or inhibiting various behaviors.

Domain specific. Domain-specific functions refer to those performed by a specific cortical region. The theory of double dissociation has been integral in determining the unique functional relationships of specific cortical areas in the ventrolateral unit (e.g., Badre & Wagner, 2007; Petrides, Alivisatos, & Evans, 1995; Petrides & Panda, 2002). Another mode of determining such relationships is through the capacity to isolate specific brain regions via functional connections to other brain regions, as seen with areas BA 45 and 47 (e.g., Petrides & Panda, 2002), as well as the need to recruit other specific brain regions to perform a given function (e.g., Garcin et al., 2012; Geddes et al., 2014). Another example might be the differential functions ascribed to the left and right aspects of the ventrolateral unit (Hkrac, Wurm, Kühn, & Schubotz, 2015). The topic of hemispheric specialization will be explored further in a subsequent section.

In actuality, an argument can be made that the ventrolateral unit supports some general functions (e.g., attention), which are not the sole domain of this unit. By contrast, there are specific functions dependent on discrete aspects of the ventrolateral unit. We will address this topic further in the next section.

The Ventrolateral Unit and Executive Functions

One of the most remarkable features of the ventrolateral unit is its involvement in mediating affective and sensory experiences, both to and from long-term storage. Indeed the ventrolateral unit performs a key function. It allows us to simultaneously consider massive amounts of information and focus on that which is the most relevant. First it appears to bias how information is recalled, as well as what is recalled, and what information is selected from long-term memories (Bardre & Wagner, 2007; Geddes et al., 2014). This process is essential when wading through ambiguous or conflicting information (Novick et al., 2009). Part of the process is influenced by the ventrolateral unit's tendency to look for similarities, patterns, and familiarities (Novick et al., 2009), which some suggest affects the storage, retrieval, and selection of episodic memories

(Badre & Wagner, 2007; Lee, Blumenfeld, & D'Esposito, 2013; Schott et al., 2011). Perhaps the ventrolateral unit can be considered to act as a higher order orienting and fine-turning device, assisting with our ability to attend to, make sense of, and use present information in the context of past experiences. The more cognitive demands conflict, or are ambiguous, the more we need the ventrolateral unit to facilitate access to relevant information and inhibit responsiveness to irrelevant information, in order to make the most appropriate behavioral response.

One example of this fine-tuning capacity is evident in the further processing of emotions, which Kujiwara and colleagues (2009) suggest makes it possible to experience "higher order" emotions such as relief. In order to demonstrate this capacity, Kujiwara et al. devised a gambling task, focusing on tangible gains and the affective experience. They found that participants who thought they made the greatest financial gains were just as likely to report feelings of joy and happiness as those who reported experiencing mere "relief." This helps explain the complex process involved in reward related behaviors.

The ventrolateral unit also helps us navigate the basic emotions of fear and anger (Morandotti et al., 2013) by turning our attention to situations that evoke these affective states and then evaluating current danger based on past experiences (Kohno et al., 2015). Kohno and colleagues suggest that this emotional regulation capacity works, in part, because it keeps us alert to potentially aversive situations. However, the evaluation of danger can be highly subjective and is actually shaped in the context of previous experiences, so that the ventrolateral unit's orientation and evaluation areas can be viewed as having subjective components.

The ventrolateral unit has also been associated with the capacity to create and follow rules (Garcin et al., 2007). The preceding paragraphs alluded to this capacity, wherein information congruent with past experiences (e.g., patterns) is more salient (particularly if it helps us avoid negative experiences) and is reinforced when we are emotionally or sensorially rewarded by acting consistently with this pattern. Following this line of reasoning, it makes sense that the capacity for analogical reasoning is among the ventrolateral unit's many functions. We can see how the orienting and selecting functions of the ventrolateral unit are essential to certain behaviors, such as navigating relationships, performing well at work, or engaging in hobbies. In the next section, we will consider these functions in further detail by looking more closely at roles that are specific to different aspects of the ventrolateral unit.

Hierarchical Organization Across Anterior, Mid-, and Posterior Ventrolateral Regions

The ventrolateral unit has been divided functionally into three regions: anterior; mid; and posterior (e.g., Badre & Wagner, 2007). This arrangement may constitute a hierarchal relationship in which the most anterior regions mediate more abstract functions, while the more posterior aspects serve more concrete functions (e.g., Garcin et al., 2012; Pandya & Yeterian, 1996). For example, Badre and Wagner (2007) use the term "functional coupling" to describe how communication takes place between the ventrolateral unit and the occipital and temporal lobes when recalling concrete visual perceptual information that exists only in the abstract once the precipitating stimulus is no longer present. Overall, depending on the task demands, still more cortical areas are recruited to support organizing information for storage, facilitating recall of similar information, and selecting among items of information.

Anterior ventrolateral. The anterior region receives sensory and affective information via its connections with posterior sensory areas and limbic regions. It is tasked with locating information that may be more remote and abstract (Hrkac, Wurm, Kuhn, & Schubotz, 2015f). Hrkac and colleagues suggest that a lack of congruency between the information and the goal increases activation in the anterior region (i.e., inferior frontal gyrus), which they suggest is a precursor to creativity.

We often search for congruencies when attempting to retrieve information, such that our recall of episodic memories is biased. Badre and Wagner (2007) refer to this as a "controlled retrieval mechanism." We can consider how this might work in relation to higher order emotions such as relief. As mentioned above, Fujiwara and colleagues (2009) examined the experience of relief during a gambling task. They found that participants were more likely to make certain behavioral responses that appeared counterfactual (on the surface), but actually corresponded to the feeling of relief. In fact participants who thought they made considerable financial gains (in terms of absolute value) reported levels of joy and happiness similar to those who experienced "relief" vs. financial gain. Thus, experiencing relief was arguably just as rewarding as one of the strongest secondary reinforcers.

Mid-ventrolateral. Receiving information from most areas of the PFC (Pandya & Yeterian, 1996), the ventrolateral unit helps to minimize conflict between multiple sources of information, such as filtering through episodic memories (Badre & Wagner, 2007). Thus when there is competition among items of information recalled from memory, the mid region of the ventrolateral unit helps to select from among the information recalled that which is most congruent with goal directed behavior.

Posterior ventrolateral. The posterior aspect of the ventrolateral unit is tasked with finding congruencies related to information being encoded, retrieved, and selected. It makes sense that along the hierarchy this information is often more concrete in nature, knowing that this region receives the majority of information from somatosensory areas (Pandya & Yeterian, 1996).

Hemispheric Specialization

The regional specialization of the ventrolateral unit extends to hemispheric specialization, with the left and right hemispheres mediating different aspects of executive functions. Many investigators have suggested that the left aspect of the ventrolateral unit is more involved with verbal or linguistic functions, whereas the right plays a more integral role in processing perceptual information (e.g., Garcin et al., 2009; Geddes et al., 2014).

Given that the ventrolateral region includes Broca's area, it is not surprising that some of its functions involve language. In fact, some investigators claim that specific neuronal activity demonstrated in areas of the ventrolateral region of non-human primates may be evidence of the ontological precursor to human speech (Hage & Nieder, 2015). Others indicate it is likely implicated in nonverbal behaviors observed in primates (Pandya & Yeterian, 1996).

A number of researchers have found that lesions of Broca's area result in only transitory or minimal symptoms, which (some suggest) is typical of Broca's aphasia (e.g., Novick et al., 2008). Regardless of the duration or extent of the damage, insult to this area significantly impairs the ability to filter through verbal incongruences or ambiguities (Badre & Wagner, 2007). Others have found similar impairments in the capacity to decipher the meaning of abstract words, wherein the meaning of a word is context dependent (Hoffman, Jefferies, & Ralph, 2010). For example, the meaning of the word "chance" varies according to the context in which it is used: "It's down to chance"; "I'll do it when I get a chance;" and "take a chance;" which respectively suggest situations where luck, opportunity, and risk, are respectively conveyed (Hoffman et al., 2010). Hoffman and colleagues suggest this is related to executive functions of the ventrolateral unit, which mediates access to semantic information.

Spence and colleagues (2008) have provided a different perspective on hemispheric specialization related to language. They demonstrated that the increased cognitive demands involved in lying resulted *not only* in increased activity in BA 45 and 47 in the left hemisphere, but also simultaneously recruited the right hemisphere (Spence, Kaylor-Hughes, Farrow, & Wilkinson, 2008).

Wais and colleagues (2012) found an increase of activity in the left mid-ventrolateral unit in the presence of visual distractions. Consistent with the main task of the mid-region, which appears to be selecting among competing information, Wais et al. proposed that the increased activity allows for the selection of mnemonic information, as opposed to attending to a stimulus in the external environment.

Conclusion

As we can see, the ventrolateral functional structural unit is involved in many facets of executive functions, including those related to attention, memory, and reasoning. Due to the ventrolateral unit's rich connections with nearly all aspects of the prefrontal cortex, as well as with secondary sensory areas, association cortices, and the limbic regions, it is tasked with sifting through massive amounts of sensory and affective information. The ventrolateral unit helps to guide and organize our thinking by orienting us to the most relevant information. This is due to its ability to make an appraisal of the current information based on the relevance to patterns from previous experiences. The greater the cognitive demands, the more we need the ventrolateral unit to facilitate access to relevant information and inhibit responsiveness to irrelevant information. Indeed, the ventrolateral unit serves a key function in helping to guide, orient, and order our sense of reality.

Language is difficult to define because of the many subcomponents involved. At a conceptual level language comprehension and preparation do seem to be largely cerebral cortical functions, versus motor speech, which seems to involve the more sensorimotor aspects of speech production. Two key cerebral cortical areas seem to be involved with language, namely Wernicke's area in processing the sensory aspects of language (hearing and understanding words), and Broca's area, which appears to be involved in speech preparation and programming and, ultimately, producing words. Broca's area cannot simply be defined as the area for speech production. Damage to certain motor areas render the patient unable to produce speech, and most with what we call Broca's aphasia are able to produce speech, albeit labored and slow with substantial word finding difficulties. In fact, the amount of effort such individuals put into their speech reminds one of the neurological condition called abulia, noted most often among those with Parkinson's disease. Patients with abulia have the physical ability to walk and to perform other movements, but cannot will themselves to do so. In Broca's aphasia, patients' inability or difficulty in willing themselves to say specific words reduces the word flow and increases their word finding difficulties. Together, these aspects of Broca's aphasia, including the oft seen dramatic improvement, seem to indicate that the difficulties are not simply motor or sensory but more like an abulia of language.

Let us consider a second factor involved in language, of expressive language in particular. Few see language springing full-born as a method of communicating between humans. Such expressions are certainly vocalizations, but not all such vocalizations are intended for communication (though many can and do communicate). If we look at the vocalizations of infants and most mammals we see a high proportion which can be interpreted as emotional responses, such as pain or fear or possibly comfort. Taking a minor theoretical step, we can see these vocalizations as being emitted from affect, and perhaps as affect responses. There is no intent, in most cases, of declarative meaning or most likely even anything communicative (the animals given the emotional feeling would have emitted the same vocalization whether there were other conspecifics there or not). Over the course of perhaps a hundred or so millennia we humans have been able to control these emotive responses to make them very effective in communications, and, on the left side, in a very analytic manner. However, the relationships between such vocalizations and affect/emotion remain. One easily can imagine how affective input would often trigger a vocal response, especially among those with poor prefrontal control (e.g., those with ADHD and those with prefrontal trauma).

12.

EXECUTIVE FUNCTIONS OF THE ORBITAL UNIT

What comes to mind when we think of the orbital region? Perhaps things like inappropriate behavior, aggression, risk-taking behavior, or social deficits? The orbital unit may not be viewed as serving the highest of executive functions, but in regard to executive dysfunctions, it just may be.

Indeed, we seem to know more about the challenges that can arise when things go awry with the orbital unit than about its more positive contributions to behavior. Certainly, an understanding of executive dysfunctions is essential to our clinical work. We recognize that dysfunctions in this region pose some of the most noticeable, enduring, and negative consequences to the lives of our patients. However, it is also important to consider the role of the orbital unit *when things are going well.*

A main focus of this chapter is to explore the functional structural relationship of the orbital unit in relation to executive functions. I will begin this discussion by mapping the territory of the orbital unit. This is an essential first step; doing so avoids the confusion that can arise due to a number of different conceptualizations of the brain areas comprising the orbital unit. Next, I will consider the specific contribution of the orbital unit in relation to executive functions. I will conclude the chapter with a brief discussion of disorders that are most commonly associated with insult or injury to this unit.

Mapping the Territory

For the purpose of our discussion, the orbital unit includes the ventral surface of the frontal lobes, which extends rostrally toward the frontal pole and caudally to the anterior perforated substance (Chiavaras & Petrides, 2000). The surface area of this unit corresponds to Brodmann areas (BA) 11, 13, and 14, which Petrides and Pandya (as cited in Öngür, Ferry, & Price, 2003; see Figure 10.1), describe as the anterior orbital, the medial orbital, and the ventromedial convexity, respectively. It is important to make the distinction between the larger surface area of the orbitofrontal cortex, which includes the most anterior aspect (BA 10), and the lateral areas (BA 12/47), as opposed to the anatomically and functionally distinct regions that comprise the functional structural orbital unit (e.g., Rushworth et al., 2005).

Thus, in the absence of this distinction, functions that are mediated by neighboring units may be attributed to the orbital unit. To continue, the anterior orbital region (BA 11) is located within the olfactory sulcus and gyrus rectus (Öngür et al., 2003). The medial aspect (BA 13) demonstrates even more connectivity to the olfactory region, as it corresponds to the olfactory tract and the olfactory sulcus, and is attached to the olfactory stalk (Öngür et al., 2003). BA 14 is seen as a distinct region from that of the medial and more lateral aspects visible on the ventral surface area (Öngür et al., 2003).

Functionally, BA 11 receives and integrates different types of sensory information. Similarly, BA 13 and 14 receive, integrate, and send highly processed sensory and affective information to the medial and lateral brain regions (Frey & Petrides, 2002; Öngür et al., 2003; Happeny, Zalazo, & Stuss, 2004; Payne, 2011). BA 11 and 13 are "alert centers" (or sentinels) of sorts, regarded as "on the look-out" for new information (Petrides, Alivisatos, & Frey, 2002). These alert centers have also been implicated in reward-related behaviors (e.g., Tsujimoto, Genovesio, & Wise, 2010).

As mentioned, the orbital region sends highly processed information to medial and lateral brain regions. Aspects of this processed information have recently been delineated with considerable specificity by Yang and colleagues (2014). Yang et al. examined the effects of surgically induced subthalamic lesions in an effort to alleviate the suffering of those with intractable symptoms of obsessive-compulsive disorder. In doing so, they highlight two distinct patterns of cortical connectivity of the orbital unit: one sends information to the thalamus while the other sends information to the brainstem (Yang et al., 2014). Admittedly, Yang et al.'s definition of the orbital unit includes BA 12 (which we conceptualize as part of the ventrolateral unit). However, the findings are not in contradiction with our conceptualization; distinct tracts are found within each aspect of the orbital unit (i.e., BA 11, 13, 14) that uniquely extend to the thalamus and brainstem.

Figure 10.1

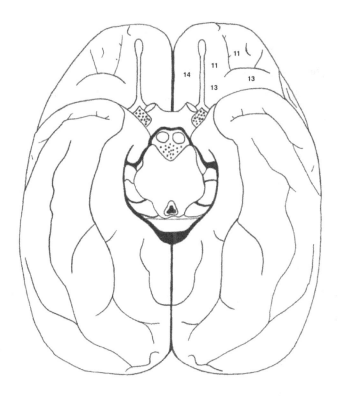

Orbital unit with Brodmann's areas denoted.

Yang et al.'s (2014) findings add to previous literature delineating regional specificity, and add support to the concept of a hierarchical organization of the frontal lobe structures. In fact, some investigators suggest that the orbital unit is a medial structure in terms of the overall hierarchy, though it is at the apex of the hierarchy when it comes to integrating information related to learning and reward (Young & Shapiro, 2011).

The Orbital Unit and Executive Functions

What are the functions mediated by the orbital region that can be contextualized in terms of executive functions? According to Soper's (2014) definition, the general components of executive functions include the capacity to receive, interpret, and respond to information in a way that is congruent with the context or goals. In the following paragraphs I will consider these overarching functions in relation to social and emotional functioning, learning, attention, and inhibiting behavior. In the final part of this discussion I will more explicitly address the role of the orbital unit in terms of sensory information.

Social-Emotional Functions. It might seem peculiar to lead a discussion of executive functions with a section on social/emotional functioning. However, despite viewpoints to the contrary (e.g., Leyfer et al., 2006), social and emotional functions are part of executive functioning. Indeed, the capacity to take in and interpret the affective states of the self and others, as well as to modulate one's affective state in order to appropriately navigate within a given social milieu (e.g., school, work, party) are part of executive functions.

Still, it is no small order to quantify the more qualitative aspects of executive functions. In order to do this, some have turned to the application and measurement of theoretical constructs, such as Premack and Woodruff's (1978) postulate of Theory of Mind (ToM), which refers to the ability to infer the mental states of others. Various approaches have been used to measure ToM, as well as other affective processes mediated by the orbital unit (e.g., Powell, Lewis, Roberts, Garcia-Finana, & Dunbar, 2012; Solbakk & Lovstad, 2004). For example, in a recent study with nonhuman primates, Poletti and Bonuccelli (2012) were able to distinguish specific aspects of ToM that are differentially mediated by orbital structures. They found that the interpretation of feelings, or "beliefs about feelings," is the domain of the orbital region, whereas beliefs about emotional experiences (i.e., "beliefs about beliefs") are mediated by the dorsolateral unit. Other approaches include measuring the capacity to identify emotions conveyed through facial expressions and evaluating apathy (e.g., Bertoux et al., 2012; Powell, Lewis, Dunbar, Garcia-Finana, & Roberts, 2010). Clearly, there is more work to be done, but it is an exciting prospect to continue to explore the social-emotional aspects of executive functions.

At this juncture we can be confident in our knowledge that the orbital unit is essential to the successful interpretation of emotions vis-à-vis their social context. One example of this capacity is demonstrated in Kolb, Pellis, and Robinson's (2004) experiment comparing the social behavior of normal rodents to those who had lesions induced in the orbital region. These investigators found that lesions in the orbital region impaired the rodents' ability to appropriately engage in the playful sparring that is part of a social ritual (Kolb et al., 2004). The impaired rodents were unable to distinguish playful cues from aggressive ones; thus they responded aggressively even to affectionate attempts to engage in the sparring ritual (Kolb et al., 2004). In addition, the rodents with intact orbital regions tended to avoid those who had impaired orbital regions, whereas those with the impairments were just as likely to approach those with impairments as those without (Kolb et al., 2004).

Because of the differences in the architecture of rodent and human brains, we must be cautious in making direct links to human behavior. Still, there is considerable evidence that the orbital unit of humans also facilitates our capacity to effectively navigate the social-emotional world. For example, the orbital unit helps us engage in prosocial behavior by facilitating our capacity to judge social situations accurately, as well as understand social hierarchy and inhibit socially maladaptive behavior (e.g., Ardila, 2008; Powell, Lewis, Roberts, Garcia-Finana, & Dunbar, 2012).

Learning

In the process of learning we develop rules and strategies that help us understand the world around us. The executive processes of the orbital unit facilitate this learning process in specific ways that differ from the contributions to learning by other functional structural units (e.g., dorsolateral). In the following discussion, we will address specific functions related to hypothetical reasoning, rule formation, and rule appraisal.

Hypothetical reasoning. The orbital unit seems to play a rather unique role in learning, which allows us to learn from the "road not taken." Indeed the orbital unit, in addition to taking in information related to our actual experiences, processes information related to the choices we did not make (Abe & Lee, 2011). This is an essential part of learning, that is, to be able to consider hypothetical situations in order to make decisions, which would be nearly impossible, highly inefficient, and quite costly to our current relationships if the only way we learned was through personally experiencing each choice that life has to offer. By comparison, the dorsolateral unit is more immediate or concrete in focus, such that it takes in information based on actual decisions (Abe & Lee, 2011). It is thought by some that the orbital unit facilitates the capacity to function more flexibly, thus allowing us to consider other possibilities as part of the larger decision-making process (Abe & Lee, 2011; Tsujimoto, Genovesio, & Wise, 2011). We might think of this as the capacity for hypothetical reasoning. Klein-Flugge, Barron, Bordersen, Dolan, and Behrens (2013) identified the medial caudal aspect of the orbital region as integral to this process of hypothetical reasoning.

Another related aspect of the learning processes of the orbital unit is demonstrated in our capacity to learn when we make the "wrong" decision (Petrides, Alivasatos, and Frey, 2002; Tsujimoto, Genovesio, & Wise, 2011). This process is nuanced by the affective experience that can accompany making a bad decision (Abe & Lee, 2011; Petrides, 2000). For example, the experience of regret can help us to make better decisions in the future (Abe & Lee, 2011; Klein-Flugge et al., 2013; Petrides, 2000). We can see how the orbital unit's capacity for hypothetical reasoning would be extremely useful when encountering new situations, which we will take up further in the next section.

Abstract functions. Each time we encounter a new situation it would be exhausting to have to create a set of rules in order to understand and navigate that situation. The functions of the orbital region aid us in this regard. For example, Tsujimoto et al. (2011) indicate that BA 11 and 13 are integrally involved in the creation of rules and strategies. Importantly, this process appears independent from the rule related functions of the dorsolateral unit (Tsujimoto et al., 2011), some of which were discussed in Chapter 8.

Tsujimoto and colleagues were able to isolate specific regions in the brains of nonhuman primates that encode information related to abstract rules. Mainly, these regions function to update information, such that rules that were not helpful to goal-related behavior were disregarded (Petrides, Alivisatos, & Frey, 2002; Tsujimoto et al., 2011). In the next section we will further examine how this process seems to work.

Rule appraisal. Some suggest that the structures of the limbic region, such as the amygdala, are involved in making connections between behavior and outcome. By contrast, the orbital region reigns over refining those rules when they are no longer adaptive (Happaney et al., 2004). This effect has been demonstrated multiple times in cognitive aspects of executive functioning, such as reversal learning tasks (Poletti & Bonuccelli, 2012). Rule appraisal depends not only on cognitive functions, but also involves social and emotional aspects of behavior (Happaney et al., 2004).

I will share an example from Soper (2014) to illustrate how essential rule appraisal is to function:

> A patient with a wound of the frontal lobes, when working in the carpenter's shop of the hospital for the purpose of rehabilitation, inadvertently continued to

plane a piece of wood until nothing remained of it. Even then he did not stop planing, but continued to plane the bench itself.

We can see how rule appraisal and the capacity to update our working models are essential to making the appropriate behavioral response. In the next section, we will consider how rule appraisal is related to the inhibition of behavior.

Inhibition of Behavior

Solbakk and Lovstad (2014) offer a unique interpretation of the orbital unit and its capacity to inhibit behavior. They suggest that since one of the primary functions of the orbital unit is to process novel information in order to update the rules related to functioning, the primary function of the orbital region is to process novel information. This is done through a process of recognizing the information and then updating the value of the information (Solbakk et al., 2014). When the process fails to function properly, resulting in a behavioral misstep, it is due to the failure to accurately monitor the information and/or the failure to recognize a change in reward value for a given source of information (Solbakk & Lovstad, 2014). Others have also found that failure to update information after a failed response leads to impaired decision-making, which has been associated with an increase in risk-taking behavior not due merely to impulsivity (e.g., Payne, 2011).

Soper (2014) provides yet another example of the consequences of failing to take in all of the available information in order to make an appropriate behavioral response: A minister had a massive prefrontal resection, but his recovery was so complete that he was given his parish back. He seemed to be functioning well until the day he started telling dirty stories at a funeral.

Sensory Functions of the Orbital Unit

Despite the overwhelming attention paid to affective functions moderated by the orbital region, there is considerable evidence that sensory information is utilized as another source of information to guide behavior. It is likely not surprising, given that the orbital region is situated within the olfactory region, that the orbital functions are associated with olfaction (Poellinger et al., 2001). Some investigators suggest that BA 13 is a secondary olfactory cortex and have linked the activation of this region to mental imagery associated with certain scents (Djordjevic, Zatorre, Petrides, Boyle, & Jones-Gotman, 2005). In animal studies, activation of the olfactory region has been linked to executive types of tasks, such as facilitating awareness of rule contingencies (Dolan, 2007) and increasing motivation due to anticipation of receiving a reward (e.g., Kahnt, Heinzle, Park, Haynes, & Romo, 2010). Some suggest that the olfactory region is controlled by the orbital region and directly related to executive functions (Poellinger et al., 2001). Others contend that olfactory input influences executive functions only in certain situations (Bowman, Kording, & Gottfried, 2012). For example, Bowman et al. demonstrated that when individuals were engaged in executive tasks that required them to make a decision when presented with ambiguous information, they used their sense of smell to guide this process.

Gottfried (2010) and others (e.g., Klein-Flugge, Barron, Brodersen, Dolan, & Behrens, 2013) suggest that sensory information is integral to the establishment of the patterns of behavior that we integrate with reward value, helping to guide future behavior in terms of optimizing reward. In fact, Klein-Flugge and colleagues were able to identify single neurons in human primates that encode the reward value of specific information. They also found that rewards that are more abstract in nature were encoded in more anterior regions of the brain, whereas rewards tied to sensory information were encoded in posterior areas of the orbital region (Klein-Flugge et al., 2013). Some suggest reward contingencies function as a type of working memory of the orbital region. This is also evidenced by the encoding of single cell neurons in the orbital unit of human primates (Kahnt et al., 2010).

In addition to olfaction, the orbital region (BA 11) has been linked with the capacity to encode visual and auditory information (Frey, Kostopoulos, & Petrides, 2002). The capacity to encode visual information in conjunction with the ventrolateral region has been associated with noticing information that is congruent with as well as different from expectations (Petrides et al., 2002).

In a study with nonhuman primates, Tremblay and Shultz (2002) demonstrated that in a paradigm involving visual information, BA 11 and 13 appeared to play a role in the decision-making progress, both by further processing sensory input and by juxtaposing this information with expectations of receiving a reward based on past experience (memory). Similarly, Frey and colleagues (2002) showed that BA 11 was involved in processing visual as well as auditory information, which served to increase the saliency of the information for later recall.

Psychopathology

Dysfunction of or damage to the orbital unit has been associated with various mental health conditions and/or neurological disorders, such as obsessive compulsive disorder (OCD), autism spectrum disorder (ASD), antisocial behavior, and borderline personality disorder (BPD). In the paragraphs that follow we will briefly discuss the neuropsychological features of ASD, OCD, and antisocial behavior, including behavioral and anatomical indicators. The remainder of the discussion will center on the neuropsychology of BPD.

Numerous studies and meta-analyses show that damage to the orbital region can lead to a range of social dysfunctions, such as impairments in ToM, understanding facial expressions, emotional processing, and empathy (e.g., Baron-Cohen & Ring, 1994; Cozolino, 2002; Decety & Chaminade, 2003; Fumagalli & Priori, 2012; Rankin, 2002, Spikeman et al., 2012). For example, Spikeman et al. found an association between deficits in social cognition and individuals who had sustained a traumatic brain injury (TBI) to the orbital region. Similarly, others have found structural differences in the orbital region that result in behavioral impairments in aspects of social cognition. Sabbagh (2004) and others (e.g., Rowe, Bullock, Polkey, & Morris, 2001; Stuss & Anderson, 2004) found an association between deficits in ToM and lesions of the right orbital unit.

Many have suggested that deficits in ToM are a hallmark of ASD (e.g., Ozonoff, Pennington, & Rogers, 1991; Soper, Wolfson, & Canavan, 2008). Now we have the neuroscience to back up the behavioral evidence, as more recently impairments in the orbital region and related structures are associated with ASD (Noggle, Dean, & MacNeill, 2012). Still, others suggest that the neuroanatomical evidence thus far implicates primarily structures of the limbic region, including the ACC (Soper et al., 2008). However, behavioral evidence collected on measures of executive function such as those requiring cognitive flexibility (Soper et al., 2008) suggest involvement of the orbital region. Indeed, another feature of ASD is related to lack of cognitive flexibility, manifested in restricted, repetitive, and/or ritualistic behaviors (American Psychiatric Association, 2013). As with ASD, impairments in social functioning, ritualistic and repetitive behaviors, and executive dysfunctions are features of OCD (American Psychiatric Association, 2013) associated with anatomical differences in and physiological impairment of the orbital unit (e.g., Cozolino, 2002; Rankin, 2002).

Other disorders, such as acquired psychopathy and antisocial personality disorder, have also been related to impairment in the orbital unit (Cozolino, 2002). One feature of these disorders are aggressive acts. Gansler et al. (2009) examined differences in gray matter volume, and were able to account for aggression (but not impulsivity). Other investigators indicate that aggression associated with the orbital region can be attributed to executive dysfunctions, wherein the orbital region does not respond quickly enough in interpreting social situations (Gansler et al., 2009). Others, too, have noted impairment in the ability to process social information that impedes the capacity to adequately respond to emotional information. This, of course, is secondary to challenges in interpreting the information (Levens, Devinsky, & Phelps, 2011).

Arguably, borderline personality disorder is marked by significant impairment in social-emotional functioning. BPD has also been linked to dysfunctions in the orbital region and related neural structures. These dysfunctions have been associated with chronic exposure to trauma, such as what may have been endured in chaotic families or via child abuse (Brendel, Stern, & Silbersweig, 2005; Minzenberg, Fan, New, Tang, & Siever, 2008; Schmahl, McGlashan, & Bremner, 2002; Stone, 2013), as well as risk factors related to biology and genetics. Distinct differences in individuals with BPD have also been found in the orbital region circuitry and related subcortical structures. For example, some investigators have found differences in the volume of specific limbic structures, that is, the amygdala and hippocampus (Brambilla et al., 2004; Brendel et al., 2005; New, Perez-Rodriguez, & Ripoll, 2012; Rossi et al., 2010; Schmahla et al., 2003) and variations in the responsiveness of these structures (Buchheim et al., 2008), which are "critically intertwined with the functions" of the orbital unit (Zald & Kim, 2001).

In addition to these differences, other researchers (e.g., Chanen et al., 2008) suggest there are differences in the grey matter volume within the orbital region of individuals with BPD. Similarly, Soloff et al. (2011) identified reduced volume in the orbital unit as well as diminished metabolic efficiency, which they suggest are correlated with suicidal behaviors of individuals with BPD. Walterfang and colleagues (2010) also found reduced grey matter volume, as well as a reduction in volume of the white matter tracts at the genu of the corpus callosum. They found an association between these structural differences and an increase in externalizing behaviors in individuals with BPD.

Still other investigators suggest that behavioral impairments (e.g., difficulty regulating emotional responses) are due to deficiencies in neural pathways between the orbital unit and limbic regions (e.g., Brendel et al., 2005; New, Perez-Rodriguez, Ripoll, 2012). Some suggest that apparent functional impairment of orbital neurocircuitry is due to inadequately developed circuits, and thus the circuits are not equipped to assist with processing affective input (e.g., Cozolino, 2002; Schore, 1997). Others too have focused on the (e.g., Brendel et al., 2005) functional structural relationship between the limbic region and the orbital unit, suggesting that the orbital unit does not respond to increased activation of the amygdala.

Thus, it is not available to process and integrate the affective input (Brendel et al., 2005). When this information is poorly integrated, an individual will have difficulty selecting the appropriate response, which Brendel suggests is particularly difficult when responding to an affect that is negative in valence. New and colleagues (2007) have suggested an integrative model in which the orbital, ventrolateral, and ACC regions each assist in the "downregulation" of the amygdala, whereas the dorsolateral prefrontal cortex modulates top-down or higher-order modulation. This suggests that the orbital, ventrolateral, and medial/ACC regions are involved in further processing of affective input and helping to inhibit an emotionally reactive response. Together, the orbital, ventrolateral, and medial/ACC work to inhibit the effect of information from lower brain regions (e.g., the limbic), which enables access to the more cognitive aspects of executive functions to remain on course.

Happaney et al. (2004) offer a different perspective on the function of the orbital unit, indicating that it is involved in the "reappraisal" of affective or motivational stimuli, which have been learned previously through affective pairing via the amygdala. Using a go/no-go learning task, they demonstrated that individuals with BPD have deficits in reversal learning and extinction. They explained that this is related to difficulties that individuals with BPD have in social contexts, more specifically in responding and adapting to changes while at the same time being able to appreciate the "gestalt" of the context and/or interactions as part of the considerations in motivating behavior. This suggests that individuals with BPD may miss crucial information that can disconfirm their hypotheses and may remain stuck in a dysfunctional pattern of interpersonal relatedness, whereby they continue to respond based on past behavior and situations as they are unable to consider the larger landscape and relevance of current information.

Conclusion

Although the orbital unit may still not be the first brain region that springs to mind for executive functions, this chapter may provide a greater appreciation for the important functions mediated by this region. In the context of Soper's definition, the orbital region takes in sensory and affective information, which is then interpreted based on various rules.

Thus, the region is essential to our capacity to successfully navigate social situations and keep our emotions in check. Part of this process involves interpreting immediate information in the context of abstract rules that have been created in response to real and hypothetical events. This flexibility appears to facilitate the capacity for hypothetical reasoning, which is much more efficient than needing to encounter every situation in order to know how to appropriately respond to the rapidly changing world around us. We can also see how failure to learn the rules in a way that is congruent to the situation or update the rules based on new information can cause significant impairments in functioning, the direst of which impair our relationships with others.

13.

EXECUTIVE FUNCTIONS OF THE MEDIAL/ACC UNIT

The medial/ACC functional structural unit might be thought of as the essential counterpart to the dorsolateral functional structural unit. Interestingly, its functions are sometimes described in nearly identical terms. For example, some investigators suggest that it is involved in monitoring, selecting, and guiding goal-directed behavior (e.g., Harmelen et al., 2014; Holroyed & Yeung, 2012; Kawai, Yamada, Sato, Takada, & Matsumoto, 2015; Shenhav, Botvinick, Cohen, 2013; van Noordt & Segalowitz, 2012). Others indicate that the medial/ACC plays a role in working memory (e.g., Fuster, 2008; Osaka et al., 2004) and attention (Garcia-Cabezas & Barbas, 2014).

Additionally, there are those who suggest it is involved in anticipating future events (e.g., Straube, Schmidt, Weiss, Mentzel, & Miltner, 2009), particularly events or consequences that are negative or aversive (Clauss, Cowan, & Blackford, 2011). Still others focus on its involvement in social-emotional functioning (e.g., Burklund, Eisenberger, & Lieberman, 2007; Etkin, Egner, & Kalisch, 2011; Frith & Amodio, 2006), such as moderating affective responses (e.g., Nieuwenhuis, Ridderinkhof, Blom, Band, & Kok, 2001). Indeed, some of the functions ascribed to this region sound strikingly similar to executive functions attributed not only to the dorsolateral unit, but also to other functional structural units (such as the role of the orbital unit in social-emotional functions). Despite the similarity in terms, the manner in which the medial/ACC contributes to such functions is unique.

In the paragraphs that follow, I will describe the unique contribution of the medial/ACC region to frontal lobe functions by framing the discussion around Soper's (2014) definition of executive functions (i.e., "the ability to take into account and integrate all of the available information and to produce the most appropriate motor output"). After delineating the areas of the brain comprising the medial/ACC functional structural unit, I will examine the type of information received by this unit (in order to be taken into account in the context of behavior). Next, I will examine how this information is interpreted and how it then influences motor behavior. Lastly, I will briefly touch upon the psychological disorders associated with dysfunctions of the medial/ACC functional structural unit.

Mapping the Territory

The functional structural medial/ACC unit has been apportioned in a variety of ways according to various theories and approaches (e.g., Drevets, Price, & Furey, 2008; Etkin et al., 2011; Öngür, Ferry, & Price, 2003; van Noordt & Segalowitz, 2012). In an effort to bring clarity to the larger discussion, I will use a common language by defining this unit in terms of Brodmann areas and descriptions of its cortical and subcortical connections. The medial/ACC cortical "surface" areas include BA 24 and aspects of BA 32, which correspond to the rostral or anterior aspects of the cingulate gyrus and are associated with affective functions (Shackman et al., 2011; see Figure 11.1).

Figure 11.1

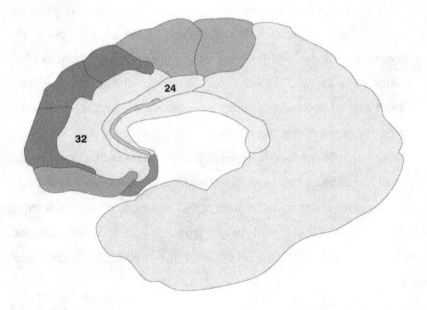

Medial/ACC with Brodmann's areas denoted.

The medial/ACC of nonhuman (e.g., Barbas, 1995) and human primates (e.g., Zald & Kim, 2013) shares information through its rich connections to and from the other functional structural units of the prefrontal cortex (i.e., dorsolateral, ventrolateral, and orbital) and subcortical structures.

A major source of information (i.e., affective, mnemonic) arises from its connections with structures in the limbic region, for example the amygdala and hippocampus (Etkins et al., 2011; Zald & Kim, 2001), which some suggest are related to its role in forming emotional memories (Medalla & Barbas, 2011). Pandya and Yeterian (1996) delineated major efferent connections from the medial/ACC to the dorsolateral and ventrolateral regions. In terms of connections with the dorsolateral unit, BA 24 sends affective input to aspects of BA 8, 9/46, and 6 (Pandya & Yeterian, 1996). Zald and Kim (2001) indicate that there are reciprocal connections between the medial/ACC and BA 8, 9, 10, and 46 (Zald & Kim, 2001), whereas others have delineated this further by suggesting that it is BA 32 of the medial/ACC that shares reciprocal connections with BA 8, 9, and 10 (Koski & Paus, 2000). BA 9 is unique to other dorsolateral cortical areas comprising the dorsolateral unit in that its lateral aspect receives an abundant amount of affective input from BA 24 and 32 (Pandya & Yeterian, 1996).

In addition to the communication between the medial/ACC and the dorsolateral unit, information is sent and received between the medial/ACC and the ventrolateral unit. Pandya and Yeterian (1996) delineated these connections in human and nonhuman primates, showing that information from BA 24 is sent to BA 44 and 45, whereas information BA 32 is sent to BA 47. Others suggest (Zald and Kim, 2001) that BA 47 shares reciprocal connections with BA 24. The medial/ACC appears in general thought to be more sparsely connected to areas of the orbital unit (Barbas & Pandya, 1989), although Zald and Kim (2001) indicate that BA 11 of the orbital region shares reciprocal connections with BA 24 and 32.

The medial/ACC receives mnemonic and sensory information from other brain regions, such as the temporal lobes, insula (Medalla & Barbas, 2012), and association cortices (Bowman, Kording, & Gottfried, 2012), as well as state information (i.e., arousal/alertness) from the brainstem (Mega & Cummings, 2001). In addition to the highly processed sensory input, there is some indication that reciprocal connections may exist between the olfactory cortex and the medial/ACC (Garcia-Cabezas & Barbas, 2014). In fact, in nonhuman primates information from the medial/ACC is sent to the primary olfactory cortex (Garcia-Cabezas & Barbas, 2014).

The physiological functioning of the medial/ACC and the dorsolateral unit is complementary in that when one is activated the other is inhibited (Medalla & Barbas, 2012). This suggests the medial/ACC is involved in moderating the interference of nonessential affective and mnemonic input between the medial/ACC and dorsolateral unit (Medalla & Barbas, 2012). Stated differently, the medial/ACC may facilitate attention during cognitively demanding tasks (e.g., Pessoa, 2008).

The Medial/ACC Unit and Executive Functions

In the next section we will consider the specific frontal lobe functions mediated by the medial/ACC unit. In particular, we will explore executive functions of the medial /ACC in terms of the information that is taken into account (i.e., received), how the information is interpreted (processed), and its influence on the motor response.

Information "taken into account" or received. The medial/ACC receives an abundant amount of information from other structures in the limbic region related to emotions or affect (e.g., Etkin, Egner, & Kalisch, 2011; Zald & Kim, 2001). It is also said to receive and further process mnemonic information (Etkin et al., 2011; Kennerly & Wallis, 2009), which some suggest is a mechanism for consolidating emotional memories (Medalla & Barbas, 2011). Others suggest the medial/ACC receives highly processed sensory information (Bowman et al., 2012; Egner, Jamieson, & Gruzelier, 2005). In the next section, we will explore how the affective, sensory, and mnemonic information is interpreted or made sense of by the medial/ACC unit.

Interpretation and integration of information. The way in which information is interpreted by the medial/ACC further delineates the specific contribution of this unit to executive functions. Affective appraisal seems to be a main interpretive strategy of the medial/ACC. It probably comes as no surprise that our appraisal of specific information is colored by our emotions. For example, what comes to mind when you think of home cooking? Whether you responded "wonderful", "horrible," or somewhere in between, it is likely that your appraisal was minimally influenced (if at all) by nutritive value, and possibly somewhat impacted by the sensory experience related to eating a home-cooked meal. However, the strongest influence was probably your affective appraisal, meaning that it is related to your overall emotional experiences of having a home-cooked meal. Indeed, it likely no surprise that our affective appraisal can influence our sensory experiences. In fact, some suggest that pairing affective information with sensory input can improve our performance on various tasks (Pessoa, 2009).

By contrast, depending on our experiences as well as other individual differences (e.g., biological, genetic), the capacity to adaptively utilize affective input can vary considerably. For example, there is compelling evidence that exposure to chronic stress or traumatic events can affect the size, shape, and reactivity of neural structures, which can have a deleterious effect on affective evaluation (e.g., Cozolino, 2002; Harmelen et al., 2014; Schore, 2011). Negative (and positive) experiences (memories) influence how we interpret phenomena such as social behavior (Dolk, Liepelt, Villringer, Prinz, & Ragert, 2012), which in turn affects future appraisals (Harmelen et al., 2014; Shore, 2011).

Other factors shown to influence how information is interpreted in the medial/ACC region are genetics (Herringa et al., 2013) and biology (Zald, 2003). For example, some suggest that we are born with biological differences in our capacity to tolerate sensory input, which is mediated by affective appraisal of such stimuli (e.g., Greenspan, Weider, & Simon, 1998). In relation to genetics, Herringa et al. (2013) examined brain differences in monozygotic twins and found genetic differences that were associated with susceptibility for developing posttraumatic stress disorder.

Together these differences (e.g., experiences, biology, genetics) can affect one's ability to navigate social situations, wherein the capacity to accurately appraise the affective information is impacted. For example, Burklund et al. (2007) examined the relationship between personal sensitivity to rejection and the subjective appraisal of facial expressions. They found a negative correlation between rejection sensitivity and facial expressions depicting disgust (Burklund et al., 2007). Others have also found that the medial/ACC seems particularly sensitive to situations that can lead to negative outcomes (Etkin et al., 2011; Pessoa, 2009). Thus, in some situations the interpretation can be thought of as ego-syntonic.

However, the medial/ACC unit also seems to pick up on information that appears out of place or incongruent with subjective experience, although only in certain situations (e.g., Aulicka et al., 2014; Desmet & Brass, 2015). For example, Aulicka and colleagues (2014) found that unusual actions (e.g., turning off a light switch with one's elbow) activated the medial/ACC region only when the person performing the action appeared confused or conflicted. If the action was incongruent with the subjective experience of the observer, but the actions of the actor appeared purposeful, the medial/ACC unit showed no increased response (Aulicka et al., 2014). It seems that the medial/ACC unit interprets information, in part, based on subjective experience, and in part on the observed experience of others. Thus, it seems the medial/ACC unit utilizes the affective information of the self and others to make sense of information that is confusing or incongruent with experience. Desmet and Brass (2015) offer a different account of the conflict resolution paradigm. They suggest that it is BA 10 that is alerted to information that is incongruent with subjective experiences, whereas the medial/ACC (BA 32) notices when *what we expect* will happen does not actually occur.

Some suggest an even broader capacity of the medial/ACC, which entails the simultaneous consideration of multiple sources of information (Kennerly, Behrens, & Wallis, 2011). For example, in a study with nonhuman primates, Kennerly and Wallis (2009) demonstrated that the medial/ACC interpreted the value of a given reward, which varied in relation to the pleasure provided by the reward and the amount of effort required to gain access to the reward. In nonhuman primates, this expanded evaluative capacity is thought of as a more general evaluative function, as opposed to the single neuron or specific encoding associated with the evaluative process of the orbital region (Kawai et al., 2015; Kennerley et al., 2011). This suggests that the executive functions of the medial/ACC involve a more general capacity that allows us to simultaneously consider multiple sources of information and inhibit our response to information that impedes goal-directed behavior.

To conclude, the medial/ACC appears to engage in a more general evaluative function, which is influenced by subjective experience, biology, and genetics. This evaluative function helps us determine which information is most relevant in order to guide our behavioral response, which implies that the medial/ACC plays a role in motivation.

Contribution to motor output. In this section, we will address how the medial/ACC interpretative functions influence motor output. Kukleta, Bob, Brazdil, Roman and Rektor (2010) and others (Etkin et al., 2011) suggest that the medial/ACC region's capacity for conscious evaluation of current information, nuanced by subjective experiences, affords "top-down" control of the limbic region. This is thought of as an integrative function that allows emotional information to be put into context, which in humans and nonhuman primates appears to influence the decision-making process (Kawai et al., 2015; Kukleta et al., 2010).

There are some rather interesting interpretations of how this integrative function is thought to play out. It seems that the medial/ACC helps us learn from negative and positive experiences by integrating the information in order to guide our future behavior (e.g., Etkin et al., 2006; Medalla & Barbas, 2011). For example, in a study in nonhuman primates, Kawai et al. (2015) artificially increased the activity of the animal's ACC, which thwarted their capacity to effectively evaluate and integrate the negative outcomes (no reward) observed by watching the behavior of the other primates. Conversely, when this manipulation of the medial/ACC regions did not occur, the animals were able to improve their performance based on observing the behaviors of their peers (Kawai et al., 2015). It seems that the medial/ACC is involved in our ability to learn from our own experiences as well as from observing the experiences of others.

Some researchers have identified what might be thought of as an enhancing capacity, wherein the medial/ACC region not only inhibits the intrusion of affective input, but strategically comes online to facilitate performance on various tasks. For example, Osaka and colleagues (2004) demonstrated that individuals who are particularly adept in working memory show increased activity in aspects of the medial/ACC unit when engaged in such tasks. Interestingly, the medial/ACC region was not activated when those with lower capacity for working memory were engaged in similar tasks (Osaka et al., 2014). Osaka et al. suggest that engagement of the medial/ACC during taxing working memory tasks is indicative of the capacity to use a "strategy" for engaging in certain cognitive tasks.

The medial/ACC unit is also implicated in "mindfulness" behaviors and hypnosis, which may be thought of as other types of volitional behaviors. For example, Chiesa and Serretti (2010) demonstrated increased activity in BA 24 during mindfulness training, which was associated with subjective reports of increased conscious awareness of emotions and the capacity to control negative appraisals. Egner et al. (2005) have suggested that induction of hypnotic states causes a decoupling of the medial/ACC from other regions of the frontal lobes (primarily the dorsolateral), which following hypnosis temporarily interferes with performance of cognitive executive tasks (Egner et al., 2005). This suggests that the medial/ACC unit may be capable of producing an analgesic effect by inhibiting attention to sensory and mnemonic information (Egner et al. 2005).

Psychopathology

As mentioned earlier, changes in the medial/ACC which are regarded as secondary to combat trauma and/or childhood maltreatment can lead to a variety of symptoms, such as rumination, hypervigilance, and dissociation (Hermelen et al., 2014; Herringa, Phillips, Fournier, Kronhaus, & Germain, 2013), as well as anxiety (Klumpp, Post, Angstadt, Fitzgerald, & Phan, 2013). Depressive disorders have also been implicated in dysfunction of the medial/ACC region (BA 24; Drevets et al., 2008).

Njomboro, Deb, and Humphreys (2012) examined the impact of apathy on tests of executive function. They were able to demonstrate that patients with damage to the ACC can perform executive tasks involving sensory and mnemonic input (Wisconsin Card Sorting Task). However, when the task (Iowa Gambling Task) involved risk akin to the affective aspects of real-life decision-making, the "apathetic" subjects did not fare as well (Njomboro et al., 2012). Njomboro et al. suggest that impairment of the ACC thwarts the ability to use affective information as a motivating and guiding factor.

Conclusion

Perhaps the medial/ACC contribution to executive functions is two-fold. On the one hand, the medial/ACC facilitates cognitive aspects of executive functions by inhibiting emotional intrusions and evaluating current information in light of past experience, which in turn guides decision-making. On the other hand, it seems to inhibit cognitive aspects of executive functions which, paradoxical to traditional conceptions of executive functions, allows us to override the influx of information in the environment (sensory) and internally (memories, affective) and attend to lower order functions (breathing, heart beating). This suggests that the medial/ACC is integral to filtering the signal to noise ratio, though how signal vs. noise are defined varies according to context.

CONCLUSIONS AND SUMMARY

The problem of clearly defining executive functions is one that still plagues neuropsychology; however, efforts to name increasing numbers of functions and correlate them to specific brain areas does little to advance an understanding of how these specialized areas function, especially outside the sensory processing and basic motor functions. In essence, this approach describes the outcome of brain dysfunction – the deficits – without addressing the underlying processes. By contrast, adherence to newer whole-brain thinking, in which executive functions cannot be fractionated and the role of the prefrontal lobes is not differentiated in this way, may also stymie advancement of theoretically based assessment and treatment of prefrontal lobe dysfunction. These approaches generate more complex constructs and theories that describe outcome behaviors without consideration of the context of the pathology.

Due to the complex nature of executive tasks, dysfunction can be observed in almost all behavior (Lezak et al., 2012). It is often difficult to discern the nature of the difficulty if not considering how a person is failing at a task or having difficulty. There are many ways to make a mistake depending on how the information is being processed. This type of information tells us more about the etiology of the problem rather than simply naming and describing the difficulty. Thus, it is imperative that examination of the qualitative aspects of dysfunction informs neuropsychological theory and assessment.

Goldberg (2009) provides a clear metaphor for this concept. He states that the frontal lobes function much like the conductor of an orchestra whose job it is to organize the tasks of each section of the orchestra in order to produce a cohesive result, namely the music. If the conductor is impaired in some way the various sections of the orchestra may still possess the ability to create music, but without the direction of the conductor the result may very well be unorganized cacophony.

In this metaphor, executive functions are represented by the music. There is a great variety of music that can be created by the interaction of the conductor and the orchestra, so if there is a problem it could manifest in various ways. Without a clear understanding of the role of the conductor as separate from each section in the orchestra, we are left describing the problems in the music with little recourse to remediate the difficulty. The conductor and the orchestra are both needed in order to create the music and if there is dysfunction in the system it behooves us to have a theory to explain the process between the conductor and the various sections of the orchestra in order to be able to determine and remedy the problem.

The current argument is not intended to advocate for a complete paradigm shift in neuropsychological conceptualization. It is important to understand the correlations between structure and function, but this approach needs to be considered in conjunction with contextual theories about process. Clarification of executive theories and the correlated brain areas is important when considering rehabilitation of those with dysexecutive issues given poor clinical outcomes and difficult management (Burgess, 1997).

Thus, study of executive functioning as a phenomenon of the frontal areas holds promise for practical application to real-life problems and is not just theoretically interesting. Indeed, there is currently a dearth of executive functioning therapies available for those impacted by damaged frontal lobes or connecting pathways (Levine et al., 2011). Reasons cited for the lack of valid treatment protocols pertain to research vulnerabilities such as lack of control groups, treatment protocols that are not theoretically based, differences in patient pathology, and few outcome measures (Levine et al., 2011). Conceptualization of executive functions as organizing and integrating all of the available information prior to choosing and implementing a behavioral response would place these abilities squarely in the prefrontal areas. This would help to clarify the role of the prefrontal lobes, which would provide an opportunity to further study how brain systems work together to process information. It would then be possible to build cohesive neuropsychological theory to inform assessment and treatment of executive dysfunction.

In this book we have covered a considerable amount of territory in the taking apart and putting together of the frontal lobes. Fractionation is but one approach that allows us to consider unique contributions of each functional-structural unit, which ideally fosters a better understanding of the system as a whole. Still, fractionation, such as used here, must be applied carefully because there can be pitfalls, as in making mind-body associations. Some are well known errors, such as the theories that the planum temporale is significant for language and that all that is hippocampal pertains to memory. However, where functional-structural relationships are reasonably well established (as in the reinforcement system) conclusions drawn regarding neural substrates will probably head us in the correct direction and provide a better understanding of how the systems work and what functions they serve. Thus fractionation is not a reduction of theory; rather it is a tool that helps to further develop the overall theory of frontal lobe functions.

Another tool is analogous reasoning. Indeed, there are a number of comparisons that have been used to describe prefrontal or executive functions. For example, Goldberg (2002) and Bennett (2014) analogize frontal lobe functions to a symphony orchestra, wherein each component (e.g., sheet music, musicians, conductor, instruments) must work together to create the music. Luria's (1966) example of physiological systems (e.g., respiratory) as informative for understanding brain function is another way we might think about executive functions. Namely, as each component in the system further processes information, it plays some part in moderating the overall response. Whether by fractionation or analogy or another method, once we understand the role of each individual part, we have the building blocks for creating an understanding of the system as a whole.

In our case, the building blocks include the cortical and subcortical structures related to the major frontal units. We have considered how these building blocks have developed over the course of evolution and over the course of an individual life. As we began to piece the system together, we considered the various modes and methods of communication, within and between the structures. It seems that this is an essential piece for understanding frontal lobe functions. The unique contribution of each structure must be understood in terms of the information sent and received, which is elucidated by examining where the information came from and where it is going. This has enabled us to take a closer look at the facilitatory and inhibitory functions that underlie the process of prefrontal or executive functions. This approach has also allowed us to rely less on descriptions of executive dysfunction and take a more process-oriented approach.

Before we continue, we will briefly summarize the executive process ascribed to each of the four functional-structural units. Beginning with the dorsolateral unit, we find ourselves in agreement with many who have come before. Thus, we regard the executive processes of the dorsolateral unit as involving the most complex of the frontal lobe functions. The dorsolateral unit (BA 8, 9, 9/46, 10, 46) integrates highly processed sensory information from other cortical areas, as well as affective and mnemonic information from the other functional structural units. The array of information is registered in the form of abstract rules, which inform cognitive aspects of executive functions, including planning and modulating a behavioral (motor) response. Thus, together, the dorsolateral unit enables us to interpret highly processed information in order to apply a rule or a strategy, which allows us to process the information further and to make new connections that further our understanding (e.g., insight), and guide our behavior.

The ventrolateral unit (BA 44,45, and 47) is integral to this process, as it mediates the encoding, recall, and selection of information sent to the dorsolateral unit by focusing on the most relevant information and filtering out the rest. It sifts through preprocessed sensory (Kohno et al., 2015) and affective (Price, 1991) information (Novick et al., 2009), as well as information from the supplementary motor area and nearly all other areas of the prefrontal cortices (Pandya & Yeterian, 1996), looking for patterns and similarities to determine what is most relevant (Novick et al., 2009). Facilitated by the ventrolateral unit, we are more likely to attend to, store, and recall information that is related to familiar patterns (e.g., Badre & Wagner, 2007). As such, the ventrolateral unit appears to filter out irrelevant information, by fine-tuning our attention to current information (sensory and affective) that is consistent with previous experiences, which assists to guide our thinking.

In concert with the dorsolateral and ventrolateral units, the orbital unit (BA 11, 13, and 14) keeps track of and continually updates various rules for how and how not to respond. Similarly to the other regions, it receives highly processed sensory and affective information though, unlike the ventrolateral unit, the orbital unit seeks out new information (Petrides et al., 2002). It is integral to our ability to understand our own emotional experiences and that of others (Bertoux et al., 2012) in order to function in social settings and in the context of relationships. The orbital unit utilizes this information to guide decision-making behavior in relation to our past experiences (insight) and anticipation of outcomes (foresight) that helps to modulate (including inhibit) current behavior.

Lastly, the medial/ACC unit (BA 24 and 32) sends and receives information between the dorsolateral, ventrolateral, and orbital units. It also receives sensory, affective, and mnemonic information from posterior and limbic regions (Medalla & Barbas, 2012), as well as input related to arousal from the brainstem (Mega & Cummings, 2001). It works to interpret and evaluate a current situation, both through the lens of subjective and intersubjective experiences, and alerts us to information that is incongruent with our expectations. The medial/ACC modulates the influence of affective and mnemonic input, in support of more cognitive aspects of executive functioning.

We hope that we have been able to expand the notion of executive functions, specifically through the identification and description of basic processes, also mediated by frontal lobe units, but traditionally not referred to when speaking of executive functions (Bennett, 2014; Stuss, 2011). As mentioned in a preceding chapter, we contend that prefrontal lobe functions are in fact synonymous with executive functions. Perhaps an example can better illustrate this point: We recognize that should we need to solve a complex mathematical equation we will need to apply rules and strategies which, because of the cognitive demands, will rely heavily on the dorsolateral unit. Imagine that while you a working on this problem a good friend walks into the room, looks upset, and begins to share some crushing personal news. If we were to continue to focus on the equation rather than attending to the friend, this could indicate that we have challenges in terms of normal frontal lobe functions. That is, in order to make the most appropriate behavioral response we need to be able to take in and interpret all of the relevant information, which necessarily involves the contribution of all four functional-structural units. It is this elusive element of the coming together of the various parts of the frontal lobe that extends beyond "integration" of functions. It is conveyed in the romantic science of Luria, wherein his prolific prose poetically exemplifies some of the most complex brain functions and provides an engaging story to describe human functional-structural experience, simultaneously expanding possibilities and our understanding of life and science.

As somewhat of an epilogue that should be mentioned, in many ways the foregoing is a translation of much of what is going on in what we call executive functions. The language we use here is, for the most part, the common language of man, which helps us exist in our social environment. It is not the language of neuropsychology or neuroscience. For example, we can come to a consensus definition of language, executive functions, intelligence, memory, and many other terms we use in trying to understand the brain and its behavior. However, most of these terms are not definitive enough to describe exactly what is going on in the brain. Therefore, using the consensus terms we have available brings us to a much closer understanding of what is going on between the ears. However, on occasion these terms will lead us astray, and in fact have led some to try to define executive functions, for example, by content, in a manner which suggests they do not exist. There are good and solid scientists who have drawn conclusions that disagree at times with those drawn here. The naming of disruptions, which has been the bailiwick of description and definition in the apraxias for decades has produced difficulties, whereas the more recent comprehensions through an understanding of process has opened doors unimaginable before that approach. In the future we hope that better approaches will advance our understandings even further.

REFERENCES

Abe, M., & Hanakawa, T. (2009). Functional coupling underlying motor and cognitive functions of the dorsal premotor cortex. *Behavioral Brain Research,* 198, 13–23. doi:10.1016/j.bbr.2008.10.046

Abe, H., & Lee, D. (2011). Distributed coding of actual and hypothetical outcomes in the orbital and dorsolateral prefrontal cortex. *Neuron,* 70(4), 731-741. doi:10.1016/j.neuron.2011.03.026

Adams, K. M. (1980). In search of Luria's battery: A false start. *Journal of Consulting and Clinical Psychology, 48,* 511-516. doi: 10.1037/0022-006X.48.4.511

Adesope, O. O., Lavin, T., Thompson, T., & Ungerleider, C. (2010). A systematic review and meta-analysis of the cognitive correlates of bilingualism. *Review of Educational Research, 80*(2), 207-245. doi:10.3102/0034654310368803

Akert, K., Gruesen, R. A., Woolsey, C. N., & Meyer, D. R. (1961). Klüver-Bucy syndrome in monkeys with neocortical ablations of temporal lobe. *Brain, 84*(3), 480-498.

Albert, D., & Steinberg, L. (2011). Judgment and decision making in adolescence. *Journal of Research on Adolescence, 21*(1), 211-224.

Alexander, G. E., Delong, M. R., and Strick, P. L. (1986). Parallel organization of functionally segregated circuits linking basal ganglia and cortex. *Annual Review of Neuroscience, 9,* 357–381. doi: 10.1146/annurev.ne. 09.030186.002041

Alexander-Bloch, A., Raznahan, A., Bullmore, E., & Giedd, J. (2013). The convergence of maturational change and structural covariance in human cortical networks. *The Journal of Neuroscience, 33*(7), 2889-2899.

Alsop, D. C., Atlas, S., Detre, J. A., Shin, R. K., Grossman, M., & D'Esposito, M. (1995). The neural basis of the central executive system of working memory. *Nature,* 378(6554), 279-281. doi:10.1038/378279a0

Alvarez, J. A., & Emory, E. (2006). Executive function and the frontal lobes: A meta-analytic review. Neuropsychology Review, 16(1), 17-42. doi:10.1007/s11065-006-9002-x

Amiez, C., Kostopoulos, P., Cham- pod, A. S., & Petrides, M. (2006). Local morphology predicts functional organization of the dorsal premotor region in the human brain. *Journal of Neuroscience.* 26, 2724–2731. doi: 10.1523/JNEUROSCI.4739-05.

Anderson, V. (2001). Assessing executive functions in children: biological, psychological, and developmental considerations. *Pediatric rehabilitation, 4*(3), 119-136.

Arain, M., Haque, M., Johal, L., Mathur, P., Nel, W., Rais, A., ... & Sharma, S. (2013). Maturation of the adolescent brain. *Neuropsychiatry Disease and Treatment, 9,* 449-61.

Ardila, A. (2008). On the evolutionary origins of executive functions. Brain and Cognition, 68(1), 92-99. doi:10.1016/j.bandc.2008.03.003

Ardila, A. (2013). Development of metacognitive and emotional executive functions in children. *Applied Neuropsychology: Child, 2,* 82-87.

Armistead, M. K., Strawn, B. D., & Wright, R. W. (Eds.). (2009). *Wesleyan Theology and Social Science: The Dance of Practical Divinity and Discovery.* Cambridge Scholars Publishing

Arnold, S. E., & Trojanowski, J. Q. (1996). Recent advances in defining the neuropathology of schizophrenia. *Acta neuropathologica, 92*(3), 217-231.

Atmaca, M., Onalan, E., Yildirim, H., Yuce, H., Koc, M., Korkmaz, S., & Mermi, O. (2011). Serotonin transporter gene polymorphism implicates reduced orbito-frontal cortex in obsessive–compulsive disorder. *Journal of Anxiety Disorders, 25*(5), 680-685. doi:10.1016/j.janxdis.2011.03.002

Augustine, J. R. (1996). Circuitry and functional aspects of the insular lobe in primates including humans. *Brain research reviews, 22*(3), 229-244.

Aulická, Š. R., Jurák, P., Chládek, J., Daniel, P., Halámek, J., Baláž, M., & Rektor, I. (2014). Subthalamic nucleus involvement in executive functions with increased cognitive load: A subthalamic nucleus and anterior cingulate cortex depth recording study. Journal of Neural Transmission, 121(10), 1287-1296. doi:10.1007/s00702-014-1191-5.

Averbeck, B. B., Lehman, J., Jacobson, M., & Haber, S. N. (2014). Estimates of projection overlap and zones of convergence within frontal-striatal circuits. *The Journal of Neuroscience* : The Official Journal of the Society for Neuroscience, 34(29), 9497-9505. doi:10.1523/JNEUROSCI.5806-12.2014

Baddeley, A. (1986). *Working memory*. Oxford: Oxford University Press.

Baddeley, A. (2003). Working memory: Looking back and looking forward. *Nature Reviews Neuroscience*, 4(10), 829-839. doi:10.1038/nrn1201.

Baddeley, A. (2012). Working memory: theories, models, and controversies. *Annual review of psychology, 63*, 1-29.

Badre, D. (2008). Cognitive control, hierarchy, and the rostro–caudal organization of the frontal lobes. *Trends in Cognitive Sciences, 12*(5), 193- 200.doi:10.1016/j.tics.2008.02.004

Badre, D., Hoffman, J., Cooney, J. W., & D'Esposito, M. (2009). Hierarchical cognitive control deficits following damage to the human frontal lobe. *Nature neuroscience, 12*(4), 515-522.

Badre, D., & Wagner, A. D. (2007). Left ventrolateral prefrontal cortex and the cognitive control of memory. *Neuropsychologia, 45*(13), 2883-2901. doi:10.1016/j.neuropsychologia.2007.06.015

Baeken, C., Schrijvers, D. L., Sabbe, B. G. C., Vanderhasselt, M. A., & De Raedt, R. (2012). Impact of one HF-rTMS session on fine motor function in right-handed healthy female subjects: a comparison of stimulation over the left versus the right dorsolateral prefrontal cortex. *Neuropsychobiology, 65*(2), 96-102.

Bailey, P., & von Bonin, G. (1951). *The isocortex of man*. University of Illinois Press.

Balsters, J. H., Cussans, E., Diedrichsen, J., Phillips, K. A., Preuss, T. M., Rilling, J. K.,   & Ramnani, N. (2010). Evolution of the cerebellar cortex: the selective expansion of prefrontal-projecting cerebellar lobules. *Neuroimage, 49*(3), 2045-2052.

Banyas, C. A. (1999). Evolution and phylogenetic history of the frontal lobes. *The human frontal lobes*, 83-106.

Barbas, H, & Pandya, D. N. (1991). Patterns of connections of the prefrontal cortex in the rhesus monkey associated with cortical architecture. In

Frontal lobe function and dysfunction, Levin, Harvey S. (Ed); Eisenberg, Howard M. (Ed); Benton, Arthur L. (Ed), (pp. 35-58). New York, NY, US: Oxford University Press.

Barbey, A., Colom, R., & Grafman, J. (2013). Dorsolateral prefrontal contributions to human intelligence. *Neuropsychologia*, 51(7), 1361-1369. doi:10.1016/j.neuropsychologia.2012.05.017

Barceló, F., & Knight, R. T. (2002). Both random and perseverative errors underlie WCST deficits in prefrontal patients. *Neuropsychologia, 40*(3), 349-356.

Barnea-Goraly, N., Menon, V., Eckert, M., Tamm, L., Bammer, R., Karchemskiy, A., & Reiss, A. L. (2005). White matter development during childhood and adolescence: a cross-sectional diffusion tensor imaging study. *Cerebral cortex*, *15*(12), 1848-1854.

Barrett, A. M. (2010). Rose-colored answers: Neuropsychological deficits and patient-reported outcomes after stroke. *Behavioural Neurology, 22,* 17-23. doi: 10.3233/BEN-2009-0250

Barrett, K. (1991). Treating organic abulia with bromocriptine and lisuride: Four case studies. *Journal of Neurology, Neurosurgery & Psychiatry, 54*, 718-721. doi:10.1136/jnnp.54.8.718

Bell, M. A., & Wolfe, C. D. (2007). Changes in brain functioning from infancy to early childhood: Evidence from EEG power and coherence during working memory tasks. *Developmental neuropsychology, 31*(1), 21-38.

Benjamin, L. (2009). A history of psychology: Original sources and contemporary research. Malden, MA: Blackwell.

Bennett, T. L. (2014). *Theory of executive processing as a prefrontal lobe function* (Doctoral dissertation). Permalink.

Bertoux, M., Volle, E., Funkiewiez, A., de Souza, L., Leclercq, D., & Dubois, B. (2012). Social cognition and emotional assessment (SEA) is a marker of medial and orbital frontal functions: A voxel-based morphometry study in behavioral variant of frontotemporal degeneration. *Journal of the International Neuropsychological Society*, 18(6), 972-985. doi:10.1017/S1355617712001300

Beurze, S. M., De Lange, F. P., Toni, I., & Medendorp, W. P. (2007). Integration of target and effector information in the human brain during reach planning. *Journal of Neurophysiology*. 97, 188–199.

doi:10.1152/jn.00456.2006.

Bhandage, A. K., Jin, Z., Bazov, I., Kononenko, O., Bakalkin, G., Korpi, E. R., &

Bianchi, L. (1895). The functions of the frontal lobes. *Brain, 18,* 497-522. doi:
10.1093/brain/18.4.497

Birnir, B. (2014). GABA-A and NMDA receptor subunit mRNA expression is
altered in the caudate but not the putamen of the postmortem brains of
alcoholics. *Frontiers in cellular neuroscience, 8,* 415.

Bishop, D. V. M. (1997). Cognitive neuropsychology and developmental
disorders: Uncomfortable bedfellows. *The Quarterly Journal of
Experimental Psychology: Section A, 50,* 899-923. doi:
10.1080/713755740

Blakemore, S. J., Burnett, S., & Dahl, R. E. (2010). The role of puberty in the
developing adolescent brain. *Human brain mapping, 31*(6), 926-933.

Blumenfeld, R. S., & Ranganath, C. (2006). Dorsolateral prefrontal cortex
promotes long-term memory formation through its role in working
memory organization. *Journal of Neuroscience,* 26(3), 916-925.
doi:10.1523/JNEUROSCI.2353-05.2006

Boring, E. G. (1957). *A history of experimental psychology.* New York, NY:
Appleton-Century-Crofts.

Bowman, N., Kording, K., & Gottfried, J. (2012). Temporal integration of
olfactory perceptual evidence in human orbitofrontal cortex.
Neuron, 75(5), 916-927. doi:10.1016/j.neuron.2012.06.035

Brendel, G. R., Stern, E., & Silbersweig, D. A. (2005). Defining the
neurocircuitry of borderline personality disorder: Functional
neuroimaging approaches. *Development and Psychopathology,* 17(4),
1197-206.

Broadhurst, P. L. (1957). Emotionality and the Yerkes-Dodson law. *Journal of
experimental psychology, 54*(5), 345.

Brocki, K. C., & Bohlin, G. (2004). Executive functions in children aged 6 to 13:
A dimensional and developmental study. *Developmental
neuropsychology, 26*(2), 571-593.

Bunge, S. A., Helskog, E. H., & Wendelken, C. (2009). Left, but not right,
rostrolateral prefrontal cortex meets a stringent test of the relational
integration hypothesis. *Neuroimage,* 46(1), 338-342.
doi:10.1016/j.neuroimage.2009.01.064.

Burgess, P. W. (1997). Theory and methodology in executive function research. In P. Rabbitt (Ed.), *Methodology of frontal and executive function*. New York, NY: Taylor & Francis Group.

Burgess, P. W. (2013). Introduction to section vi: Neuropsychology. In D. Stuss & R. Knight (Eds.), *Principles of frontal lobe function* (pp. 469-474). New York, NY: Oxford University Press.

Burgess P (2010). Rostral PFC: Gateway Between Imaginings and Happenings. Frontiers in Human Neuroscience. Conference Abstract: *The 20th Annual Rotman Research Institute Conference*, The frontal lobes.doi: 10.3389/conf.fnins.2010.14.00021.

Burklund, L. J., Eisenberger, N. I., & Lieberman, M. D. (2007). The face of rejection: Rejection sensitivity moderates dorsal anterior cingulate activity to disapproving facial expressions. Social Neuroscience, 2(3), 238-253. doi:10.1080/17470910701391711.

Bush, G., Luu, P., and Posner, M.I. (2000). Cognitive and emotional influences in anterior cingulate cortex. Trends in Cognitive Science, *4*, 215–222.

Butter, C. M. (1969). Perseveration in extinction and in discrimination reversal tasks following selective frontal ablations in macaca mulatta. *Physiology and Behavior, 4,* 163-171. doi: http://dx.doi.org.fgul.idm.oclc.org/10.1016/0031-9384(69)90075-4

Buzzell, K. A., & Amaral, J. (2007). Man, a three-brained being: Resonant aspects of modern science and the Gurdjieff teaching. Salt Lake City: Fifth Press.

Callaert, D. V., Vercauteren, K., Peeters, R., Tam, F., Graham, S., Swinnen, S. P., & Wenderoth, N. (2011). Hemispheric asymmetries of motor versus nonmotor processes during (visuo) motor control. *Human brain mapping, 32*(8), 1311-1329.

Campbell, J. J., Duffy, J. D., & Salloway, S. P. (2001). Treatment strategies for patients with dysexecutive syndromes. *The Frontal Lobes and Neuropsychiatric Syndrome*, 153-166.Carlson, N.R. (2012). *Physiology of behavior.* Upper Saddle River, NJ: Pearson.

Carmichael, S. T., & Price, J. L. (1995). Limbic connections of the orbital and medial prefrontal cortex in macaque monkeys. *Journal of Comparative Neurology, 363*, 615-641. doi: 10.1002/cne.903630408

Catani, M., Howard, R. J., Pajevic, S., & Jones, D. K. (2002). Virtual in vivo interactive dissection of white matter fasciculi in the human brain. *Neuroimage, 17*(1), 77-94. doi:10.1006/nimg.2002.1136

Chan, R. C., Shum, D., Toulopoulou, T., & Chen, E. Y. (2008). Assessment of executive functions: Review of instruments and identification of critical issues. *Archives of Clinical Neuropsychology, 23*, 201-216. doi: http://dx.doi.org.fgul.idm.oclc.org/10.1016/j.acn.2007.08.010

Chanen, A. M., Velakoulis, D., Carison, K., Gaunson, K., Wood, S. J., Yuen, H. P., & Pantelis, C. (2008). Orbitofrontal, amygdala and hippocampal volumes in teenagers with first-presentation borderline personality disorder. *Psychiatry Research: Neuroimaging,*163(2),116-125. doi:10.1016/j.pscychresns.2007.08.007

Chao, L. L., & Knight, R. T. (1998). Contribution of human prefrontal cortex to delay performance. *Journal of cognitive neuroscience, 10*(2), 167-177.

Chiavaras, M. M., & Petrides, M. (2000). Orbitofrontal sulci of the human and macaque monkey brain. *The Journal of Comparative Neurology, 422*(1), 35-54. doi:10.1002/(SICI)1096-9861(20000619)422:1<35::AID-CNE3>3.0.CO;2

Chiesa, A., & Serretti, A. (2010). A systematic review of neurobiological and clinical features of mindfulness meditations. *Psychological Medicine, 40*(8), 1239-1252. doi:10.1017/S0033291709991747

Choi, E., Yeo, B., & Buckner, R. (2012). The organization of the human striatum estimated by intrinsic functional connectivity. *Journal of Neurophysiology,* 108(8), 2242-2263. doi:10.1152/jn.00270.2012

Chow, T. W., & Cummings, J. L. (1999). Frontal-subcortical circuits. *The human frontal lobes: Functions and disorders*, 3-26.

Christensen, A. L. (1996) Alexandr Romanovich Luria (1902-1977): Contributions to neuropsychological rehabilitation. *Neuropsychological Rehabilitation: An International Journal, 6*, 279-304, doi: 10.1080/713755511

Christensen, A. L., Goldberg, E., & Bougakov, D. (Eds.). (2009). *Luria's legacy in the 21st century*. New York, NY: Oxford University Press.

Christensen, A. L., & Luriā, A. R. (1975). *Luria's neuropsychological investigation: Text.* New York: Spectrum Publications.

Clarke, H. F., Walker, S. C., Dalley, J. W., Robbins, T. W., & Roberts, A. C. (2007). Cognitive inflexibility after prefrontal serotonin depletion is behaviorally and neurochemically specific. *Cerebral Cortex, 17*(1), 18-27.and Biobehavioral Reviews, 36(1), 218236.

Clauss, J. A., Cowan, R. L., & Blackford, J. U. (2011). Expectation and temperament moderate amygdala and dorsal anterior cingulate cortex responses to fear faces. *Cognitive, Affective, & Behavioral Neuroscience,* 11(1), 13-21. doi:10.3758/s13415-010-0007-9

Cohen, Y. E., Russ, B. E., Davis, S. J., Baker, A. E., Ackelson, A. L., & Nitecki, R. (2009). A functional role for the ventrolateral prefrontal cortex in non-spatial auditory cognition. *Proceedings of the National Academy of Sciences of the United States of America, 106*(47), 20045-20050. doi:10.1073/pnas.0907248106

Colombo, B., Balzarotti, S., & Mazzucchelli, N. (2016). The influence of the dorsolateral prefrontal cortex on attentional behavior and decision making. A t-DCS study on emotionally vs. functionally designed objects. *Brain and cognition, 104*, 7-14.

Conklin, H. M., Luciana, M., Hooper, C. J., & Yarger, R. S. (2007). Working memory performance in typically developing children and adolescents: Behavioral evidence of protracted frontal lobe development. *Developmental neuropsychology, 31*(1), 103-128.

Counsell, S. J., Edwards, A. D., Chew, A. T., Anjari, M., Dyet, L. E., Srinivasan, L., & Cowan, F. M. (2008). Specific relations between neurodevelopmental abilities and white matter microstructure in children born preterm. *Brain, 131*(12), 3201-3208.

Cozolino, L. (2002). *The neuroscience of psychotherapy: building and rebuilding the human brain (norton series on interpersonal neurobiology).* WW Norton & Company.

Crivellato, E., & Ribatti, D. (2007). Soul, mind, brain: Greek philosophy and the birth of neuroscience. *Brain research bulletin, 71*(4), 327-336.

Cummings J. L. (1993). Frontal-subcortical circuits and human behavior. *.Archives of Neurology, 50,* 873-880. doi: 10.1001/archneur.1993.00540080076020

Damasio, A. (2003). Feelings of emotion and the self. *Annals of the New York Academy of Sciences, 1001,* 253-261. doi: 10.1196/annals.1279.014

Damasio, H., Grabowski, T., Frank, R., Galaburda, A. M., & Damasio, A. R. (1994). The return of Phineas Gage: Clues about the brain from the skull of a famous patient. *Science, 264*, 1102-1105.

Darby, D., & Walsh, K. W. (2005). *Walsh's neuropsychology: A clinical approach*. Churchill Livingstone.

Davis, D. D. (1958). Caudate lesions and spontaneous locomotion in the monkey. *Neurology, 8*, 135-139. doi: 10.1212/WNL.8.2.135

Dean, D. C., O'Muircheartaigh, J., Dirks, H., Waskiewicz, N., Lehman, K., Walker, L., & Deoni, S. C. (2014). Modeling healthy male white matter and myelin development: 3 through 60 months of age. *Neuroimage, 84*, 742-752.

Decety, J. (2010). The neurodevelopment of empathy in humans. *Developmental neuroscience, 32*(4), 257-267.

Delis, D. C., Kaplan, E., & Kramer, J. H. (2001). *Delis-Kaplan Executive Function System (D-KEFS) examiner's manual*. San Antonio, TX: The Psychological Corporation.

Delis, D. C., Kramer, J. H., Kaplan, E., & Ober, B. A. (1987). *The California Verbal Learning Test*. New York: Psychological Corporation.

Demerens, C., Stankoff, B., Logak, M., Anglade, P., Allinquant, B., Couraud, F., & Lubetzki, C. (1996). Induction of myelination in the central nervous system by electrical activity. *Proceedings of the National Academy of Sciences, 93*(18), 9887-9892.

Deoni, S. C., Dean, D. C., O'Muircheartaigh, J., Dirks, H., & Jerskey, B. A. (2012). Investigating white matter development in infancy and early childhood using myelin water faction and relaxation time mapping. *Neuroimage, 63*(3), 1038-1053.

Desmet, C., & Brass, M. (2015). Observing accidental and intentional unusual actions is associated with different subregions of the medial frontal cortex. Neuroimage, 122, 195-202. doi: 10.1016/j.neuroimage.2015.08.018

D'Esposito, M., & Postle, B. (2015). The cognitive neuroscience of working memory. (pp. 115-142). *PALO ALTO: ANNUAL REVIEWS*. doi: 10.1146/annurev-psych-010814-015031.

D'Esposito M, Postle B, Rypma B. 2000. Prefrontal cortical contributions to working memory: evidence from event-related fMRI studies. *Experimental Brain Research*, 133:3–11

Dias, R., Robbins, T. W., & Roberts, A. C. (1996a). Dissociation in prefrontal

cortex of affective and attentional shifts. *Nature, 380*, 69-72.
doi:10.1038/380069a0

Dias, R., Robbins, T. W., & Roberts, A. C. (1996b). Primate analogue of the
Wisconsin Card Sorting Test: Effects of excitotoxic lesions of the
prefrontal cortex in the marmoset. *Behavioral Neuroscience, 110*, 872.
doi: 10.1037/0735-7044.110.5.872

Dias, R., Robbins, T. W., & Roberts, A. C. (1997). Dissociable forms of
inhibitory control within prefrontal cortex with an analog of the
Wisconsin Card Sort Test: Restriction to novel situations and
independence from "on-line" processing. *The Journal of Neuroscience,
17*, 9285-9297.

Djordjevic, J., Zatorre, R. J., Petrides, M., Boyle, J. A., & Jones-Gotman, M.
(2005). Functional neuroimaging of odor imagery. *Neuroimage, 24*(3),
791-801. doi:10.1016/j.neuroimage.2004.09.035

Dobbins, I. G., & Wagner, A. D. (2005). Domain-general and domain-sensitive
prefrontal mechanisms for recollecting events and detecting novelty.
Cerebral Cortex, 15(11), 1768–1778.

Dolan, R. J. (2007). The human amygdala and orbital prefrontal cortex in
behavioural regulation. *Philosophical Transactions of the Royal Society
of London B: Biological Sciences, 362*(1481), 787-799.

Dolk, T., Liepelt, R., Villringer, A., Prinz, W., & Ragert, P. (2012).
Morphometric gray matter differences of the medial frontal cortex
influence the social simon effect. *Neuroimage, 61*(4), 1249-1254.
doi:10.1016/j.neuroimage.2012.03.061

Drevets, W. C., Price, J. L., & Furey, M. L. (2008). Brain structural and
functional abnormalities in mood disorders: Implications for
neurocircuitry models of depression. *Brain Structure and
Function, 213*(1), 93-118. doi:10.1007/s00429-008-0189-x.

Dubois, B., Pillon, B., & McKeith, I. G. (2007). Parkinson's disease with and
without dementia and Lewy body dementia. In B. L. Miller & J. L.
Cummings (Eds.), *The human frontal lobes: Functions and disorders,
(2nd ed.; pp. 472-504). New York: Guilford University Press.

Duke, L. M., & Kaszniak, A. W. (2000). Executive control functions in
degenerative dementias: A comparative review. *Neuropsychology
Review, 10*, 75-99. doi: 10.1023/A:1009096603879

Durston, S., Davidson, M. C., Tottenham, N., Galvan, A., Spicer, J., Fossella, J. A., & Casey, B. J. (2006). A shift from diffuse to focal cortical activity with development. *Developmental science*, *9*(1), 1-8.

Edgin, J. O., Inder, T. E., Anderson, P. J., Hood, K. M., Clark, C. A., & Woodward, L. J. (2008). Executive functioning in preschool children born very preterm: relationship with early white matter pathology. *Journal of the International Neuropsychological Society*, *14*(01), 90-101.

Egner, T., Jamieson, G., & Gruzelier, J. (2005). Hypnosis decouples cognitive control from conflict monitoring processes of the frontal lobe. *Neuroimage*, 27(4), 969-978. doi:10.1016/j.neuroimage.2005.05.00

Einarsson, E., Pors, J., & Nader, K. (2015). Systems reconsolidation reveals a selective role for the anterior cingulate cortex in generalized contextual fear memory expression. *Neuropsychopharmacology*, 40(2), 480-487. doi:10.1038/npp.2014.197

Elwood, R. W. (1995). The California Verbal Learning Test: Psychometric characteristics and clinical application. NeuropsychoPessoa, L. (2009). How do emotion and motivation direct executive control? *Trends in Cognitive Sciences,* 13(4), 160-166. doi:10.1016/j.tics.2009.01.006logy Review, 5, 173-201. doi: 10.1007/BF02214761

Etkin, A., Egner, T., & Kalisch, R. (2011). Emotional processing in anterior cingulate and medial prefrontal cortex. *Trends in Cognitive Sciences*, 15(2), 85-93. doi:10.1016/j.tics.2010.11.004.

Etkin, A., Egner, T., Peraza, D. M., Kandel, E. R., & Hirsch, J. (2006). Resolving emotional conflict: A role for the rostral anterior cingulate cortex in modulating activity in the amygdala. *Neuron*, 51(6), 871-882. doi:10.1016/j.neuron.2006.07.029.

Ferrer, E., Whitaker, K. J., Steele, J. S., Green, C. T., Wendelken, C., & Bunge, S. A. (2013). White matter maturation supports the development of reasoning ability through its influence on processing speed. *Developmental science*, *16*(6), 941-951.

Ferrier, D. (1886). *The functions of the brain*. London: UK: Smith, Elder.

Filley, C. M. (2009). The frontal lobes. *Handbook of clinical neurology*, *95*, 557-570.

Filskov, S. B., & Goldstein, S. G. (1974). Diagnostic validity of the Halstead-

Reitan neuropsychological battery. *Journal of Consulting and Clinical Psychology*, *42*, 382. doi: 10.1037/h0036712

Finger, S. (2001). *Origins of neuroscience: a history of explorations into brain function*. Oxford University Press, USA.

Fitzgerald, P. J. (2011). A neurochemical yin and yang: does serotonin activate and norepinephrine deactivate the prefrontal cortex?. *Psychopharmacology*, *213* (2-3), 171-182.

Floden, D., Alexander, M. P., Kubu, C. S., Katz, D., & Stuss, D. T. (2008). Impulsivity and risk-taking behavior in focal frontal lobe lesions. *Neuropsychologia*, 46(1), 213-223. doi:10.1016/j.neuropsychologia.2007.07.020

Flynn, J. R. (2013). *James Flynn: Why our IQ levels are higher than our grandparents'*. Retrieved from Ted.com: http://www.ted.com/talks/james_flynn_why_our_iq_levels_are_higher_than_our_grandparents.html

Folger, T. (2012). Can we keep getting smarter? *Scientific American*, *307*, 44-47. doi:10.1038/scientificamerican0912-44

Franceschi, M., Anchisi, D., Pelati, O., Zuffi, M., Matarrese, M., Moresco, R. M., ... & Perani, D. (2005). Glucose metabolism and serotonin receptors in the frontotemporal lobe degeneration. *Annals of neurology*, *57*(2), 216-225.

Franz, E. A., & Gillett, G. (2011). John Hughlings Jackson's evolutionary neurology: a unifying framework for cognitive neuroscience. *Brain*, *134*(10), 3114-3120.

Freud, S.(1895). Project for a scientific psychology. *Standard Edition* 1:295-397.

Frey, S., Kostopoulos, P., & Petrides, M. (2004). Orbitofrontal contribution to auditory encoding. *Neuroimage*, 22(3), 1384-1389. doi:10.1016/j.neuroimage.2004.03.018

Fried, P. J., Rushmore, R. J., Moss, M. B., Valero-Cabré, A., & Pascual-Leone, A. (2014). Causal evidence supporting functional dissociation of verbal and spatial working memory in the human dorsolateral prefrontal cortex. *European Journal of Neuroscience*, 39(11), 1973-1981. doi:10.1111/ejn.12584

Frith, C. D., & Amodio, D. M. (2006). Meeting of minds: The medial frontal cortex and social cognition. Nature Reviews Neuroscience, 7(4), 268-

277. doi:10.1038/nrn1884.

Frye, D., Zelazo, P. D., & Palfai, T. (1995). Theory of mind and rule-based reasoning. *Cognitive Development,* 10(4), 483-527. doi:10.1016/0885-2014(95)90024-1

Fujiwara, J., Tobler, P. N., Taira, M., Iijima, T., & Tsutsui, K. (2009). A parametric relief signal in human ventrolateral prefrontal cortex.*Neuroimage, 44*(3), 1163 1170. doi: 10.1016/j.neuroimage.2008.09.050

Fulton, J. F. (1943). *Physiology of the nervous system.* New York, NY: Oxford University Press.

Fuster, J. (2008). *The prefrontal cortex.* Academic Press: London.

Fuster, J. M. (2015). *The Prefrontal Cortex* (Fifth Edition). Academic Press, London.

Fuster, J. M. , Bauer, R. H., & Jervey, J. P., (1985). Functional interactions between inferotemporal and prefrontal cortex in a cognitive task. *Brain Research,* 330:299–307

Gansler, D. A., McLaughlin, N. C. R., Iguchi, L., Jerram, M., Moore, D. W., Bhadelia, R., & Fulwiler, C. (2009). A multivariate approach to aggression and the orbital frontal cortex in psychiatric patients. *Psychiatry Research: Neuroimaging,* 171(3), 145-154. doi:10.1016/j.pscychresns.2008.03.007

García-Cabezas, M. Á., & Barbas, H. (2014). A direct anterior cingulate pathway to the primate primary olfactory cortex may control attention to olfaction. Brain Structure and Function, 219(5), 1735-1754. doi:10.1007/s00429-013-0598-3

Garcin, B., Volle, E., Dubois, B., & Levy, R. (2012). Similar or different? the role of the ventrolateral prefrontal cortex in similarity detection. *Plos One, 7*(3), e34164. doi:10.1371/journal.pone.0034164

Gathercole, S. E., Pickering, S. J., Ambridge, B., & Wearing, H. (2004). The structure of working memory from 4 to 15 years of age. *Developmental psychology, 40*(2), 177.

Geddes, M., Tsuchida, A., Ashley, V., Swick, D., & Fellows, L. (2014). Material-specific interference control is dissociable and lateralized in human prefrontal cortex. *Neuropsychologia, 64,* 310-319. doi:10.1016/j.neuropsychologia.2014.09

Geschwind, N., & Levitsky, W. (1968). Human brain: Left-right asymmetries in temporal speech region. *Science, 161*, 186-187.

Gibson, K. R. (1991). Myelination and behavioral development: A comparative perspective on questions of neoteny, altriciality and intelligence. *Brain maturation and cognitive development: Comparative and cross-cultural perspectives*, 29-63.

Glasser, M. F., Goyal, M. S., Preuss, T. M., Raichle, M. E., & Van Essen, D. C. (2014). Trends and properties of human cerebral cortex: correlations with cortical myelin content. *Neuroimage, 93*, 165-175.

Glozman, J. M. (1999). Russian neuropsychology after Luria. *Neuropsychology Review, 9*, 33-44. doi: 10.1023/A:1025690920712

Glozman, J. M. (2007). AR Luria and the history of Russian neuropsychology. *Journal of the History of the Neurosciences, 16*, 168-180. doi: 10.1080/09647040600550368

Goldberg, E. (2001). *The executive brain: Frontal lobes and the civilized mind.* New York, NY: Oxford University Press.

Goldberg, E. (2009). *The new executive brain: Frontal lobes in a complex world.* New York, NY: Oxford University Press.

Goldberg, E., & Bougakov, D. (2000). *International handbook of neuro-psychological rehabilitation.* New York, NY: Plenum Publishers.

Goldberg, E., & Bougakov, D. (2009). Neuropsychology and AR Luria's concept of higher cortical functions in the beginning of the 3rd millennium. In A. L. Christensen, E. Goldberg, & D. Bougakor (Eds.), *Luria's legacy in the 21st century* (pp. 17-22). New York, NY: Oxford University Press.

Goldberg, E., & Costa, L. D. (1981). Hemisphere differences in the acquisition and use of descriptive systems. *Brain and language, 14*, 144-173.

Goldberg, E., Harner, R., Lovell, M., Podell, K., & Riggio, S. (1994). Cognitive bias, functional cortical geometry, and the frontal lobes: Laterality, sex, and handedness. *Journal of Cognitive Neuroscience, 6*, 276-296. doi:10.1162/jocn.1994.6.3.276

Goldberg, E., & Podell, K. (2000). Adaptive decision making, ecological validity, and the frontal lobes. *Journal of Clinical and Experimental Neuropsychology, 22*, 56-68. doi: 10.1076/1380-3395(200002)22

Golden, C. J., Hammeke, T. A., & Purish, A. D. (1978). Diagnostic validity of a standardized neuropsychological battery derived from Luria's neuropsychological tests. *Journal of Consulting and Clinical Psychology*, 46, 1258-1265. doi: 10.1037/0022-006X.46.6.1258

Goldman-Rakic, P. S. (1995). Cellular basis of working memory. *Neuron, 14*(3), 477-485.

Gottfried, J. A. (2010). Central mechanisms of odour object perception. *Nature Reviews Neuroscience, 11*(9), 628-641.

Gould, G. M., & Pyle, W. L. (1896). *Anomalies and curiosities of medicine.* New York, NY: Bell.

Grafman, J., & Litvan, I. (1999). Importance of deficits in executive functions. *The Lancet, 354*, 1921-1923.

Graybiel, A. M. (2008). Habits, rituals, and the evaluative brain. *Annual Review of Neuroscience.* 31, 359–387. doi: 10.1146/ annurev.neuro.29.051605. 112851

Green, J. B. (2009). Chapter twelve science, theology, and Wesleyans. *Wesleyan Theology and Social Science: The Dance of Practical Divinity and Discovery*, 177.

Greenspan, S. I., Wieder, S., & Simons, R. (1998). *The child with special needs: Encouraging intellectual and emotional growth.* Addison-Wesley/ Addison Wesley Longman.

Gross, C. G. (1999). *Brain, vision, memory: Tales in the history of neuroscience.* MIT Press.

Gross, C. G. (1963). Locomotor activity following lateral frontal lesions in rhesus monkeys. *Journal of Comparative and Physiological Psychology, 56*, 232-236. doi:http://dx.doi.org/10.1037/h0048041

Grossmann, T., Parise, E., & Friederici, A. (2010). The detection of communicative signals directed at the self in infant prefrontal cortex. *Frontiers in Human Neuroscience*, 4, 201.

Gunzler, S. A., Schoenberg, M. R., Riley, D. E., Walter, B., & Maciunas, R. J. (2011). Parkinson's disease and other movement Disorders. In *The Little Black Book of Neuropsychology* (pp. 567-646). Springer U.S.

Hage, S., & Nieder, A. (2015). Audio-vocal interaction in single neurons of the monkey ventrolateral prefrontal cortex. *Journal of Neuroscience, 35*(18), 7030-7040. doi:10.1523/JNEUROSCI.2371-14.2015

Hale, J. B., & Fiorello, C. A. (2004). *School neuropsychology: A practitioner's handbook.* Guilford Press.

Halgren, E. (1992). Emotional neurophysiology of the amygdala within the context of human cognition. Halgren, Eric and Aggleton, John P. (Ed), (1992). *The amygdala: Neurobiological aspects of emotion, memory, and mental dysfunction.* (pp. 191-228). New York, NY, US: Wiley-Liss, xii, 615 pp.

Halsband, U., & Freund, H. J. (1990). Premotor cortex and conditional motor learning in man. *Brain* 113(Pt 1), 207–222. doi: 10.1093/brain/113.1.207

Halsband, U., & Passingham, R. E. (1982). The role of premotor and parietal cortex in the direction of action. *Brain Research.* 240, 368–372. doi:

Halsband, U., & Passingham, R. E. (1985). Premotor cortex and the conditions for movement in monkeys (*Macaca fascicularis*). *Behav. Brain Res.* 18, 269–277. doi: 10.1016/0166-4328(85)90035-X

Halstead, C. W. (1947). *Brain and intelligence: A quantitative study of the frontal lobes.* Chicago, IL: University of Chicago Press.

Hanakawa, T., Honda, M., Sawamoto, N., Okada, T., Yonekura, Y., & Fukuyama, H., et al. (2002). The role of rostral Brodmann area 6 in mental- operation tasks: an integrative neuroimaging approach. *Cerebral Cortex* 12, 1157-1170. doi:10.1093/cer cor/12.11.1157

Happaney, K., Zelazo, P. D., & Stuss, D. T. (2004). Development of orbitofrontal function: Current themes and future directions. *Brain and Cognition,* 55(1), 1-10. doi:10.1016/j.bandc.2004.01.001

Harlow, J. M. (1868). Recovery from the passage of an iron bar through the head. *Publications of the Massachusetts Medical Society, 2,* 327-346.

Harmelen, A. V., Hauber, K., Moor, B. G., Spinhoven, P., Boon, A. E., Crone, E. A., & Elzinga, B. M. (2014). Childhood emotional maltreatment severity is associated with dorsal medial prefrontal cortex responsivity to social exclusion in young adults: E85107. PLoS One, 9(1). doi:10.1371/journal.pone.0085107.

Harrison, D. W. (2015). Confabulation of Speech, Faces, and Places. In *Brain Asymmetry and Neural Systems* (pp. 365-375). Springer International Publishing.

Hayman, L. A., Rexer, J. L., Pavol, M. A., Strite, D., & Meyers, C. A. (1998). Kluver-Bucy syndrome after bilateral selective damage of amygdala and its cortical connections. *The Journal of Neuropsychiatry and Clinical*

Neurosciences, 10(3), 354.

Hebb, D. O. (1945). Man's frontal lobes: A critical review. *Archives of Neurology and Psychiatry, 54*, 10. doi:10.1001/archneurpsyc.1945. 02300070020002

Hedden, T., & Gabrieli, J. D. E. (2010). Shared and selective neural correlates of inhibition, facilitation, and shifting processes during executive control. *Neuroimage, 51*(1), 421-431. doi:10.1016/j.neuroimage.2010.01.089

Heekeren, H. R., Marrett, S., Ruff, D. A., Bandettini, P. A., & Ungerleider, L. G. (2006). Involvement of human left dorsolateral prefrontal cortex in perceptual decision making is independent of response modality. *Proceedings of the National Academy of Sciences, 103*(26), 10023-10028.

Heilman, K. M., Meador, K. J., & Loring, D. W. (2000). Hemispheric asymmetries of limb-kinetic apraxia: A loss of deftness. *Neurology, 55*, 523-526. doi: 10.1212/WNL.55.4.523

Herder, J. G. (1772). 1969 Essay on the origin of speech. *On language: Plato to von Humboldt, Holt, Rinehart and Winston. New York*, 147-166.

Herringa, R., Phillips, M., Fournier, J., Kronhaus, D., & Germain, A. (2013). Childhood and adult trauma both correlate with dorsal anterior cingulate activation to threat in combat veterans. *Psychological Medicine, 43*(7), 1533-1542. doi:10.1017/S0033291712002310

Hoeft, F., Barnea-Goraly, N., Haas, B. W., Golarai, G., Ng, D., Mills, D., ... & Reiss, A. L. (2007). More is not always better: increased fractional anisotropy of superior longitudinal fasciculus associated with poor visuospatial abilities in Williams syndrome. *The Journal of Neuroscience, 27*(44), 11960-11965.

Hoeft, F., Barnea-Goraly, N., Haas, B. W., Golarai, G., Ng, D., Mills, D., ... & Reiss, A. L. (2007). More is not always better: increased fractional anisotropy of superior longitudinal fasiculus associated with poor visuospatial abilities in Williams syndrome. *The Journal of Neuroscience, 27*(44), 11960-11965.

Hoffman, J. L. (1949). Clinical observations concerning schizophrenic patients treated by prefrontal leucotomy. *New England Journal of Medicine, 241*, 233-236. doi: 10.1056/NEJM194908112410604

Honer, W. G., Prohovnik, I., Smith, G., & Lucas, L. R. (1988). Scopolamine reduces frontal cortex perfusion. Journal of Cerebral Blood Flow & Metabolism, 8, 635-641. doi:10.1038/jcbfm.1988.110

Horton, A. M., & Soper, H. V. (2008). Neuropsychology of children's memory. In J. Reed & J. Warner (Eds.), *Child neuropsychology* (pp. 218-234). New York, NY: Wiley-Blackwell.

Hrkać, M., Wurm, M. F., Kühn, A. B., & Schubotz, R. I. (2015). Objects Mediate Goal Integration in Ventrolateral Prefrontal Cortex during Action Observation. *PloS one, 10*(7), e0134316.

Hoffman, P., Jefferies, E., & Lambon Ralph, M. A. (2010). Ventrolateral prefrontal cortex plays an executive regulation role in comprehension of abstract words: Convergent neuropsychological and repetitive TMS evidence. *The Journal of Neuroscience: The Official Journal of the Society for Neuroscience, 30*(46), 15450-15456. doi:10.1523/JNEUROSCI.3783-10.2010

Hoffmann, M. (2013). The human frontal lobes and frontal network systems: an evolutionary, clinical, and treatment perspective. *ISRN neurology, 2013*.

Holroyd, C., & Yeung, N. (2012). Motivation of extended behaviors by anterior cingulate cortex. *Trends in Cognitive Sciences*, 16(2), 122-128. doi:10.1016/j.tics.2011.12.008.

Homberg, J. R. (2012). Serotonin and decision making processes. *Neuroscience & Biobehavioral Reviews, 36*(1), 218-236.

Horton, A. M., Jr., & Horton, A. M., III. (2008). Overview of clinical neuropsychology. In A. M. Horton, Jr. & D. Wedding (Eds.), The neuropsychology handbook (3rd ed., pp. 3–30). New York: Springer Publishing Company.

Hoshi, E. (2015). Cortico-basal ganglia networks subserving goal-directed behavior mediated by conditional visuo-goal association. *Neural Circuits: Japan*, 67.

Howells, F. M., Stein, D. J., & Russell, V. A. (2012). Synergistic tonic and phasic activity of the locus coeruleus norepinephrine (LC-NE) arousal system is required for optimal attentional performance. *Metabolic brain disease, 27*(3), 267-274.

Hrkać M, Wurm MF, Kühn AB, Schubotz RI (2015) Objects Mediate Goal Integration in Ventrolateral Prefrontal Cortex during Action Observation.

PLoS ONE 10(7): e0134316.doi:10.1371/journal.pone.0134316

Huang, H., Shu, N., Mishra, V., Jeon, T., Chalak, L., Wang, Z. J., & Dong, Q. (2015). Development of human brain structural networks through infancy and childhood. *Cerebral Cortex, 25*(5), 1389-1404.

Hudspeth, W. J., & Pribram, K. H. (1990). Stages of brain and cognitive maturation.

Huizinga, M., Dolan, C. V., & van der Molen, M. W. (2006). Age-related change in executive function: Developmental trends and a latent variable analysis. *Neuropsychologia, 44*(11), 2017-2036.

Ilinsky, I. A., Jouandet, M. L., & Goldman-Rakic, P. S. (1985). Organization of the nigrothalamocortical system in the rhesus monkey. *Journal of Comparative Neurology, 236,* 315-330. doi: 10.1002/cne.902360304

Irle, E., & Markowitsch, H. J. (1984). Differential effects of prefrontal lesions and combined prefrontal and limbic lesions on subsequent learning performance in the cat. *Behavioral Neuroscience, 98,* 884-897. doi: 10.1037/0735-7044.98.5.884

Isaac, W., & Devito, J. L. (1958). Effect of sensory stimulation on the activity of normal and prefrontal-lobectomized monkeys. *Journal of Comparative and Physiological Psychology, 51,* 172-174. doi:http://dx.doi.org/10.1037/h0041433

Jääskeläinen, I. (Ed.). (2012). *Introduction to cognitive neuroscience.* Bookboon.

Jacobson, S., & Trojanowski, J. Q. (1975). Corticothalamic neurons and thalamocortical terminal fields: an investigation in rat using horseradish peroxidase and autoradiography. *Brain Research, 85*(3), 385-401.

Jacobsen, C. F. (1931). A study of cerebral function in learning: The frontal lobes. *Journal of Comparative Neurology, 52,* 271-340. doi: 10.1002/cne.900520205

Jacobsen, C. F. (1935). Functions of frontal association area in primates. *Archives of Neurology & Psychiatry, 33,* 558-569. doi:10.1001/archneurpsyc.1935.02250150108009

Jacobsen, C. F. (1936). Studies of cerebral function in primates. In the functions of the frontal association areas in monkeys. *Comparative Psychology Monographs, 13,* 1-60. Retrieved from http://search.proquest.com/docview/615061609?accountid=10868

Jacobsen, C. F., & Nissen, H. W. (1937). Studies of cerebral function in primates.

IV the effects of frontal lobe lesions on the delayed alternation habit in monkeys. *Journal of Comparative Psychology, 23*, 101. doi: 10.1037/h0056632

Jarbo, K., & Verstynen, T. (2015). Converging structural and functional connectivity of orbitofrontal, dorsolateral prefrontal, and posterior parietal cortex in the human striatum. *Journal of Neuroscience*, 35(9), 3865-3878. doi:10.1523/JNEUROSCI.2636-14.2015

Jellison, B. J., Field, A. S., Medow, J., Lazar, M., Salamat, M. S., & Alexander, A. L. (2004). Diffusion tensor imaging of cerebral white matter: A pictorial review of physics, fiber tract anatomy, and tumor imaging patterns. *AJNR. American Journal of Neuroradiology, 25*(3), 356.

Jerison, H. J. (1990). Fossil evidence on the evolution of the neocortex. In *Comparative Structure and Evolution of Cerebral Cortex, Part I* (pp. 285-309). Springer US.

Jerison, H. J. (2007). What fossils tell us about the evolution of the neocortex. *Evolution of Nervous System. New York, Elsevier.*

Jones, E. G. , & Powell, T. P. S. (1970). An anatomical study of converging sensory pathways within the cerebral cortex of the monkey. *Brain*, 93, 793-820.

Jonides, J., Smith, E. E., Koeppe, R. A., Awh, E., Minoshima, S., & Mintun, M. A. (1993). Spatial working-memory in humans as revealed by PET. *Nature, 363,* 623-625. doi: http://dx.doi.org.fgul.idm.oclc.org/10.1038/363623a0

Jung, R. E., & Haier, R. J. (2007). The Parieto-Frontal Integration Theory (P-FIT) of intelligence: converging neuroimaging evidence. *Behavioral and Brain Sciences, 30*(02), 135-154.

Kaas, J. H. (2005). From mice to men: the evolution of the large, complex human brain. *Journal of biosciences, 30*(2), 155-165.

Kahnt, T., Heinzle, J., Park, S. Q., Haynes, J., & Romo, R. (2010). The neural code of reward anticipation in human orbitofrontal cortex. *Proceedings of the National Academy of Sciences of the United States of America*, 107(13), 6010-6015. doi:10.1073/pnas.0912838107

Kalisch, R. (2009). The functional neuroanatomy of reappraisal: Time matters. *Neuroscience and Biobehavioral Reviews*, 33(8), 1215-1226. doi:10.1016/j.neubiorev.2009.06.003

Kamali, A., Flanders, A. E., Brody, J., Hunter, J. V., & Hasan, K. M. (2014). Tracing superior longitudinal fasciculus connectivity in the human brain using high resolution diffusion tensor tractography. *Brain Structure and Function, 219*(1), 269-281.

Kandel, E., Schwartz, J.H., Jessel, T.M., Siegelbaum, S.A., & Hudspeth, A.J. (2013). *Principles of neural science.* Columbus, OH: McGraw-Hill.

Katon, W. (2010). Depression and diabetes: unhealthy bedfellows. *Depression and anxiety, 27*(4), 323-326.

Katsuki, F., & Constantinidis, C. (2013). Time course of functional connectivity in primate dorsolateral prefrontal and posterior parietal cortex during working memory: E81601. *PLoS One,* 8(11) doi:10.1371/journal.pone.0081601.

Kaufer, D. (2007). The dorsolateral and cingulate cortex. *The human frontal lobes: Functions and disorders, 2,* 44-58.

Kawai, T., Yamada, H., Sato, N., Takada, M., & Matsumoto, M. (2015). Roles of the lateral habenula and anterior cingulate cortex in negative outcome monitoring and behavioral adjustment in nonhuman primates. Neuron, 88(4), 792-804. doi:10.1016/j.neuron.2015.09.030

Kennard, M. A. (1945). Focal autonomic representation in the cortex and its relation to sham rage. *Journal of Neuropathology & Experimental Neurology, 4*(3), 295-304.

Kennerley, S. W., Behrens, T. E., & Wallis, J. D. (2011). Double dissociation of value computations in orbitofrontal and anterior cingulate neurons. *Nature neuroscience,* 14(12), 1581-1589.

Kennerley, S., & Wallis, J. (2009). Evaluating choices by single neurons in the frontal lobe: Outcome value encoded across multiple decision variables. European Journal of Neuroscience, 29(10), 2061-2073. doi:10.1111/j.1460-9568.2009.06743.x

Kilgus, M. D., Maxmen, J. S., & Ward, N. G. (2015). *Essential Psychopathology & Its Treatment.* WW Norton & Company.

Klein-Flugge, M., Barron, H., Brodersen, K., Dolan, R., & Behrens, T. (2013). Segregated encoding of reward-identity and stimulus-reward associations in human orbitofrontal cortex. *Journal of Neuroscience,* 33(7), 3202-3211. doi:10.1523/JNEUROSCI.2532-12.2013

Klumpp, H., Post, D., Angstadt, M., Fitzgerald, D. A., & Phan, K. L. (2013).
Anterior cingulate cortex and insula response during indirect and direct
processing of emotional faces in generalized social anxiety
disorder. *Biology of Mood & Anxiety Disorders*, 3(1), 7-7.
doi:10.1186/2045-5380-3-7

Koenigsberg, H.W., Fan, J., Ochsner, K.N., Liu, X., Guise, K.G., Pizzarello, S.,
Dorantes, C., Guerreri, S., Tecuta, L., Goodman, M., New, A., & Siever,
L.J., (2009). Neural correlates of the use of psychological distancing to
regulate disorder. *Biological Psychiatry*, 66, 854–863.

Kohno, S., Noriuchi, M., Iguchi, Y., Kikuchi, Y., & Hoshi, Y. (2015). Emotional
discrimination during viewing unpleasant pictures: Timing in human
anterior ventrolateral prefrontal cortex and arnygdala.*Frontiers in
Human Neuroscience, 9*doi:10.3389/fnhurn.2015.00051

Kolb, B., Pellis, S., & Robinson, T. E. (2004). Plasticity and functions of the
orbital frontal cortex. *Brain and Cognition*, 55(1), 104-115.
doi:10.1016/S0278-2626(03)00278-1

Kolb, B., & Whishaw, I. Q. (2009). *Fundamentals of human neuropsychology*.
Macmillan.

Kong, F., Hu, S., Xue, S., Song, Y., & Liu, J. (2015). Extraversion mediates the
relationship between structural variations in the dorsolateral prefrontal
cortex and social well-being. *Neuroimage*, 105, 269-275.
doi:10.1016/j.neuroimage.2014.10.062

Korkman, M. (1999). Applying Luria's diagnostic principles in the
neuropsychological assessment of children. *Neuropsychology Review*, *9*,
89-105. doi: 10.1023/A:1025659808004

Koski, L., & Paus, T. (2000). Functional connectivity of the anterior cingulate
cortex within the human frontal lobe: a brain-mapping meta-analysis. In
Executive Control and the Frontal Lobe: Current Issues (pp. 55-65).
Springer Berlin Heidelberg.

Koziol, L. F., & Budding, D. E. (2009). *Subcortical structures and cognition:
Implications for neuropsychological assessment*. Springer Science &
Business Media.

Koziol, L. F. (2013). Introduction. *Applied Neuropsychology: Child, 2*, 81.

Kukleta, M., Bob, P., Brázdil, M., Roman, R., & Rektor, I. (2010). The level of
frontal-temporal beta-2 band EEG synchronization distinguishes anterior

cingulate cortex from other frontal regions. *Consciousness and Cognition, 19*(4), 879-886. doi:10.1016/j.concog.2010.04.007

Lawicka, W. A., Mishkin, M., & Kreiner, J. (1966). Delayed response deficit in dogs after selective ablation of the proreal gyrus. *Acta Biologiae Experimentalis, 26*, 309-322. Retrieved from http://search.proquest.com/docview/615478652?accountid=10868

Lee, T. G., Blumenfeld, R. S., & D'Esposito, M. (2013). Disruption of dorsolateral but not ventrolateral prefrontal cortex improves unconscious perceptual memories. *The Journal of Neuroscience : The Official Journal of the Society for Neuroscience, 33*(32), 13233-13237. doi:10.1523/JNEUROSCI.5652-12.2013

Levens, S. M., Devinsky, O., & Phelps, E. A. (2011). Role of the left amygdala and right orbital frontal cortex in emotional interference resolution facilitation in working memory. *Neuropsychologia, 49*(12), 3201-3212. doi:10.1016/j.neuropsychologia.2011.07.021

Levine, B., Schweizer, T. A., O'Connor, C., Turner, G., Gillingham, S., Stuss, D. T., & Robertson, I. H. (2011). Rehabilitation of executive functioning in patients with frontal lobe brain damage with goal management training. *Frontiers in human neuroscience, 5,* 1-9. doi: 10.3389/fnhum.2011.00009

Levy, R., & Goldman-Rakic, P. S. (2000). Segregation of working memory functions within the dorsolateral prefrontal cortex. *Experimental Brain Research, 133*(1), 23-32. doi:10.1007/s002210000397

Leyfer, O. T., Folstein, S. E., Bacalman, S., Davis, N. O., Dinh, E., Morgan, J., & Lainhart, J. E. (2006). Comorbid psychiatric disorders in children with autism: Interview development and rates of disorders. *Journal of Autism and Developmental Disorders, 36*(7), 849-861. doi:10.1007/s10803-006

Lezak, M. (1983). *Neuropsychological assessment.* New York, NY: Oxford University Press.

Lezak, M. D., Howieson, D. B., Bigler, E. D., & Tranel, D. (2012). *Neuropsychological assessment (5th ed.).* New York, NY: Oxford University Press.

Liddell, B. J., Brown, K. J., Kemp, A. H., Barton, M. J., Das, P., Peduto, A., ... & Williams, L. M. (2005). A direct brainstem–amygdala–cortical 'alarm' system for subliminal signals of fear. *Neuroimage, 24*(1), 235-

243.

Lilja, Å., Hagstadius, S., Risberg, J., Salford, L. G., Smith, G. J., & Ohman, R. (1992). Frontal lobe dynamics in brain tumor patients: A study of regional cerebral blood flow and affective changes before and after surgery. Cognitive and Behavioral Neurology, 5, 294-300.

Liu, C., Tang, Y., Ge, H., Wang, F., Sun, H., Meng, H., & Zhang, Z. (2014). Increasing breadth of the frontal lobe but decreasing height of the human brain between two Chinese samples from a Neolithic site and from living humans. *American journal of physical anthropology*, *154*(1), 94-103.

Luciana, M., Conklin, H. M., Hooper, C. J., & Yarger, R. S. (2005). The development of nonverbal working memory and executive control processes in adolescents. *Child development*, *76*(3), 697-712.

Luk, G., Bialystok, E., Craik, F. I., & Grady, C. L. (2011). Lifelong bilingualism maintains white matter integrity in older adults. *The Journal of Neuroscience*, *31*(46), 16808-16813.

Luria, A. R. (1966). *Higher cortical functions in man (2ⁿᵈed.).* New York, NY: Basic Books.

Luria, A. R. (1973). *The working brain: An introduction to neuropsychology.* New York, NY: Basic Books.

Luria, A. R. (1976). *Cognitive development: Its cultural and social foundations.* Cambridge, MA: Harvard University Press.

Luria, A. R., & Majovski, L. V. (1977). Basic approaches used in American and Soviet clinical neuropsychology. *American Psychologist*, *32*, 959. doi: 10.1037/0003-066X.32.11.959

MacLean, P. D. (1990). *The triune brain in evolution: Role in paleocerebral functions.* Springer Science & Business Media.

Makris, N., Kennedy, D., McInerney, S., Sorensen, A., Wang, R., Caviness, V., & Pandya, D. (2005;2004;). Segmentation of subcomponents within the superior longitudinal fascicle in humans: A quantitative, in vivo, DT-MRI study. *Cerebral Cortex, 15*(6), 854-869. doi:10.1093/cercor/bhh186.

Manger, P. R., Spocter, M. A., & Patzke, N. (2013). The evolutions of large brain size in mammals: the 'over-700-gram club quartet'. *Brain, behavior and evolution, 82*(1), 68-78.

Mannella, F., & Baldassarre, G. (2015). Selection of cortical dynamics for motor behaviour by the basal ganglia. *Biological Cybernetics, 109*(6), 575-595. doi:10.1007/s00422-015-0662-6

Marin, R. S. (1991). Apathy: A neuropsychiatric syndrome. *The Journal of Neuropsychiatry and Clinical Neurosciences, 3*, 243-254.

Marzo, A., Totah, N. K., Neves, R. M., Logothetis, N. K., & Eschenko, O. (2014). Unilateral electrical stimulation of the rat Locus Coeruleus elicits bilateral response of norepinephrine neurons and sustained activation of the mPFC. *Journal of neurophysiology*, jn-00920.

Medalla, M., & Barbas, H. (2010). Anterior cingulate synapses in prefrontal areas 10 and 46 suggest differential influence in cognitive control. *The Journal of Neuroscience, 30*(48), 16068-16081.

Mega, M. S., & Cummings, J. L. (1997). *The cingulate and cingulate syndromes.* Woburn, MA: Butterworth-Heinemann. Retrieved from http://search.proquest.com/docview/619148524?accountid=10868

Mesulam, M. M. (Ed.). (1985). *Principles of behavioral neurology* (No. 26). Oxford University Press, USA.

Mettler, F. A. (1944). Physiologic effects of bilateral simultaneous frontal lesions in the primate. *Journal of Comparative Neurology and Psychology, 81*, 105-136. doi: http://dx.doi.org/10.1002/cne.900810202

Mettler, F. A., & Mettler, C. C. (1942). The effects of striatal injury. *Brain: A Journal of Neurology, 65,* 242-255. doi: 10.1093/brain/65.3.242

Meyer, J. S., & Barron, D. W. (1960). Apraxia of gait: A clinico-physiological study. *Brain, 83*, 261-284. doi: 10.1093/brain/83.2.261

Miller E. K., & Cohen J. D. 2001. An integrative theory of prefrontal cortex function. *Annual Review Neuroscience*, 24:167–202.

Miller, B. L., & Cummings, J. L. (Eds.). (2007). *The human frontal lobes: Functions and disorders.* Guilford Press.

Miller, B. L., Cummings, J. L., McIntyre, H., Ebers, G., & Grode, M. (1986). Hypersexuality or altered sexual preference following brain injury. *Journal of Neurology, Neurosurgery & Psychiatry, 49*(8), 867-873.

Miller, G. A., Galanter, E. & Pribram, K. H. *Plans and the Structure of Behavior.* New York: Holt, Rinehart & Winston.

Miller, M. H., & Orbach, J. (1972). Retention of spatial alternation following frontal lobe resections in stump-tailed macaques. *Neuropsychologia, 10,*

291-298.

Milner, B. (1964). Some effects of frontal lobectomy in man. In J. Warren & K. Akert (Eds.), *The frontal granular cortex and behavior* (pp.313-334). New York, NY: McGraw-Hill.

Minzenberg, M. J., Fan, J., New, A. S., Tang, C. Y., & Siever, L. J. (2008) Frontolimbic structural changes in borderline personality disorder. *American Journal of Psychiatry*, 42(9):727-733.

Mischel, W., Ebbesen, E. B., & Raskoff Zeiss, A. (1972). Cognitive and attentional mechanisms in delay of gratification. *Journal of personality and social psychology*, *21*(2), 204.

Montgomery, M. (2013). *An introduction to language and society*. Routledge.

Moes, E., Duncanson, H., & Armengol, C. G. (2013). Process-focused assessment of arousal and attention. In L. Ashendorf, R. Swenson, & D. Libson (Eds.), *The Boston process approach to neuropsychological assessment: A practitioner's guide* (pp. 39-64). New York, NY: Oxford University Press.

Molnár, Z. (2011). Evolution of cerebral cortical development. Brain, Behavior and Evolution, 78(1), 94-107. doi:10.1159/000327325

Moniz, E. (1937). Prefrontal leucotomy in the treatment of mental disorders. *American Journal of Psychiatry*, *93*, 1379-1385.

Morandotti, N., Dima, D., Jogia, J., Frangou, S., Sala, M., De Vidovich, G... Brambilla, P. (2013). Childhood abuse is associated with structural impairment in the ventrolateral prefrontal cortex and aggressiveness in patients with borderline personality disorder. *Psychiatry Research-Neuroimaging, 213*(1), 18-23. doi:10.1016/j.pscychresns.2013.02.002

Morey, R. A., Hariri, A. R., Gold, A. L., Hauser, M. A., Munger, H. J., Dolcos, F., & McCarthy, G. (2011). Serotonin transporter gene polymorphisms and brain function during emotional distraction from cognitive processing in posttraumatic stress disorder. BMC Psychiatry, 11(1), Article 76-Article 76. doi:10.1186/1471-244X-11-76

Morrot, G., Bonny, J., Lehallier, B., & Zanca, M. (2013). fMRI of human olfaction at the individual level: Interindividual variability. *Journal of Magnetic Resonance Imaging*, 37(1), 92-100. doi:10.1002/jmri.23802

Mulder, H., Pitchford, N. J., Hagger, M. S., & Marlow, N. (2009). Development of executive function and attention in preterm children: a systematic review. *Developmental neuropsychology, 34*(4), 393-421.

Murphy, F., Smith, K., Cowen, P., Robbins, T., & Sahakian, B. (2002). The effects of tryptophan depletion on cognitive and affective processing in healthy volunteers. *Psychopharmacology, 163*(1), 42-53. doi:10.1007/s00213-002-1128-9

Nakayama, Y., Yamagata, T., Tanji, J., and Hoshi, E. (2008). Transformation of a virtual action plan into a motor plan in the premotor cortex. *Journal of Neuroscience, 28*, 10287–10297. doi: 10.1523/JNEUROSCI.2372-08.2008

Nauta, W. J. (1972). Neural associations of the frontal cortex. *Acta Biologiae Experimentalis, 32*, 125-140.

Netter, F. H. (2010). *Atlas of human anatomy*. Elsevier Health Sciences.

New, A. S., Perez-Rodriguez, M. M., & Ripoll, L. H. (2012). Neuroimaging and borderline personality disorder. *Psychiatric Annals, 42*(2), 65-71. doi:10.3928/00485713-20120124-07

Nieuwenhuis, S., Ridderinkhof, K.R., Blom, J., Band, G. P., & Kok, A. (2001). Error-related brain potentials are differentially related to aware- ness of response errors: evidence from an antisaccade task. *Psychophysiology*, 38:752–756.

Nieuwenhuys, R. (2009). Analysis of the structure of the brain stem of mammals by means of a modified D'arcy thompson procedure. *Brain Structure & Function, 214*(1), 79-85. doi:10.1007/s00429-009-0223-7

Nieuwenhuys, R. (2013). The myeloarchitectonic studies on the human cerebral cortex of the vogt-vogt school, and their significance for the interpretation of functional neuroimaging data. *Brain Structure & Function, 218*(2), 303-352. doi:10.1007/s00429-012-0460-z

Njomboro, P., Deb, S., & Humphreys, G. W. (2012). Apathy and executive functions: Insights from brain damage involving the anterior cingulate cortex. *BMJ Case,* Reports, 2012.

Noback, C. R., Strominger, N. L., Demarest, R. J., & Ruggiero, D. A. (2005). Basic Neurophysiology. *The Human Nervous System: Structure and Function*, 41-75.

Nobler, M. S., Sackeim, H. A., Prohovnik, I., Moeller, J. R., Mukherjee, S., Schnur, D. B., & Devanand, D. P. (1994). Regional cerebral blood flow in mood disorders, III: Treatment and clinical response. Archives of

General Psychiatry, 51, 884. doi:
10.1001/archpsyc.1994.03950110044007

Novick, J. M., Kan, I. P., Trueswell, J. C., & Thompson-Schill, S. L. (2009). A
case for conflict across multiple domains: Memory and language
impairments following damage to ventrolateral prefrontal cortex.
Cognitive Neuropsychology, 26(6), 527-567.
doi:10.1080/02643290903519367

O'Muircheartaigh, J., Dean, D. C., Ginestet, C. E., Walker, L., Waskiewicz, N.,
Lehman, K., ... & Deoni, S. C. (2014). White matter development and
early cognition in babies and toddlers. *Human brain mapping, 35*(9),
4475-4487.

Offringa, R., Brohawn, K. H., Staples, L. K., Dubois, S. J., Hughes, K. C., Pfaff,
D. L.. . Shin, L. M. F. (2013). Diminished rostral anterior cingulate
cortex activation during trauma-unrelated emotional interference in
PTSD. *Biology of Mood and Anxiety Disorders, 3*(1), Article 10-Article
10. doi:10.1186/2045-5380-3-10

Öngür, D., Ferry, A. T., & Price, J. L. (2003). Architectonic subdivision of the
human orbital and medial prefrontal cortex. *The Journal of Comparative
Neurology*, 460(3), 425-449. doi:10.1002/cne.10609

Osaka, N., Osaka, M., Kondo, H., Morishita, M., Fukuyama, H., & Shibasaki, H.
(2004). The neural basis of executive function in working memory: An
fMRI study based on individual differences. *Neuroimage*, 21(2), 623-
631. doi:10.1016/j.neuroimaging.2003.09.069.

Ozonoff, S., Pennington, B. F., & Rogers, S. J. (1991). Executive function
deficits in high-functioning autistic individuals: relationship to theory of
mind. *Journal of child Psychology and Psychiatry, 32*(7), 1081-1105.

Pandya, D. N., & Yeterian, E. H. (1996). Morphological correlations of human
and monkey frontal lobe. *In Neurobiology of decision-making* (pp. 13-
46). Springer Berlin Heidelberg.

Paus, T. (2010). Growth of white matter in the adolescent brain: myelin or axon?.
Brain and cognition, 72(1), 26-35.

Payne, C. (2011). *The Role of the Amygdala and Orbital frontal Cortex in
Processing Socially Relevant Crossmodal Signals* (Doctoral
dissertation). Permalink.

Perach-Barzilay, N., Tauber, A., Klein, E., Chistyakov, A., Ne'eman, R., &

Shamay-Tsoory, S. (2013). Asymmetry in the dorsolateral prefrontal cortex and aggressive behavior: A continuous theta-burst magnetic stimulation study. *Social Neuroscience, 8*(2), 178-188. doi:10.1080/17470919.2012.720602

Perecman, E. E. (1987). The frontal lobes revisited. In *Based on a conference sponsored by the Institute for Research in Behavioral Neuroscience in 1985.*. The IRBN Press.

Perecman, E. (1987). Consciousness and the meta-functions of the frontal lobes: Setting the stage. In The frontal lobes revisited. New York, NY: The IRBN Press.

Pessoa, L. (2009). How do emotion and motivation direct executive control? *Trends in Cognitive Sciences, 13*(4), 160-166. doi:10.1016/j.tics.2009.01.006

Petrides, M. (1982). Motor conditional associative-learning after selective prefrontal lesions in the monkey. *Behavior Brain Research, 5*, 407–413. doi: 10.1016/0166-4328(82)90044-4

Petrides, M. (1986). The effect of periarcuate lesions in the monkey on the performance of symmetrically and asymmetrically reinforced visual and auditory go, no-go tasks. *Journal of Neuroscience. 6*, 2054–2063.

Petrides, M. (1991) Monitoring of selections of visual stimuli and the primate frontal cortex. Philosophical Transactions of the Royal Society B: Biological Sciences, 246:293–298.

Petrides, M. (1994) Frontal lobes and working memory: evidence from investigations of the effects of cortical excisions in non- human primates. In: Boller F, Grafman J (Eds.) *Handbook of neuropsychology*, Vol. 9. Elsevier, Amsterdam, pp. 59–82

Petrides, M. (2000). The role of the mid-dorsolateral prefrontal cortex in working memory. *Experimental Brain Research*, 133(1), 44-54. doi:10.1007/s002210000399.

Petrides, M. (2005). Lateral prefrontal cortex: architectonic and functional organization. *Philosophical Transactions of the Royal Society of London B: Biological   Sciences, 360*(1456), 781-795.

Petrides, M., Alivisatos, B., Meyer, E., & Evans, A. C. (1993). Functional activation of the human frontal cortex during the performance of verbal working memory tasks. *Proceedings of the National Academy of*

Sciences, 90(3), 878-882.

Petrides, M., Alivisatos, B., & Evans, A. C. (1995). Functional activation of the human ventrolateral frontal cortex during mnemonic retrieval of verbal information. *Proceedings of the National Academy of Sciences of the United States of America, 92*(13), 5803-5807. doi:10.1073/pnas.92.13.5803

Petrides, M., Alivisatos, B., & Frey, S. (2002). Differential activation of the human orbital, midventrolateral, and mid-dorsolateral prefrontal cortex during the processing of visual stimuli. Proceedings of the National Academy of Sciences of the United States of America, 99(8), 5649-5654. doi:10.1073/pnas.072092299

Petrides, M., & Pandya, D. N. (1999). Dorsolateral prefrontal cortex: Comparative cytoarchitectonic analysis in the human and the macaque brain and corticocortical connection patterns. *The European Journal of Neuroscience,* 11(3), 1011.

Petrides, M., & Pandya, D. N. (2002). Comparative cytoarchitectonic analysis of the human and the macaque ventrolateral prefrontal cortex and corticocortical connection patterns in the monkey .*The European Journal of Neuroscience, 16*(2), 291-310. doi:10.1046/j.1460-9568.2001.02090.x

Pontius, A. A., & Yudowitz, B. S. (1980). Frontal lobe system dysfunction in some criminal actions as shown in the narratives test. *The Journal of Nervous and Mental Disease, 168,* 111-117.

Poellinger, A., Thomas, R., Lio, P., Lee, A., Makris, N., & Kwong, K. (2001). Activation and habituation in olfaction: An fMRI study. Radiology, 221, 485-485.

Polderman, T. J., Derks, E. M., Hudziak, J. J., Verhulst, F. C., Posthuma, D., & Boomsma, D. I. (2007). Across the continuum of attention skills: a twin study of the SWAN ADHD rating scale. *Journal of Child Psychology and Psychiatry,* 48(11), 1080-1087.

Poletti, M., & Bonuccelli, U. (2012). Orbital and ventromedial prefrontal cortex functioning in Parkinson's disease: Neuropsychological evidence. *Brain and Cognition,* 79(1), 23-33. doi:10.1016/j.bandc.2012.02.002

Postle, B. R., D'Esposito, M., & Corkin, S. (2005). Effects of verbal and nonverbal interference on spatial and object visual working memory.

Memory & Cognition, 33(2), 203-212. doi:10.3758/BF03195309.

Possin, K. L., Chester, S. K., Laluz, V., Bostrom, A., Rosen, H. J., Miller, B. L., & Kramer, J. H. (2012). The frontal-anatomic specificity of design fluency repetitions and their diagnostic relevance for behavioral variant frontotemporal dementia. *Journal of the International Neuropsychological Society, 18*, 1-11.

Possin, K. L., & Kramer, J. H. (2013). Error analysis of the Delis-Kaplan Executive Function System. In L. Ashendorf, R. Swenson, & D. Libon (Eds.), *The Boston process approach to neuropsychological assessment: A practitioner's guide.* New York, NY: Oxford University Press.

Powell, J. L., Lewis, P. A., Dunbar, R. I. M., García-Fiñana, M., & Roberts, N. (2010). Orbital prefrontal cortex volume correlates with social cognitive competence. *Neuropsychologia, 48*(12), 3554-3562. doi:10.1016/j.neuropsychologia.2010.08.004

Powell, J., Lewis, P. A., Roberts, N., García-Fiñana, M., & Dunbar, R. I. M. (2012). Orbital prefrontal cortex volume predicts social network size: An imaging study of individual differences in humans. Proceedings: Biological Sciences, 279(1736), 2157-2162. doi:10.1098/rspb.2011.2574

Premack, D., & Woodruff, G. (1976). Does the chimpanzee have a theory of mind? Behavioral and Brain Sciences, 4, 515–526.

Pribram, K. H. (1987). The subdivisions of the frontal cortex revisited., (pp. 11-39). New York, NY, US: The IRBN Press, xv, 309 pp.

Pribram, K. H., Ahumada, A., Hartog, J., & Roos, L. (1964). A progress report on the neurological processes disturbed by frontal lesions in primates. In J. Warren & K. Akert (Eds.), *The frontal granular cortex and behavior* (pp. 28-55). New York, NY: McGraw-Hill.

Pribram, K. H., Mishkin, M., Rosvold, H. E., & Kaplan, S. J. (1952). Effects on delayed-response performance of lesions of dorsolateral and ventromedial frontal cortex of baboons. *Journal of Comparative and Physiological Psychology, 45*, 565-575. doi:http://dx.doi.org/10.1037/h0061240

Price, J. L. (1999). Prefrontal cortical networks related to visceral function and mood. *Annals of the New York Academy of Sciences, 877*(1), 383-396.

Raedt, R. (2012). Impact of one HF-rTMS session on fine motor function in

right-handed healthy female subjects: A comparison of stimulation over
the left versus the right dorsolateral prefrontal cortex.
Neuropsychobiology, 65(2), 96. doi:10.1159/000329699.

Rankin, K. (2007). Social cognition in frontal injury. *The human frontal lobes:
Functions and disorders*, *2*, 345-360.

Raznahan, A., Lerch, J. P., Lee, N., Greenstein, D., Wallace, G. L., Stockman,
M., ... & Giedd, J. N. (2011). Patterns of coordinated anatomical change
in human cortical development: a longitudinal neuroimaging study of
maturational coupling. *Neuron*, *72*(5), 873-884.

Rempel-Clower, N. L., & Barbas, H. (1998). Topographic organization of
connections between the hypothalamus and prefrontal cortex in the
rhesus monkey. *Journal of Comparative Neurology*, *398*(3), 393-419.

Reitan, R. M. (1964). Psychological deficits resulting from cerebral lesions in
man. In J. Warren & K. Akert (Eds.), *The frontal granular cortex and
behavior* (pp. 295-312). New York, NY: McGraw-Hill.

Reitan, R. M. (1974). Assessment of brain-behavior relationships. In P.
McReynolds (Ed.), *Advances in psychological assessment (Vol. 3)*. San
Francisco, CA: Jossey-Bass.

Reitan, R. M. (1976). Neuropsychology: The vulgarization Luria always wanted.
Contemporary Psychology, 21, 737-739.

Reitan, R. M., & Davison, L. A. (1974). *Clinical neuropsychology: Current
status and applications.* New York, NY: Winston-Wiley.

Richtee, C. P., & Hines, M. (1938). Increased spontaneous activity produced in
monkeys by brain lesions. *Brain*, *61*, 1-16. doi: 10.1093/brain/61.1.1

Risberg, J. (1980). Regional cerebral blood flow measurements: Methodology
and applications in neuropsychology and psychiatry. Brain and
Language, 9, 9-34. doi:
http://dx.doi.org.fgul.idm.oclc.org/10.1016/0093-934X(80)90069-3

Riva, D., Cazzaniga, F., Esposito, S., & Bulgheroni, S. (2013). Executive
functions and cerebellar development in children. *Applied
Neuropsychology: Child, 2*, 97-103.

Romine, C. B., & Reynolds, C. R. (2005). A model of the development of frontal
lobe functioning: Findings from a meta-analysis. *Applied
neuropsychology*, *12*(4), 190-201.

Rossi, R., Pievani, M., Lorenzi, M., Boccardi, M., Beneduce, R., Bignotti, S., &

Frisoni, G. B. (2013). Structural brain features of borderline personality and bipolar disorders. Psychiatry Research, 213(2), 83.

Rousseau, J. J. (1754). 1992. *Discourse on the Origin of Inequality*. London.

Rushworth, M. F. S., Buckley, M. J., Gough, P. M., Alexander, I. H., Kyriazis, D., McDonald, K. R., & Passingham, R. E. (2005). Attentional selection and action selection in the ventral and orbital prefrontal cortex. *Journal of Neuroscience*, 25(50), 11628-11636. doi:10.1523/JNEUROSCI.2765-05.2005

Sacks, O. (1990). Luria and "romantic science". *Contemporary neuropsychology and the legacy of Luria*, 181-194.

Salloway, S. P., Malloy, P. F., & Duffy, J. D. (2001). *The frontal lobes and neuropsychiatric illness*. Washington, DC: American Psychiatric.

Salthouse, T. A. (2005). Relations between cognitive abilities and measures of executive functioning. *Neuropsychology*, *19*, 532. doi: 10.1037/0894-4105.19.4.532

Sanides, F. (1968). The architecture of the cortical taste nerve areas in squirrel monkey (Saimiri sciureus) and their relationships to insular, sensorimotor and prefrontal regions. *Brain research*, *8*(1), 97-124.

Sbordone, R. J. (2010). Neuropsychological tests are poor at assessing the frontal lobes, executive functions, and neurobehavioral symptoms of traumatically brain-injured patients. *Psychological Injury and Law*, *3*, 25-35. doi: 10.1007/s12207-010-9068-x

Schiebinger, L. (1993). Why mammals are called mammals: gender politics in eighteenth-century natural history. *The American historical review*, *98*(2), 382-411.

Schluter, N. D., Rushworth, M. F., Passingham, R. E., & Mills, K. R. (1998). Temporary interference in human lateral premotor cortex suggests dominance for the selection of movements. A study using transcranial magnetic stimulation. Conditional visuo-goal association and brain networks. *Brain,* 121(Pt 5), 785–799. doi: 10.1093/brain/121.5.785

Schmahl, C. G., Vermetten, E., Elzinga, B. M., & Douglas Bremner, J. (2003). Magnetic resonance imaging of hippocampal and amygdala volume in women with childhood abuse and borderline personality disorder. Psychiatry Research: Neuroimaging, 122(3), 193-198. doi:10.1016/S0925-4927(03)00023-4.

Schmithorst, V. J., & Yuan, W. (2010). White matter development during adolescence as shown by diffusion MRI. *Brain and cognition, 72*(1), 16-25.

Schoenemann, P. T. (2006). Evolution of the size and functional areas of the human brain. *Annual Review of Anthroplogy, 35*, 379-406.

Schore, A.N. (1997). A Century After Freud's Project: Is A Rapprochement Between Psychoanalysis And Neurobiology At Hand?. *Journal of the American Psychoanalytic Associaiton.*, 45:807-840

Schott, B. H., Niklas, C., Kaufmann, J., Bodammer, N. C., Machts, J., Schütze, H.. . Mishkin, M. (2011). Fiber density between rhinal cortex and activated ventrolateral prefrontal regions predicts episodic memory performance in humans. *Proceedings of the National Academy of Sciences of the United States of America, 108*(13), 5408-5413. doi:10.1073/pnas.1013287108

Semendeferi, K., Damasio, H., Frank, R., & Van Hoesen, G. W. (1997). The evolution of the frontal lobes: a volumetric analysis based on three-dimensional reconstructions of magnetic resonance scans of human and ape brains. *Journal of human evolution, 32*(4), 375-388.

Semendeferi, K., Lu, A., Schenker, N., & Damásio, H. (2002). Humans and great apes share a large frontal cortex. *Nature neuroscience, 5*(3), 272-276.

Shackman, A. J., Salomons, T. V., Slagter, H. A., Fox, A. S., Winter, J. J., & Davidson, R. J. (2011). The integration of negative affect, pain and cognitive control in the cingulate cortex. *Nature Reviews Neuroscience, 12*(3), 154-167.

Shaikh, M. B., & Siegel, A. (1994). Neuroanatomical and neurochemical mechanisms underlying amygdaloid control of defensive rage behavior in the cat. *Brazilian journal of medical and biological research= Revista brasileira de pesquisas medicas e biologicas/Sociedade Brasileira de Biofisica...[et al.], 27*(12), 2759-2779.

Shallice, T. (1982). Specific impairments of planning. *Philosophical Transactions of the Royal Society of London Biological Sciences, 298*, 199-209. doi: 10.1098/rstb.1982.0082

Shallice, T. (1988). *From neuropsychology to mental structure*. New York, NY: Cambridge University Press.

Shenhav, A., Botvinick, M., & Cohen, J. (2013). The expected value of control:

An integrative theory of anterior cingulate cortex function.Neuron, 79(2), 217-240. doi:10.1016/j.neuron.2013.07.007.

Siegel, D. J. (2015). *The developing mind: How relationships and the brain interact to shape who we are*. Guilford Publications.

Siddiqui, S. V., Chatterjee, U., Kumar, D., & Goyal, N. (2008). Neuropsychology of the prefrontal cortex. *Indian Journal of Psychiatry, 50,* 202-208. doi: 10.4103/0019-5545.43634

Simpson, D. (2005). Phrenology and the neurosciences: contributions of FJ Gall and JG Spurzheim. *ANZ journal of surgery, 75*(6), 475-482.

Sironi, V. A. (2011). The mechanics of the brain. *Progress in Neuroscience, 1,* 15-26.

Skranes, J., Vangberg, T. R., Kulseng, S., Indredavik, M. S., Evensen, K. A. I., Martinussen, M., & Brubakk, A. M. (2007). Clinical findings and white matter abnormalities seen on diffusion tensor imaging in adolescents with very low birth weight. *Brain, 130*(3), 654-666.

Smaers, J. B., Steele, J., Case, C. R., Cowper, A., Amunts, K., & Zilles, K. (2011). Primate prefrontal cortex evolution: human brains are the extreme of a lateralized ape trend. *Brain, behavior and evolution, 77*(2), 67-78.

Smallwood, J., Brown, K. S., Baird, B., Mrazek, M. D., Franklin, M. S., & Schooler, J. W. (2012). Insulation for daydreams: A role for tonic norepinephrine in the facilitation of internally guided thought: E33706. *PLoS One, 7*(4)   doi:10.1371/journal.pone.0033706

Smirni, D., Turriziani, P., Mangano, G. R., Cipolotti, L., & Oliveri, M. (2015). Modulating memory performance in healthy subjects with transcranial direct current stimulation over the right dorsolateral prefrontal cortex. *PloS one, 10*(12), e0144838.

Snyder, K., Wang, W. W., Han, R., McFadden, K., & Valentino, R. J. (2012). Corticotropin-releasing factor in the norepinephrine nucleus, locus coeruleus, facilitates behavioral flexibility. *Neuropsychopharmacology, 37*(2), 520-530.

Solbakk, A., & Løvstad, M. (2014). Effects of focal prefrontal cortex lesions on electrophysiological indices of executive attention and action control. Scandinavian Journal of Psychology, 55(3), 233-243. doi:10.1111/sjop.12106

Solms, M., & Meintjes, E. M. (2011). The neural substrates of mindfulness: An fMRI investigation. *Social Neuroscience, 6*(3), 231-242. doi:10.1080/17470919.2010.513495

Soloff, P. H., Pruitt, P., Sharma, M., Radwan, J., White, R., & Diwadkar, V. A. (2012). Structural brain abnormalities and suicidal behavior in borderline personality disorder. Journal of Psychiatric Research, 46(4), 516-525. doi:10.1016/j.jpsychires.2012.01.003

Soper, H. V. (1974). Analysis of spatial dysfunction following posterior parietal and principal sulcus cortex lesions in the monkey (Doctoral Dissertation, University of Connecticut). *Dissertation Abstracts*, 5679B. (University Microfilms N. 75-10, 671.)

Soper, H. V. (1982). The pulvinar and visual information processing in the monkey. *Society for Neuroscience Abstracts, 8*, 313.

Soper, H. V. (1983). *Prefrontal cortex function in humans.* Unpublished manuscript. Clinical Psychology Department, Fielding Graduate University, Santa Barbara, CA.

Soper, H. V. (2010, May). Executive functioning. *Neuroweek.* Lecture conducted from Fielding Graduate University, Ventura, CA.

Soper, H. V., Wolfson, S., & Canavan, F. (2008). Neuropsychology of autism spectrum disorders. In A. M. Horton Jr., & D. Wedding (Eds.), *The neuropsychology handbook* (pp. 681-704). New York, NY: Springer.

Soper, H. V. (2014, May). Executive Functioning. *Neuroweek.* Lecture conducted from Fielding Graduate University, Ventura, CA.

Spear, L. P. (2013). Adolescent neurodevelopment. *Journal of Adolescent Health, 52*(2), S7-S13.

Spence, S. A., Kaylor-Hughes, C., Farrow, T. F. D., & Wilkinson, I. D. (2008). Speaking of secrets and lies: The contribution of ventrolateral prefrontal cortex to vocal deception. *Neuroimage, 40*(3), 1411-1418. doi:10.1016/j.neuroimage.2008.01.035

Srebro, B. (1999). Ivan Divac in memoriam. *Acta Neurobiologiae Experimentalis, 59*(2).

Stanley, S. M. (1992). An ecological theory for the origin of Homo. *Paleobiology*, 237-257.

Stein, D. J., Miczek, K. A., Lucion, A. B., & de Almeida, R. M. M. (2013). Aggression-reducing effects of F15599, a novel selective 5-HT1A receptor agonist, after microinjection into the ventral orbital prefrontal cortex, but not in infralimbic cortex in male mice. *Psychopharmacology, 230*(3), 375-387.

Steinberg, L. (2005). Cognitive and affective development in adolescence. *Trends in cognitive sciences, 9*(2), 69-74.

Stone, M. H. (2013). A new look at borderline personality disorder and related disorders: hyper-reactivity in the limbic system and lower centers. *Psychodynamic psychiatry, 41*(3), 437.

Stone, V. E., Baron-Cohen, S., & Knight, R. T. (1998). Frontal lobe contributions to theory of mind. *Journal of cognitive neuroscience, 10*(5), 640-656.

Straube, T., Schmidt, S., Weiss, T., Mentzel, H. J., & Miltner, W. H. R. (2009). Dynamic activation of the anterior cingulate cortex during anticipatory anxiety. *Neuroimage,* 44, 975–981.

Stuss, D. T., & Benson, D. F. (1986). *The Frontal Lobes*. Raven Press: *New York.*

Stuss, D. T., & Alexander, M. P. (2000). Executive functions and the frontal lobes: A conceptual review. *Psychological Research, 63,* 289-298. doi: 10.1007/s004269900007

Stuss, D. T., & Knight, R. T. (2002). *Principles of frontal lobe functioning.* Cary, NC: Oxford University Press.

Stuss, D. T., Levine, B., Alexander, M. P., Hong, J., Palumbo, C., Hamer, L., Murphy, K. J., & Isukawa, D. (2000). Wisconsin Card Sorting Test performance in patients with focal frontal and posterior brain damage: Effects of lesion location and test structure on separable cognitive processes. *Neuropsychologia 38,* 388–402. doi: http://dx.doi.org.fgul.idm.oclc.org/10.1016/S0028-3932(99)00093-7

Stuss, D. T., Van Reekum, R., & Murphy, K. J. (2000). Differentiation of states and causes of apathy. In J. Borod (Ed.), *The neuropsychology of emotion.* New York, NY: Oxford University Press.

Stuss, D. T. (2011). Functions of the frontal lobes: Relation to executive functions. *Journal of the International Neuropsychological Society, 17*(5), 759-765. doi:10.1017/S1355617711000695

Swinnen, S., & P. Wenderoth, N. (2011). Hemispheric asymmetries of motor versus nonmotor processes during (visuo)motor control. *Human Brain Mapping,* 32(8), 1311-1329. doi:10.1002/hbm.21110.

Teitelbaum, H. (1964). A comparison of effects of orbitofrontal and hippocampal

lesions upon discrimination learning and reversal in the cat.
Experimental Neurology, 9, 452-462. doi:
http://dx.doi.org.fgul.idm.oclc.org/10.1016/0014-4886(64)90053-6

Teuber, H. L. (1955). Physiological psychology. *Annual Review of Psychology, 6*, 267-296.

Teuber, H. L. (1959). Some alterations in behavior after cerebral lesions in man. In A. Bass (Ed.), *Evolution of nervous control from primitive organisms to man* (pp. 157-194). Washington, DC: American Association for the Advancement of Science.

Thorn, C. A., Atallah, H., Howe, M., & Graybiel, A. M. (2010). Differential dynamics of activity changes in dorsolateral and dorsomedial striatal loops during learning. *Neuron, 66*(5), 781-795.

Tierney, A. J. (2000). Egas Moniz and the origins of psychosurgery: A review commemorating the 50th anniversary of Moniz's Nobel Prize. *Journal of the History of the Neurosciences, 9*, 22-36. doi: 10.1076/0964-704X(200004)9:1;1-2;FT022.

Trampel, R., Ott, D. V., & Turner, R. (2011). Do the congenitally blind have a stria of Gennari? First intracortical insights in vivo. *Cerebral Cortex, 21*(9), 2075-2081.

Tremblay, L., & Schultz, W. (2000). Modifications of reward expectation-related neuronal activity during learning in primate orbitofrontal cortex. *Journal of neurophysiology, 83*(4), 1877-1885.

Trevarthen, C. B. (1968). Two mechanisms of vision in primates. *Psychologische Forschung, 31*(4), 299-337.

Tsujimoto, S., Genovesio, A., & Wise, S. P. (2010). Comparison of strategy signals in the dorsolateral and orbital prefrontal cortex. The Journal of Neuroscience : The Official *Journal of the Society for Neuroscience*, 31(12), 4583-4592.

Ungerleider, L. G. (2006). Involvement of human left dorsolateral prefrontal cortex in perceptual decision making is independent of response modality. *Proceedings of the National Academy of Sciences of the United States of America*, 103(26), 10023-10028. doi:10.1073/pnas.0603949103.

Van Noordt, S., & Segalowitz, S. (2012). Performance monitoring and the medial prefrontal cortex: A review of individual differences and context effects as a window on self-regulation. *Frontiers in Human Neuroscience*, 6, 197. doi:10.3389/fnhum.2012.00197

Vasung, L., Fischi-Gomez, E., & Hüppi, P. S. (2013). Multimodality evaluation of the pediatric brain: DTI and its competitors. *Pediatric radiology*, *43*(1), 60-68.

Velayos, J. L., & Reinoso-Suarez, F. (1982). Topographic organization of the brainstem afferents to the mediodorsal thalamic nucleus. *Journal of Comparative Neurology*, *206*, 17-27.

Villablanca, J. R., Marcus, R. J., & Olmstead, C. E. (1976). Effects of caudate nuclei or frontal cortical ablations in cats: Neurology and gross behavior. *Experimental Neurology, 52*, 389-420. doi: http://dx.doi.org.fgul.idm.oclc.org/10.1016/0014-4886(76)90213-2

Vogt, B. A., Hof, P. R., Zilles, K., Vogt, L. J., Herold, C., & Palomero-Gallagher, N. (2013). Cingulate area 32 homologies in mouse, rat, macaque and human: Cytoarchitecture and receptor architecture. *Journal of Comparative Neurology*, 521(18), 4189-4204. doi:10.1002/cne.23409

Volle, E., Gilbert, S., Benoit, R., & Burgess, P. (2010). Specialization of the rostral prefrontal cortex for distinct analogy processes. *Cerebral Cortex, 20*(11), 2647-2659. doi:10.1093/cercor/bhq012

Wais, P. E., Kim, O. Y., & Gazzaley, A. (2012). Distractibility during episodic retrieval is exacerbated by perturbation of left ventrolateral prefrontal cortex. *Cerebral Cortex, 22*(3), 717-724. doi:10.1093/cercor/bhr160

Wakana, S., Jiang, H., Nagae-Poetscher, L. M., van Zijl, Peter C M, & Mori, S. (2004). Fiber tract-based atlas of human white matter anatomy. *Radiology, 230*(1), 77-87. doi:10.1148/radiol.2301021640

Walker, S. C., Robbins, T. W., & Roberts, A. C. (2009). Differential contributions of dopamine and serotonin to orbitofrontal cortex function in the marmoset. *Cerebral Cortex, 19* (4), 889-898.

Wallis, J. D., & Miller, E. K. (2003). From rule to response: neuronal processes in the premotor and prefrontal cortex. *Journal of Neurophysiology, 90*, 1790–1806. doi: 10.1152/jn.00086.2003

Walsh, C. A., Morrow, E. M., & Rubenstein, J. L. (2008). Autism and brain development. *Cell, 135*(3), 396-400.

Walsh, K. (1985, April). *Clinical evaluation in neuropsychology.* Paper presented at the Thirteenth Annual Meeting of the International Neuropsychology

Society, San Diego, CA.

Warren, J. M., Coutant, L. W., & Cornwell, P. R. (1969). Cortical lesions and response inhibition in cats. *Neuropsychologia, 7,* 245-257. doi: http://dx.doi.org.fgul.idm.oclc.org/10.1016/0028-3932(69)90005-0

Warren, J. M., Warren, H. B., & Akert, K. (1972). The behavior of chronic cats with lesions in the frontal association cortex. *Acta Biologiae Experimentalis, 32,* 361-392.

Wasserman, T., & Wasserman, L. D. (2012). The sensitivity and specificity of neuropsychological tests in the diagnosis of attention deficit hyperactivity disorder. *Applied Neuropsychology: Child, 1,* 90-99.

Wasserman, T., & Wasserman, L. D. (2013). Toward an integrated model of executive functioning in child. *Applied Neuropsychology: Child, 2,* 88-96

Wolff, J. J., Gu, H., Gerig, G., Elison, J. T., Styner, M., Gouttard, S., ... & Evans, A. C. (2012). Differences in white matter fiber tract development present from 6 to 24 months in infants with autism. *American Journal of Psychiatry, 169*(6), 589-600.

Wortis, H., & Maurer, W. S. (1942). " Sham rage" in man. *American Journal of Psychiatry, 98*(5), 638-644.

Wynn, T., & Coolidge, F. (2008). Why not cognition?. *Current Anthropology, 49*(5), 895-897.

Yang, J. C., Papadimitriou, G., Eckbo, R., Yeterian, E. H., Liang, L., Dougherty, D. D., & Makris, N. (2015;2014;). Multi-tensor investigation of orbitofrontal cortex tracts affected in subcaudate tractotomy. *Brain Imaging and Behavior,* 9(2), 342-352. doi:10.1007/s11682-014-9314-z

Yohe, L. R., Suzuki, H., & Lucas, L. R. (2012). Aggression is suppressed by acute stress but induced by chronic stress: Immobilization effects on aggression, hormones, and cortical 5-HT1B/striatal dopamine D2 receptor density. *Cognitive, Affective, & Behavioral Neuroscience, 12*(3), 446-459.

York, G. K., & Steinberg, D. A. (2011). Hughlings Jackson's neurological ideas. *Brain, 134*(10),3106-3113.

Young, J., & Shapiro, M. (2011). Dynamic coding of goal-directed paths by orbital prefrontal cortex. Journal of Neuroscience, 31(16), 5989-6000. doi:10.1523/JNEUROSCI.5436-10.20

Zald, D. H. (2003). The human amygdala and the emotional evaluation of sensory stimuli. *Brain Research Reviews, 41*(1), 88-123.

Zald, D. H., & Kim, S. W. (1996). Anatomy and function of the orbital frontal cortex, I: anatomy, neurocircuitry, and obsessive-compulsive disorder. *Journal of Neuropsychiatry ClinicalNeuroscience,* 8:125–138.

Zhang, J. (2003). Evolution of the human ASPM gene, a major determinant of brain size. *Genetics, 165*(4), 2063-2070.

Zhang, Z., Matos, S. C., Jego, S., Adamantidis, A., & Séguéla, P. (2013). Norepinephrine drives persistent activity in prefrontal cortex via synergistic α1 and α2 adrenoceptors. *PLoS One, 8*(6), e66122.

Ziegler, W. (2008). Apraxia of speech. *Handbook of clinical neurology, 88,* 269-285. doi: http://dx.doi.org.fgul.idm.oclc.org/10.1016/S0072-9752(07)88013-4

ABOUT THE AUTHORS

Henry V. Soper received his B.A. from Yale University (awarded Normal Hall, 1965; and Robert R. Chamberlain Awards), and his M.A. and Ph.D. from the University of Connecticut. He also has two NIH Postdoctoral Fellowships (ADAMHA) and (NIMH), and served as Chief Fellow, Neuropsychology, at the University of California, Los Angeles; received the Wilmont Sweeney Juvenile Justice Award; and served as reviewer, *Perceptual and Motor Skills Psychological* Reports, and on the Editorial Board of *Applied Neuropsychology* and *The Encyclopedia of Neuropsychological Disorder*. He is also a Fellow of the National Academy of Neuropsychology and Psychonomic Society. He has published over 150 abstracts, papers, chapters, and books in the neurosciences, neuropsychology, medicine and psychology.

K. Drorit Gaines, Ph.D., received an academic excellence scholarship to UCLA and completed a Bachelor's Degree in Business Economics and Accounting. She received her Ph.D. from Fielding Graduate University in Clinical Psychology, with a specialization in Clinical Neuropsychology and completed her post-doctoral experience in neuropsychology at the Veterans Affairs of Greater Los Angeles and UCLA Longevity Center. Dr. Gaines received awards from the American Psychological Association, Society of Nuclear Medicine and Molecular Imaging, Veterans Affairs of greater Los Angeles, and Fielding Graduate University. Dr. Gaines currently serves as an expert on the Criminal Panel for the Los Angeles Superior Court, Principal Investigator at the VA West Los Angeles, Clinical Faculty, vl., at UCLA Department of Pediatrics, Adjunct Faculty at Fielding Graduate University, Secretary and Board Member of the National Academy of Neuropsychology Foundation, Journal Reviewer for Applied Neuropsychology, and CEO of Neuro Health, LLC. She is the author of *Combating Dementia in Thirty Days*.

Robin E. Kissinger, Ph.D., is a licensed clinical psychologist, who serves as the Postdoctoral Autism Fellow at The University of Southern California, Keck School of Medicine, University Center for Excellent for Developmental Disabilities in the California Leadership Education in Neurodevelopmental Disabilities (CA-LEND) program at Children's Hospital, Los Angeles (CHLA). Her fellowship work specializes in the assessment, diagnosis, and treatment of children - birth to 5 years, with neurodevelopmental disorders and co-occurring mental health conditions. At CHLA, Dr. Kissinger's research involves a National Institute of Health (NIH) National Institute of Neurological Disorders (NINDS) funded project on the differential diagnosis of children with autism and co-occurring genetic disorders.

Tonya Comstock, Ph.D., knew from early in her academic career that she wanted to focus on brain behavior relationships. After earning a Master's of Science degree in Counseling Psychology at California Lutheran University in 2007 she set her sights on earning her Ph.D. in Clinical Psychology and emphasizing in Neuropsychology at Fielding Graduate University. After graduating in 2014 much of her career has focused on helping teams who work with those with severe and persistent mental illness. She was able to bring the neuropsychological perspective to difficult cases in the form of assessment and consultation. After relocating to Seattle in 2016 she had the opportunity to work with persons with chronic pain. Working on a team with physiatrists, psychologists, physical therapists, nurses, occupational therapists, and vocational counselors, Dr. Comstock helps people with injuries and pain increase fulfillment in their lives. Dr. Comstock is thrilled to have participated in this project and feels grateful to be involved in the dialogue of this important topic.